LIVING WITH GRIEF:

BEFORE AND AFTER THE DEATH

EDITED BY
Kenneth J. Doka

Foreword by
J. William Worden

HOSPICE FOUNDATION
OF AMERICA

This book is part of Hospice Foundation of A

Supported in part by the Foundation for End-of-Li

This book is part of HFA's *Living With Grief®* series.

Ordering information:

Call Hospice Foundation of America: 800-854-3402

Or write:
Hospice Foundation of America
1621 Connecticut Avenue, NW #300
Washington, DC 20009

Or visit HFA's Web site:
www.hospicefoundation.org

Managing Editor: Amy Tucci
Assistant Managing Editor: Keith Johnson
Cover Design: Patricia McBride
Typesetting and Design: Page Designs

Publisher's Cataloging-in-Publication Data
(Prepared by Quality Books Inc.)

    Living with grief : before and after the death / edited by
    Kenneth J. Doka ; foreword by J. William Worden.
      p. cm. -- (Living with grief series)
      Includes bibliographical references and index.
      LCCN 2006939001
      ISBN-13: 978-1-893349-08-7
      ISBN-10: 1-893349-08-X

      1. Grief. 2. Loss (Psychology) 3. Bereavement--
    Psychological aspects. 4. Death--Psychological aspects.
    I. Doka, Kenneth J. II. Hospice Foundation of America.
    III. Title: Before and after the death. IV. Series:
    Living with grief.

    BF575.G7L595 2007   155.9'37
                        QBI06-600719

To my new granddaughter,
Luzelenia
"Lucy"
And her strong, protective, older brother,
Kenny
And to their parents, Michael and Angelina
Who manage it all!

■

And to all hospice, palliative care,
and bereavement care professionals
Who assist those in grief
Before and after death

Kenneth J. Doka

■

▪ Contents ▪

■ FOREWORD ■

J. William Worden

Thirty-five years ago, a group of us began offering workshops for mental health professionals on grief counseling at the University of Chicago. These workshops, limited to 100 attendees, were so popular that we had to offer them twice per year for nearly a decade. It has been 25 years since my book, *Grief Counseling and Grief Therapy*, appeared in its first edition. Over this three decade period, it has been exciting for me to see new ideas and concepts emerge that help us understand how we ourselves, and our clients, adapt to loss. It has also been discouraging to see how some seemingly useful concepts get jettisoned merely for the sake of publishing something new and different. I applaud the Hospice Foundation of America for sponsoring this book and teleconference so that we may re-explore the foundations of our knowledge and some of our fundamental assumptions in order to provide the highest levels of practice for clients and patients.

Over these past three decades, there have been three emerging concepts that I have found very useful:

1. Continuing Bonds. Freud's earlier notion of emotional disengagement with the deceased was not adequate to the data. The idea of continuing bonds came, in part, from our longitudinal research of bereaved children and their families in the Harvard Child Bereavement Study. We found that many of these children remained connected with their dead parent over the two years that we studied them. Continuing bonds were helpful for most of these children but they were not for some. Stroebe and others have explored reasons why such bonds are supportive for some but maladaptive for others. Klass furthered our thinking on continuing bonds with his important research on bereaved parents, resulting in a seminal book.

2. Disenfranchised Grief. Grief is not a solo phenomenon but is experienced in a social setting. This social setting gives one permission to grieve and offers rituals for how to express one's grief. Doka emphasized this idea in his concept of disenfranchised grief in which the mourner's loss is not socially sanctioned, making it difficult for them to grieve. Doka developed an idea that we had written about earlier called "socially unspeakable losses" and "socially negated losses" and took it much further. This importance of grieving as a social phenomenon has been a touchstone for research on family adaptation to loss.

3. Meaning Making. This is another important concept that has come to the fore. Grief is not just an emotional reaction to a loss but also involves a cortical struggle to find meaning in the loss and how the loss relates to one's current life. Neimeyer has written extensively on this need and on ways to help mourners with this task. Nadeau has made meaning making a family task and her research shows how families go about this with varying success.

Looking forward, where do we go from here? I want to suggest several needs that will help make our field become even more effective.

- We need more cross-cultural research. The experience of grief and the expression thereof is, in part, culturally determined. Parkes, Martinson, Klass, and others have drawn our attention to this but more work is needed. The International Work Group (IWG) is currently engaged in some of these cross cultural investigations. One of my Sudanese graduate students recently conducted a well-crafted study of the refugee children of Darfur, looking at the experience of grief, trauma, and depression among these displaced children. Western concepts don't always apply here.

- We need better research with more careful replication. As an example, someone once wrote that bereaved children have a lot of difficulty in school. This notion was then repeated in other publications without further validation or without carefully comparing bereaved children with their matched non-bereaved counterparts. When careful comparisons are made, we find that bereaved children are no more compromised in school work than their non-bereaved counterparts matched for age and gender. Another example of re-quoted information that gets treated as truth is recent published discussions of the negative/iatrogenic effects of grief counseling. These original findings are not based on adequate research and should not be quoted and requoted without better research support.

- We need to be careful to not pathologize grief. There has been a rush to come up with DSM criteria that will enable mental health workers to diagnose mourners for third party payments and perhaps generate research monies. I believe that there are forms of complicated bereavement and have written about them for 25 years. However, many existing DSM diagnostic categories such as depression, anxiety disorders, and trauma will apply to some grieving individuals. A loss by death may precipitate these disorders and existing diagnostic criteria and treatment plans are sufficient to identify and treat them.

- We need to further investigate the relationship between trauma and grief. At a time when there is increasing attention on traumatic events, knowing how these two overlapping responses relate and interact is important. After a catastrophe, identifying who needs help (and what kind of help) is important, and will become increasingly more important in the future. For example, is Critical Incident Stress Debriefing helpful and for whom? EMDR can be useful for helping people dealing with trauma responses but what is its role in working with grief?

- We need to think of grieving in longer time frames. In the Harvard Child Bereavement Study, the negative sequelae of parental death did not appear for some of these children until two years after the loss. Klass, in his follow-up of bereaved parents, found that some significant changes did not occur until four years after the child died. In hospice work, we tend to follow families only for a year after the death. For some individuals and families, a longer follow-up time may be more useful.

This book is filled with excellent chapters that bring us up to date with the most current information on both pre-death and post-death interventions. These experts tell us what we currently know and point us in the direction of what we still need to investigate. Read these chapters carefully but in the final analysis, always use your own experiences of loss as a touchstone for what is true. ■

J. William Worden, Ph.D. ABPP is a Fellow of the American Psychological Association and holds academic appointments at the Harvard Medical School and the Rosemead Graduate School of Psychology. He is Co-Principal Investigator of the Harvard Child Bereavement Study based at the Massachusetts General Hospital and is the author of four books including Grief Counseling & Grief Therapy, *and* Children & Grief: When a Parent Dies.

■ ACKNOWLEDGMENTS ■

It is always a pleasure to pause and thank those who enrich our work—or our lives. First and foremost is the staff of the Hospice Foundation of America (HFA). While the staff is small, they manage to accomplish so much each year. David Abrams, the president of HFA, offers advice, counsel, and suggestions as well as editorial comments at each stage of the process. He keeps us grounded. Amy Tucci is listed as the managing editor of this book. That title does not convey the amazing effort she expends at every stage of development. Her service has been invaluable. Others in the Hospice Foundation of America provide indirect support, assisting the foundation's work so that the book can reach fruition. Included here are Sophie Viteri Berman, Bertha Ramirez, Robert Lee, Kristen Baker, Keith Johnson, Susan Belsinger, and Marcia Eaker.

I also wish to thank my administrators and colleagues at the College of New Rochelle for creating a warm and encouraging environment that allows me to write and edit. I need to thank so many there. Administrators include President Stephen Sweeny, Vice-President Joan Bailey, Dean Guy Lometti, and Assistant Dean Marie Ribarich. Mary Whalen and Vera Mezzaucella provide critical assistance. Colleagues at the College of New Rochelle as well as the Association of Death Education and the International Work Group on Dying, Death and Bereavement are always there to offer stimulation and support.

I, of course, need to acknowledge all those in my personal life who are always encouraging. My son, Michael, and his wife, Angelina, give me great joy as I watch them parent my grandson Kenny and granddaughter Lucy. My godson, Keith Whitehead, continues in college. I enjoy these new adult conversations with him. Other members of my intimate network of family, friends, and neighbors—including Kathy Dillon, my sister Dorothy, my brother Franky, and all of their families; Eric Schwarz; Dylan Rieger; Larry Laterza; Ellie Andersen; Jim, Karen, and Greg Cassa; Paul Kimbal; Don and Carol Ford; Allen and Gail Greenstein; Jim and

Mary Millar; Robert and Tracey Levy; Linda and Russell Tellier; Jill Boyer; Terry Webber; Fred and Lisa Amore; Lynn Miller; James Rainbolt; Scott and Lisa Carlson; Tom and Lorraine Carlson; Matt Atkins; Kurt Mulligan; and Don and Lucille Matthews—provide respite, friendship, and most importantly, laughter.

Finally, I need to thank all the contributing authors who met demanding deadlines with fine chapters that continue to push our field forward. And all at the Hospice Foundation of America offer our sincere thanks to all those who attend the teleconference and work in this field. It is our hope that this work will make your work easier. ■

—Kenneth J. Doka

The Dying Process: Understanding Anticipatory Grief and Anticipatory Mourning

A number of years ago, I was in the audience for a presentation of the then-new model of palliative care. The presenter enthusiastically described this new approach, noting that the palliative care team would be available from the time of diagnosis, advising on symptom control and pain management. The presenter continued to describe the range of services offered, noting that after the death, this continuum of care would continue, as a bereavement specialist would be called in to address the family's grief. Many hospice staff in the audience immediately challenged her. Grief, they reminded her, would begin not at the death but at the diagnosis.

Charles Corr opens this section by exploring the phenomenon of anticipatory grief. Corr notes that the concept often had a troubled history, implying that there was a finite grief that families experienced. The assumption was that as families grieved in anticipation of the loss, their adjustment at the time of the loss should be easier—a point not borne out in the research. Rando's work (2000) has contributed to this discussion. Rando terms *anticipatory grief* a "useful misnomer." Preferring the term *anticipatory mourning*, Rando offers a more inclusive use of the concept, applying it to the range of losses patients, families, and staff experience in the course of an illness. These losses not only include the anticipated loss due to a dire prognosis but also encompass the present changes experienced as the patient's health declines and the patient's capabilities, roles, and activities are diminished. These losses may be both tangible—such as the loss of income—and intangible—such as the death of a dream.

Elizabeth Uppman movingly portrays this anticipatory mourning in the first *Voices* piece. The *Voices* pieces scattered throughout the book illustrate how grieving individuals actually experience many of these concepts. Here Uppman powerfully and touchingly describes her grief as she contemplates the death of her young son, Gabriel.

Both Corr and Uppman illustrate the complexity of anticipatory mourning. In describing the grief process, Stroebe and Schut (1999) explain grief as entailing dual processes: reacting to the loss and adjusting to life in the face of the loss. Anticipatory mourning also entails such dual processes. On the one hand, dying persons and their families may need to respond to the losses encountered in the course of illness. On the other hand, they frequently have to adjust to the changes imposed by disease and plan for a future now altered by illness.

As dying patients struggle with their sense of loss, they also try to make sense of the life that they lived. Most individuals wish to leave a legacy—to know that their lives mattered. James Magee offers a discussion of the role of life review and reminiscence in helping individuals find that legacy. While Magee explores life review as a function of aging, it clearly is related to finitude—the sense that one's life is drawing to a close. Life review and reminiscence are critical therapies to use with dying patients, allowing them to fulfill one spiritual task of dying, "to have lived a meaningful life" (Doka, 1993). In addition to life review, there may be other strategies to support the quest for meaning. Many dying patients find it helpful to develop a moral or ethical will, reminding their heirs of the values they have hoped to model and wish to impart and perpetuate. Some dying individuals have hosted "living eulogies" where family and friends share memories and legacies while the dying individual is still able to hear them.

Recognizing that dying is not just a medical problem but a social, spiritual, and psychological challenge as well is one of the hallmark contributions of hospice care. Because patients cope with dying on so many levels, it is critical to use multiple approaches. Expressive therapies such as music or art not only facilitate life review, they can assist dying persons as they struggle with other issues such as fears and anxieties.

Another contribution of hospice is that it views the family as the unit of care. Carla Sofka's chapter examines the ways families respond to the dying process. It provides wise counsel to those who would assist.

Care does not end with the death of the patient. It continues as the family struggles with loss and grief. Professionals can offer a profound and sensitive presence at the moment of death. Here there is much that can be done. The family's needs and grief can be validated. The family can be offered the opportunity to design and participate in a moment of ritual—perhaps lighting a candle, anointing or lovingly dressing the person, saying a prayer, or offering a final blessing or farewell. Sensitive funeral directors can remove the body not only with dignity and respect but with special touches such as dressing the deceased in his or her favorite pajamas or swaddling the person in a special blanket or quilt. Hospice professionals, other health care staff, clergy, and funeral directors can offer another critical gift: assisting families with the nitty-gritty tasks that accompany a death.

This section ends, perhaps appropriately, with a discussion of the funeral. The funeral is a liminal event, a transition between life and death. Paul Irion's chapter offers sound suggestions. Irion presents a vision of a funeral service where participatory and personalized rituals address the needs of a variety of mourners, thus facilitating the grief process. Many funeral directors have made great efforts to personalize funerals. Memory boards filled with family photos, special memorial Web pages, and videos or DVDs that chronicle the life of the deceased are now common. Other funeral homes have gone even further. For example, a funeral home in the Midwest has rooms that depict a mother's kitchen and a father's game room for use during visitation times. Even caskets, cremation containers, and urns are being customized with interchangeable panels and corners, creative engravings, and drawers in which to leave mementos and notes.

Funeral services may even be moving in other directions. The New Jersey State Funeral Directors Association and the Metropolitan

(New York City) Funeral Directors Association are cooperating to test a Knowledge-Based Model of Funeral Service that offers services to families around the dying process as well as after the death. Such a model reaffirms that the funeral does not mark the end of the grieving but rather a stop in the journey. ■

REFERENCES

Doka, K. J. (1993). *Living with life-threatening illness: A guide for patients, their families, and caregivers.* Lexington, MA: Lexington Books.

Rando, T. A. (2000). *Clinical dimensions of anticipatory mourning. Theory and practice in working with the dying, their loved ones, and their caregivers.* Champaign, IL: Research Press.

Stroebe, M., & Schut, H. (1999). The dual process model of coping with bereavement: Rationale and description. *Death Studies, 23,* 197-234.

CHAPTER 1

Anticipatory Grief and Mourning
An Overview

Charles A. Corr

HISTORICAL PRELUDE

Credit for first drawing explicit attention to the concept of anticipatory grief is usually given to Erich Lindemann (1944). Since that time, many writers and researchers have addressed this topic. Research studies have come from many perspectives, focusing especially on parents of terminally ill children and reports from bereaved spouses. In particular, Fulton and colleagues (Fulton & Fulton, 1971, 1972; Fulton & Gottesman, 1980) attempted to clarify the meaning of the phrase "anticipatory grief" and put an end to erroneous assumptions that had misled many researchers. Much of this early work is reflected in books edited by Schoenberg and colleagues (1974) and by Rando (1986), as well as in Rando's (2000b) insightful review of the literature.

While many writers have used the phrases "anticipatory grief" and "anticipatory mourning" interchangeably, Futterman, Hoffman, and Sabshin (1972) appear to have been the first to distinguish them formally, at least insofar as they viewed grief and grieving as distinct components of the mourning process. Rando (1988) conceded that the phrase "anticipatory grief" is a misnomer (for reasons explained below) but insisted that the phenomenon is a reality. In a second edited book on the subject, Rando (2000a) preferred "anticipatory mourning" as the master concept.

More recently, Fulton (2003, p. 348) observed, "I have serious reservations regarding the heuristic value—either theoretical or practical—of the concepts 'anticipatory grief' and 'anticipatory mourning.'

OBJECTIVES OF THE CHAPTER

This chapter examines the distinction between anticipatory grief and anticipatory mourning, as well as the meaning of the two phrases. It describes some unhelpful assumptions that have clouded understanding of the two concepts and identifies more constructive ways of thinking about anticipatory grief and mourning. The primary objectives of this chapter are (1) to help people who are experiencing anticipatory grief and mourning better understand their own reactions and responses in the face of expected losses, and (2) to enable those providing care to function more effectively in their roles. The goal is to demonstrate the practical value of anticipatory grief and anticipatory mourning, and provide some guidelines for helping those who are experiencing anticipatory grief and mourning.

THREE EXAMPLES OF ANTICIPATORY GRIEF AND MOURNING

We can clarify experiences of anticipatory grief and anticipatory mourning through three examples: a historical report and two composite cases.

Edgar Allan Poe

In a letter dated January 4, 1848 (part of which is reproduced on page 7), Edgar Allan Poe writes about repeated episodes in which his wife ruptured blood vessels while singing. Apparently, Virginia Poe suffered from an advanced case of "consumption" or what would now be diagnosed as tuberculosis, a case so extreme that when she engaged in what for a healthy person might have been a benign activity she bled from her lungs.

Whenever this happened, his wife's bleeding led Poe to anticipate her death. Her loss seemed so likely, Poe writes, that "Her life was despaired of" and he "took leave of her forever" or gave her up for dead. Expecting her to die, Poe "underwent all the agonies of her death." That is, he experienced anticipatory grief in his reaction to the expected loss of his wife. His reactions were so extreme that he "became insane," only to renew his

EXTRACT FROM A LETTER BY EDGAR ALLAN POE OF JANUARY 4, 1848

You say—"Can you hint to me what was the terrible evil which caused the irregularities so profoundly lamented?" Yes; I can do more than hint. This "evil" was the greatest which can befall a man. Six years ago, a wife, whom I loved as no man ever loved before, ruptured a blood-vessel in singing. Her life was despaired of. I took leave of her forever & underwent all the agonies of her death. She recovered partially and I again hoped. At the end of a year the vessel broke again—I went through precisely the same scene. Again in about a year afterward. Then again-again-again & even once again at varying intervals. Each time I felt all the agonies of her death—and at each accession of the disorder I loved her more dearly & clung to her life with more desperate pertinacity. But I am constitutionally sensitive—nervous in a very unusual degree. I became insane, with long intervals of horrible sanity. During these fits of absolute unconsciousness I drank, God only knows how often or how much. As a matter of course, my enemies referred the insanity to the drink rather than the drink to the insanity. I had indeed, nearly abandoned all hope of a permanent cure when I found one in the death of my wife. This I can & do endure as becomes a man— it was the horrible never-ending oscillation between hope & despair which I could not longer have endured without the total loss of reason. In the death of what was my life, then, I receive a new but—oh God! how melancholy an existence.

Source: The Letters of Edgar Allan Poe, 1948, vol. 2, p. 356.

desperate love for her each time she recovered. In his periods of extreme grief, Poe turned to alcohol. His drinking, he explains, was the consequence of his grief, depression, and "insanity," not the other way around. This is a familiar way of trying to manage loss and grief, although not one that most counselors would recommend. What was most difficult to bear, Poe writes, was "the horrible never-ending oscillation between hope & despair which I could not longer have endured without the total loss of reason."

Paradoxically, it was only upon the actual death of his wife that Poe experienced "a permanent cure." His grief and mourning did not cease, but they altered in character. Freed from the anticipation of his wife's death and from the conflicting strains of her relapses and recoveries, Poe had now to confront the finality of her death. This meant the loss of his precious wife and his previous mode of existence, and the beginning of a new and very melancholy mode of living.

A Wife with a Life-Threatening Illness

During the 41 years of their marriage, Joan and Ned Wagner had experienced no serious health problems. When the specialist told Joan that she had a life-threatening illness, they found it hard to believe. They did not fully understand the gravity of the situation until several weeks later, when they went back to their family doctor for further consultation. As time passed, Joan grew progressively weaker and less able to engage in her former activities. She quit her job, eventually withdrew to her bed, and gradually required more and more care. Ned took a leave from work, arranged for a visiting nurse service, and tried to help as much as he could. He told one of the nurses that he had always expected to die before Joan. Now he didn't know quite what to do.

The many challenges and losses that had come into their lives led Joan and Ned to talk about the future. They realized that Joan did not have long to live and had her admitted to a hospice home care program. They agreed to use the remaining time in the best ways they could. They encouraged each of their three children and four grandchildren to visit and pray with them. They reviewed their financial situation, made funeral and burial plans, and put things in order as much as they could for Ned's future life as a widower.

They were able to anticipate some losses, while others surprised them. The hospice staff helped Joan and Ned by validating their grief reactions and offering support to each of them, by teaching them what they might expect as Joan's illness progressed, and by promising to be available whenever they were needed, both before and after Joan's death.

Joan and Ned kept a journal throughout her illness. As they read back through earlier entries, they were able to see how things had changed over time. At any given point, they could identify the losses they had already experienced, those they were currently undergoing, and—most difficult— those they would soon experience, in particular the loss they both dreaded: Joan's death. As expected or anticipated losses were realized with the passage of time, they became part of the present and then the past in this life story. Their journal recorded many losses and new challenges, many everyday incidents, and some surprises and cherished events. It was a precious time, one they tried to make as rich and meaningful as they could, a reflection of their deep love for each other.

After Joan's death, Ned told the hospice bereavement coordinator that he was surprised by the freshness and depth of his grief. He said, "We knew that Joan was dying and gradually coming closer to the end. We experienced a lot of grief during that time and we appreciated that you helped us engage in some constructive mourning processes. So we thought that when the moment of Joan's death would finally arrive, we would be well prepared for her loss. In fact, it almost seemed as if our grief increased. Well, perhaps that's not exactly right. What happened was that we encountered a new wave of grief. All of us, the children and I, cried and sobbed. It was almost as if we hadn't known that she would die. But we did. And I guess we weren't finished with our grief by a long shot."

A Child with a Life-Threatening Illness

When Carol and Joe Sullivan were told that their youngest child, Julie, had been diagnosed with a life-threatening illness, they were thunderstruck. It was all they could do to keep themselves together while they drove home and when they were with their two older children.

For Carol, the first weeks after the diagnosis were a time of intense pain and sadness. "It was a defining time in my life," she said later. "Things were never the same afterwards." Carol made an effort not to cry in front of the children but did so often when she was alone. She tried to turn to Joe to share her grief, but found that he was focused almost entirely on looking up more information about Julie's disease, seeking out second opinions, and investigating alternative therapies and other interventions that might lead to a cure. He urged Carol not to give up hope and refused to believe that Julie would die almost up to the moment of her death. Unfortunately, some of the interventions he wanted to try would have inflicted harsh side effects on Julie. Carol cooperated with Joe's ideas at first, but gradually realized that Julie didn't want such severe treatment. Unlike Joe, Carol came to acknowledge that Julie would die. As a result, she concentrated on improving the quality of Julie's life, spending time with her children, and creating memories that they could all look back on after Julie's death.

The hospice bereavement worker congratulated Carol on her realistic outlook and her ability to tolerate Joe's need to deny Julie's impending death without allowing a major rift to come between them. Carol explained that her priorities were to help Julie feel safe and be happy as long as she was with them, and to make it possible for every member of her family to go on after Julie's death. She said, however, that Joe was having a very difficult time coping with his daughter's death.

GRIEF AND MOURNING

Grief is often described as "the emotional reaction to loss." It is that, but it is more than that. Part of the problem is that the word "emotion," as Elias (1991) pointed out, can refer either to feelings alone or to a combination of feelings, behaviors, and physical components. When people experience a major loss, such as the death of someone they love, they may react to the loss not just in how they feel but in all the dimensions of their being. Their grief often includes physical, behavioral, social, psychological (cognitive and affective), and spiritual reactions. Bereaved persons often express resentment of the idea that their grief should be limited to feelings alone. Even well-meaning friends frequently underestimate the depth of a person's grief by suggesting that it can simply or easily be set aside.

The example of Edgar Allan Poe demonstrates an extreme anticipatory grief reaction. The possibility of his wife's death became so real to him on more than one occasion that, as he wrote, he "became insane." Her impending loss reached deep into his being and caused him great agony.

On the other hand, family members and care providers may assume that a person who does not express grief publicly in recognized ways (e.g., by crying) is not aware of the significance of an anticipated or actual loss. The person may be assumed not to be "dealing with" an actual or impending death when, in fact, that is not correct. How grief is experienced and expressed is very much an individual matter and is influenced by social and cultural norms.

"Mourning" refers to what one does with one's grief or, more precisely, the efforts one makes to manage grief. Trying to cope with loss is both an individual task and one that normally is aided by social support and community rituals. When the loss, grief, and bereavement are disenfranchised, as Doka (1989, 2002) has shown, opportunities are closed off for open acknowledgment, public mourning, and receiving social support as a bereaved person. One problem with anticipatory mourning is that while well-recognized forms of social ritual are designed to help bereaved persons after a death, this kind of support is typically not available before a death. People may develop their own informal rituals to support anticipatory mourning. Some ethnic and religious groups have rituals connected with caring for the dying, and hospice programs often encourage life review and funeral planning as part of coping with an expected death. However, family members may find few ways to receive social support when they are anticipating a loss through death.

Grieving persons are often told, "Be strong," "Put a smile on your face," "Pull yourself together," or "Don't dwell on bad feelings." This kind of advice is meant to urge them to manage or cope with their losses and grief reactions in certain socially approved ways. Such advice may serve the needs of those around the grieving person but may not be useful for the mourner. Rather, the grieving person needs to engage in constructive mourning processes to cope with the grief reactions and begin to develop ways of living in a world that has been changed by a current or impending loss.

Unfortunately, Edgar Allan Poe sought to cope with the anticipated loss of his wife and with his extreme grief reactions by turning to alcohol to block out or erase his pain. Attempting to manage one's losses and grief in this way is, at best, only a temporary mode of coping. It does not alter the situation; when one sobers up, all the pain remains unaltered.

FOREWARNING AND ANTICIPATION

To be forewarned about the likelihood of a possible loss is to be alerted to the fact that it might occur at some point in the future. Sudden, unexpected deaths by definition rule out the possibility of forewarning. In the cases we are considering, however, the Wagners and the Sullivans had been warned by their physicians of the likelihood of Joan's and Julie's deaths. At first, they were reluctant to accept the warnings. All of us, throughout our lives, hear warnings about things that might happen. Often we dismiss the warnings or do not take them too seriously. Sometimes we acknowledge a warning but assume that the potential loss is not as bad as it might seem or that it will not occur until some time in the distant future. In their initial reactions, the Wagners and Sullivans illustrate that forewarning does not mean that the death will be anticipated or accepted, at least not at first and, for some people, never.

This fact is important for family members and professional and volunteer care providers to understand. It helps explain why persons who are warned of the likelihood of their own death or the death of someone they love may not acknowledge the warning or act on it. For example, they may not complete advance directives, engage in end-of-life planning, or take steps to ensure that people or projects they value will be taken care of after a death. In other words, forewarning is not a sufficient condition for realistic anticipation. Anticipation depends on forewarning, but forewarning does not necessarily lead to anticipation. If one had no forewarning or reason to expect that a death or other loss might occur, one would have no reason to anticipate its occurrence. One might have a pessimistic outlook about the future or even be anxious about what might lie ahead, but that would not necessarily lead to anticipatory grief and mourning.

Forewarning eventually led Poe, Ned Wagner, and Carol Sullivan to anticipate the death of the person they loved. That anticipation led to grief reactions and coping processes. Only Joe Sullivan was unwilling until the last moment to accept the likelihood of his daughter's death. He did not fully believe the warnings he received, choosing instead to try to manage the situation by seeking ways to discount those warnings and somehow save his daughter's life.

GRIEF AND MOURNING IN RELATION TO ANTICIPATED LOSS

As noted previously, Rando (1988) suggested that the adjective "anticipatory" is not always used correctly when people speak or write about anticipatory grief and mourning. In the course of an illness or dying trajectory, those who are involved will experience a shifting series of losses. At any point in the process, some losses will already have occurred, others will be in process, and some will be in the future. Only the future losses can be said to be anticipated. Much was going on while Joan was dying; not all of it was about loss and not all the losses could be described as anticipated.

For example, when the Wagners decided to enroll Joan in a hospice program, they did so in recognition of the heightened level of care she then required and in anticipation of her approaching death. Joan needed more care because she had already experienced a number of losses—she had lost energy and become weaker, she had given up her job, and she was bedfast. These are all past losses with which Joan and Ned appeared to have come to terms. Including them in the sphere of anticipatory grief and mourning stretches the concept of "anticipation" beyond recognition.

The future was becoming clearer to Joan and Ned, but they might not have been able to fully appreciate it until they started living it. They discussed their expectations with the hospice staff. Very likely, the hospice staff tried to help them develop realistic ideas about what lay ahead, at least in the short term. As they formed those ideas, they experienced grief reactions and mourning processes related to the losses they expected. The anticipated losses included Joan's death but also losses that could be expected in the intervening weeks and months, such as increased physical discomfort, problems with memory or recognition of others, slipping into a coma, and missed opportunities to be part of treasured events.

GRIEF AND MOURNING: BEFORE AND AFTER A DEATH

A great deal of confusion exists about grief and mourning before a death and after a death. Misunderstanding of the relationship between predeath and postdeath experiences results in misinterpretation of anticipatory grief and mourning. Such misinterpretation has led some research and clinical responses astray in this field.

Fulton once characterized the misunderstood links as the "hydrological theory of grief." He meant that we act as if grief were a large bucket of tears, and that if we can pour out some of the tears before the death occurs, we will have fewer to pour out after it occurs. Thus, many researchers have focused attention on anticipatory grief and mourning in the hope that it will somehow remove or at least reduce the need for grief and mourning after the death. Although human life is not sharply divided into disconnected segments, grief and mourning address different realities before and after a death. As Fulton (2003, p. 348) wrote, "'Anticipatory grief' is not simply grief begun in advance: it is different from post-mortem grief both in duration and form."

Consider again the example of Edgar Allan Poe. His anticipatory grief involved depression, a type of insanity, and a "horrible never-ending oscillation between hope & despair." All this occurred while Virginia Poe was still alive. Her death provided Poe with "a permanent cure" and "a new but—oh God! how melancholy an existence." Because the losses he experienced and the challenges he faced before and after his wife's death were quite different, his predeath and postdeath grief and mourning also differed in significant ways.

Many people in our society die at an advanced age from degenerative or chronic diseases that involve a long dying trajectory. Family members have typically been warned that death is the likely outcome, and many experience anticipatory grief and mourning. Still, as they often report, when the death actually took place, they found themselves encountering a new reality with a new form of grief and a new need to mourn. Some were surprised when this happened, but knowledgeable care providers explained that now they were grieving and mourning the finality of death and the new losses that follow. Death and its aftermath evoke reactions and responses that family members might not have expected.

Anticipatory grief and mourning are responses to the expectation of death or loss; postmortem grief and mourning are responses to the reality of that death or loss. Once the anticipated loss has occurred, postmortem grief and mourning may last from the moment of death through the rest of the bereaved person's life.

NOT JUST DEATH

This chapter has concentrated on anticipatory grief and mourning as they are associated with expected death-related losses. The concentration was chosen with an eye to the audience for this book and the teleconference with which it is associated. However, an illness or dying trajectory may include many losses and challenges, and any of them may evoke anticipatory grief reactions and anticipatory mourning tasks or processes. Death itself need not be the sole focus of anticipatory grief and mourning.

Furthermore, anticipatory grief and mourning are not exclusively restricted to death-related events. Many experiences in life can evoke grief reactions and mourning responses. A person might be facing the amputation of a body part, the termination of a social status that has meant a great deal, the end of a relationship with a significant other, the birth of a handicapped child, the need to euthanize a cherished pet, or the threat of an approaching hurricane. What is common in all these and many other experiences of significant loss is the sense that one is about to be robbed of something that is valued, that one feels bereft, and that one must find ways to live without that which will soon be taken away. The fact of the loss, one's perception of its value, the multiple dimensions that it often entails, and the disruption or disequilibrium that it imposes on one's life are all central to grief reactions and mourning responses. Whenever one expects a loss of this type, one may experience anticipatory grief and mourning.

GUIDELINES FOR CARE PROVIDERS

On the basis of this analysis of anticipatory grief and mourning, the following 11 guidelines are suggested for anyone who is providing care to persons who are experiencing anticipatory grief and mourning.

- Be available; be present; listen. People who are experiencing anticipatory grief and mourning may or may not share with you their reactions and responses to the losses they are experiencing and anticipating, but they will never do so if you are not available, present, and actively listening. Ask questions and make observations that encourage them to share their concerns. Listen to what they say...and to what they do not say. Pay attention to verbal and nonverbal communications, to literal and symbolic disclosures.

- Meet people where they are. Acknowledge that it is acceptable for them to grieve and mourn when anticipating major losses, because these losses are important and may even be life-changing for them and their families.

- Prepare yourself to encounter grief reactions in various forms: physical, psychological (cognitive and affective), behavioral, social, and spiritual. Do not limit or fail to appreciate a person's grief reactions because of preconceptions or misunderstandings about anticipatory grief.

- Allow persons who are experiencing and expressing anticipatory grief reactions to do so in whatever ways they need; only reactions that are directly harmful to the person or to others are inappropriate.

- Allow persons who are engaged in anticipatory mourning tasks and processes to do so in whatever ways they need. Do not limit or fail to appreciate all of a person's mourning tasks and processes because of preconceptions or misunderstandings about anticipatory mourning, or lack of appreciation for familial, social, ethnic, or religious customs. Allow those who are involved in anticipatory mourning tasks and processes to do so in whatever ways they need; only tasks and processes that are directly harmful to the person or to others are inappropriate.

- Expect to encounter different perspectives. Some people may be experiencing anticipatory grief and mourning, while others may not. People may view anticipated losses in quite different ways.

- Expect the passage of time and changes in the situation to affect anticipatory grief and mourning. Ask what the primary focus of concern is for the person at the present moment. Do not be surprised if the focus of concern changes. Life is not static; neither are anticipatory grief and mourning. Assess and reassess each time you come to offer help.

- Even during an illness or dying trajectory, loss, grief, and mourning are not likely to take up the whole of a person's life. Anniversaries and holidays may be celebrated, reconciliations may be achieved, "unfinished business" and last wishes may be pursued. Dying persons and those who are anticipating other losses are human beings with their own priorities. Pressures associated with impending death may make the available time especially precious.

- Providing care and being cared for by persons who are experiencing anticipatory grief and mourning are important roles for family members and close friends, although they may benefit from support from trained volunteers and professionals.

- Much can be done to minimize distress and improve quality of life for persons who are experiencing anticipatory grief and mourning. Help is best offered on the basis of a realistic assessment of one's own strengths and limitations, and with the support of an interdisciplinary team of helpers who can draw on each other's strengths and limitations. Enabling people to grieve as they should and cope as they must is the noble work of helping in a context of life-threatening illness and anticipated losses.

- The more we can learn about anticipatory grief and mourning, the better we will be as helpers and as fellow human beings. In the long term, better understanding and appreciation are a constant goal; in the short term, heightened sensitivity and genuine caring are most highly prized. As Carl Jung once said about theories in psychology, "[W]e need certain points of view for their orienting and heuristic value; but they should always be regarded as mere auxiliary concepts that can be laid aside at any time" (Jung, 1954, p. 7).

CONCLUDING THOUGHTS

Grief reactions to anticipated death or loss are not inherently positive or negative. Everything depends on the nature of the reaction, how it is experienced, and how it is expressed. Similarly, engaging in anticipatory mourning to cope with impending death or loss is neither inherently positive nor negative. Everything depends on whether the coping tasks and processes promote productive living before and after the death or loss is realized.

For the most part, anticipatory grief and mourning are healthy and constructive experiences. As a general rule, it is better to have opportunities for anticipatory grief and mourning than to be confronted by a sudden, unanticipated death or loss. Anticipation provides opportunities to prepare for expected events, to develop productive coping strategies, and to mobilize assistance. We should not minimize opportunities for people to experience anticipatory grief and mourning. Nor should we minimize the roles of those who are privileged to foster understanding, offer support, and provide help to these persons. ■

Charles A. Corr, PhD, CT, is a member of the Board of Directors, The Hospice Institute of the Florida Suncoast, the Executive Committee of the National Donor Family Council, the ChiPPS (Children's Project on Palliative/Hospice Services) Leadership Advisory Council of the National Hospice and Palliative Care Organization, the Association for Death Education and Counseling, and the International Work Group on Death, Dying, and Bereavement (Chairperson, 1989-93). He is also professor emeritus, Southern Illinois University Edwardsville. Dr. Corr's publications include 30 books and booklets, along with more than 100 articles and chapters, in the field of death, dying, and bereavement. His most recent publication is the fifth edition of Death and Dying, Life and Living *(Thomson Wadsworth, 2006), co-authored with Clyde M. Nabe and Donna M. Corr.*

REFERENCES

Doka, K. J. (Ed.). (1989). *Disenfranchised grief: Recognizing hidden sorrow.* Lexington, MA: Lexington Books.

Doka, K. J. (Ed.). (2002). *Disenfranchised grief: New directions, strategies, and challenges for practice.* Champaign, IL: Research Press.

Elias, N. (1991). On human beings and their emotions: A process-sociological essay. In M. Featherstone, M. Hepworth, & B. S. Turner (Eds.), *The body: Social process and cultural theory* (pp. 103-125). London: Sage.

Fulton, R. (2003). Anticipatory mourning: A critique of the concept. *Mortality, 8,* 342-351.

Fulton, R., & Fulton, J. (1971). A psychosocial aspect of terminal care: Anticipatory grief. *Omega, Journal of Death and Dying, 2,* 91-100.

Fulton, R., & Fulton, J. (1972). Anticipatory grief: A psychosocial aspect of terminal care. In B. Schoenberg, A. C. Carr, D. Peretz, & A. H. Kutscher (Eds.), *Psychosocial aspects of terminal care* (pp. 227-242). New York: Columbia University Press.

Fulton, R., & Gottesman, D. J. (1980). Anticipatory grief: A psychosocial concept reconsidered. *British Journal of Psychiatry, 137,* 45-54.

Futterman, E. H., Hoffman, I., & Sabshin, M. (1972). Parental anticipatory mourning. In B. Schoenberg, A. C. Carr, D. Peretz, & A. H. Kutscher (Eds.), *Psychosocial aspects of terminal care* (pp. 243-272). New York: Columbia University Press.

Jung, C. G. (1954). The development of personality (Vol. 17). In H. Read, M. Fordham, & G. Adler (Eds.), *The collected works of C. G. Jung* (2nd ed.; 20 vols.). New York: Pantheon.

Lindemann, E. (1944). Symptomatology and management of acute grief. *American Journal of Psychiatry, 101,* 143-148.

Poe, E. A. (1948). *The letters of Edgar Allan Poe* (2 vols.). J. W. Ostrom (Ed.). Cambridge, MA: Harvard University Press.

Rando, T. A. (Ed.). (1986). *Loss and anticipatory grief.* Lexington, MA: Lexington Books.

Rando, T. A. (1988). Anticipatory grief: The term is a misnomer but the phenomenon exists. *Journal of Palliative Care, 4*(1/2), 70-73.

Rando, T. A. (Ed.). (2000a). *Clinical dimensions of anticipatory mourning: Theory and practice in working with the dying, their loved ones, and their caregivers.* Champaign, IL: Research Press.

Rando, T. A. (2000b). Anticipatory mourning: A review and critique of the literature. In T. A. Rando (Ed.), *Clinical dimensions of anticipatory mourning: Theory and practice in working with the dying, their loved ones, and their caregivers* (pp. 17-50). Champaign, IL: Research Press.

Schoenberg, B., Carr, A., Kutscher, A. H., Peretz, D., & Goldberg, I. (Eds.). (1974). *Anticipatory grief.* New York: Columbia University Press.

A Chunk of Crystal

Elizabeth Uppman

When Gabriel was nine months old, I had a moment of clarity. I was stopped at a stoplight in front of the grocery store, crying and not caring who saw me cry—sobbing, actually, in a drastic but inevitable way, like a tree when it finally falls. I had just realized that he was going to die.

At nine months, babies are supposed to suck on their mothers' car keys, swab the floor with their tummies, and holler from their cribs. The baby in the car seat behind me didn't do any of that. He stiffened his limbs and turned his head with the slow stateliness of a door closing. His large eyes, blue on the outside and gray-green near the pupils, usually looked up and left, bouncing sometimes at the edge of the eye-slit, rolling and skittering, fixing on nothing, the lids fluttering. They looked dumb as in deaf-and-dumb. They were gutted. They were heartbreaking.

Cerebral palsy will do that to a person. But cerebral palsy isn't fatal. I knew that. I was thinking of something else. The trigger, the tipping-point to my knowing, wasn't his stiffness or his gutted eyes—it was his broken thermostat. Sometimes Gabriel's temperature soared off the top of the thermometer, and I would

Continued

pour baby Tylenol down his throat and swab off his hot red cheeks. Other times I would pick him up from his crib and find him cool to the touch, like a cabbage fresh out of the crisper, and then I would wrap us both in a Mexican poncho and breathe on him and rub his arms. That day in the car, musing on these spikes and dips, I thought of how horses and dogs and mice all had brains capable of regulating their body temperature. Even snakes knew when to bask and when to find shade. But not Gabriel.

That's when I knew we would fail. We could try to control his temperature, cure his frequent infections, teach his eyes to focus, force his limbs to bend, but let's face it: the delicate biological system in the carseat behind me was careening out of control. "He can't last," I sobbed to the red light and the grocery store and the empty sky. "He can't *last.*"

Almost three years later, Gabriel died of pneumonia in the pediatric intensive care unit.

■ ■ ■

When I look back at myself sobbing at the stoplight, what strikes me most is that I never stopped to wonder how I could foretell with such certainty the death of my son. It simply came to me, like a weighty chunk of crystal, too big to turn away from. It came like a gift, actually, and I carried it with me always.

I told several people, obliquely, of my premonition, and I got a variety of reactions. A friend on the phone said, "Um, do you have anyone you could talk to? A psychologist or something?" Another began e-mailing me inspirational poems. My husband Chucho pointed out two things: my own family's legacy of longevity, and Gabriel's fighting spirit, which had brought him through many days in the intensive care unit. When Chucho saw me looking at Gabriel in a particular way, he would blurt out, "He's not going to die, okay?"

But the surgery made things worse, and the medicines didn't work, and Gabriel spent many nights in the hospital with the hissing oxygen and the kid crying down the hall. And pretty soon a doctor led Chucho and me to a windowless room where he sat us down and talked about hospice. Gabriel's death became undeniable, as true as stone.

And yet—and yet—it couldn't be true. All the books and movies about sick kids end with some kind of triumph—a cure, a breakthrough, hugs all around. A mother ought to strive for the movie ending. A mother doesn't give up. Does she? Do mothers sometimes give up?

That was my struggle. I lived for a long time in the gap between knowing he was going to die and not giving up on him. I bounced between those two perspectives like a pinball. Take the problem of the minivan. We needed one, the kind you can roll a wheelchair onto, because Gabriel was getting too heavy for me to lift. But I resisted buying one, not because I thought Gabriel would ever learn to walk but because I thought he would die before we needed it. And at the same time, I took him to physical therapy, where they did exercises to help him stand and take steps. I still didn't believe he would walk, but it would be wrong not to try.

I did those and many other contradictory things. I did them with a variety of contradictory feelings. Sometimes all of it—the braces, the doctor appointments, the expensive wheelchair— seemed like a pretend life, a show we put on to fool the gods of health and propriety. Sometimes the truth of the crystal seemed like a shameful thing to carry, a dirty secret. When I felt like that, I couldn't sit still. I yelled at a couple of nurses. I yelled at my

Continued

husband. I still regret that. "Grief" is such a quiet word; it makes you think of women in black shawls, silent and lovely. But the grieving aren't lovely. The grieving are a pain in the neck. And when everyone in the house is grieving, nobody can comfort anybody else. It's dreadful work.

And here again, I look back and wonder at how, clearly, much of that anguish came from believing that Gabriel was going to die. Why didn't I say no, to the doctors or to the gods? Why didn't I insist, like some mothers do, that *this will not happen to us?*

I couldn't. I had to let myself know what I knew. It had become precious to me, my little crystal of truth that I could neither embrace nor ignore. Perhaps it was the only thing I could count on.

■　■　■

I remember sitting with Gabriel one morning on his big bed by the window. I always did the morning feeding and meds, which shouldn't have taken long except that I couldn't do it without feeling bad about how things were turning out for us, what with the suction machine and the infernal beeping monitor and the sweet, sweet smell of the stuff we poured down his feeding tube. So I was holding Gabriel and dutifully feeling bad while he slept, his head against my arm. And I was thinking about the friend who had come to visit the week before, how she had tried to hold Gabriel but could not manage his stiffness, his arched back and rigid legs. I though of how she had turned to Chucho and me, bewildered, for help.

It was hard to hold Gabriel—just to hold him—and not invoke that stiffness. You had to keep the back of his head from pressing against anything. You had to push up on the ball of his foot to make his knee bend, and when this made him supple, you quickly tucked his hips into a tight bend and held them there. And if you managed to get his arms in front of his body and avoided touching his cheek, and if when he arched out again you started over, and if you were quiet and patient and did these things again and again, then he might eventually relax in your arms. He might sleep.

So I held him, sleeping, and I felt his heaviness and his trust, and I looked up to the ceiling where the ghosts were and I nodded. Once. Because we were doing about as good a job as we could do, Gabriel and I. We were doing our jobs, and we were doing them with the little shreds of hope that remained to us, and we just kept on doing them. Whether we would prevail or not, whether this story would turn into a made-for-TV movie or a blurb on the obituary page, it was our story. For a moment I was at peace with my knowing.

I leaned down and kissed Gabriel's hair.

■ CHAPTER 2 ■

Life Review, Paradox, and Self-Esteem

James J. Magee

The developmental benefits of life review occur because the reminiscing process gives older adults repeated opportunities to reflect on their personal history and accept responsibility for it. It is a process in which reviewers gradually reconstruct and assess their past, using their current values to weigh behavior that their memory progressively returns to consciousness. Life review focuses attention on the connections between their past and their current sense of themselves, evoking memories of formative experiences that influenced their personal development.

Life review is a normal, integrative process that occurs throughout the life cycle, peaking during the fifth decade and remaining strong thereafter. It usually proceeds circuitously through reverie, reflection, dreams, diary or journal entries, correspondence, and storytelling. The process can be spontaneous or planned, solitary or in groups. Reviewers recall long-forgotten incidents, dwell on them, and recapture the emotions that originally accompanied them, often while trying to convey these felt experiences to a listener.

These reminiscences are usually vivid, accompanied by pleasant or uncomfortable emotions of varying intensity. They may focus on any period of the life cycle and any aspect of a person's life. The underlying theme that unifies the recollections is the goal of integrating them in an acceptance of oneself here and now (Haight & Webster, 2002).

Achieving self-acceptance is a task with several dimensions. Looking toward the past, it requires readiness to take responsibility for one's life story and locate it in the historical and cultural contexts that affected it. Looking at the present, it draws on one's ability to savor the satisfactions derived throughout the life cycle and to forgive oneself for harm done and good not done. Looking toward the future, it includes the capacity to anticipate needs and plan for the most satisfying ways to meet them (Magee, 1988).

Reminiscences are often precipitated by retirement and by an increase in aging-related decrements. Retirement, by severing older adults from significant, gratifying roles and relationships, endows memories of seemingly trivial events with value beyond their original character, since these memories are the principal links to the person's previous identity (McAdams, 1993). Some older adults intentionally reminisce about former occupational and social roles to claim role parity with or superiority to those on whom they are now dependent. Others use their past as a reservoir of entertaining tales and for problem-solving precedents to help them address uncomfortable decisions that confront them in the present.

Identification with the competence and self-determination that characterized their performance in earlier decades tempers the painful constriction of personal autonomy arising from failing physical capacities and patronizing societal expectations. In addition, the increasing proximity of death enables life review to become a form of anticipatory grief work and a part of letting go (Garland, 2001).

THE ROLE OF CONFIDANTS AND FEEDBACK

Ongoing clusters of aging-related diminishments that threaten health, relationships, and empowering roles can evoke reminiscences with corresponding themes of inadequacy and disillusion. Current crises tend to elicit memories of comparable unresolved issues. For most older adults, however, the hazard of obsessive rumination precipitating prolonged and profound mood swings is usually dispelled if they can share their life review with a confidant or receive feedback from other reminiscence group members.

Those who share their memories and self-assessment with a confidant can transcend their own selective memories. A confidant, for instance, can point out the good character hidden in the shy person's memory of timorous advocacy for someone oppressed, the impatient person's disgruntled forbearance with someone inept, or the fastidious person's slender hospitality toward an unexpected guest. When the reviewer focuses on a failure of character, the confidant does not engage in debate but remarks on the reviewer's courage in getting through the scene in real life and in returning to it now, despite the discomfort involved. Finally, emotionally charged issues often lead to memories of early family relationships. A confidant who is familiar with the family lore, and may even have a close relationship with the extended family, can help the reviewer bring some closure to these issues (Kotre, 1995).

Seventy-seven-year-old Florence had been sexually inhibited throughout her life. She told a friend in their assisted living residence that she had not attended a movie or live theater show for the past 50 years because she had become so anxious about "having to monitor my reactions to plots, scenes, and dialog that might be salacious." This prompted her friend to confess that she still shyly followed her mother's example of asking the butcher for "chicken chests" rather than "chicken breasts." They could laugh, because now neither felt alone. Both had finally distinguished the differences between inhibition and modesty. They decided to start shouting out during movies shown at the residence, "Here comes a hot scene!"

Matthew was a retired fire chief. His reminiscences were replete with incidents in which he rejected his supposed "rejecters" by spitefully thwarting their authority. For instance, when he admitted to his second grade teacher, "I can't do this math problem," she replied that "can't" was not permitted in his vocabulary and held a conference with his parents. They concurred with the teacher and set aside a shelf in the living room to hold the academic trophies that they assured him he would win when he applied himself. Matthew "showed" them by forgoing college and joining the fire department directly after high school. After his parents' deaths he started taking college courses in the evenings and took the examinations that culminated in his being appointed chief. This regimen, however, made him an absentee father to his sons and left his wife an "examination widow."

He saw his distant parenting as the pattern for the current alienation between his sons and their children. Of course, whenever he offered them advice, he only "made the mess worse."

These reminiscences prompted a weekly visitor, the driver of the chief's official car, to say that he saw parallels between his family relationships and those of the chief. His own grandparents had mislabeled their children's efforts at self-expression as disloyalty or eccentricity; this attitude had, in turn, affected his parents' parenting. He encouraged Matthew to read histories, biographies, and historical fiction about political, economic, and religious issues that could have shaped his grandparents' attitudes toward his parents. What Matthew learned about the intractability of these issues and about family survival strategies over generations fed a warmer acceptance of himself and a respectful indulgence toward his children and grandchildren. "I give no lectures, just tell stories. Whenever an ancestor 'messed up,' I show how I did much the same. I leave it up to the younger folks to figure out that there may be no exemptions for them, either."

SELF-ESTEEM AND LIFE REVIEW

Like everyone else, older adults fall along a continuum of self-esteem; that is, the abiding judgment we make about our competence and worth, the lens through which we review our personal history and discern meaning in our lives (Branden, 1994). At one end are people with hearty self-esteem. Their reminiscences disclose that, as children, they internalized the positive regard their caregivers had for them and then proceeded through life with the conviction that they were inherently "good enough." For them, an experience of shame was a signal that their behavior was inconsistent with their own ideals, and they usually responded by bringing their behavior into line. As older adults, they enjoy self-confidence and self-respect, and believe that who they are and what they do continue to matter.

At the other end of the continuum are people who entered adulthood with self-esteem in tatters. Theirs is a shame transmitted over generations and embedded in their childhood's emerging, tentative self. As children, they responded to insufficiently empathic attitudes of caregivers by fusing shame and identity, and throughout life they have lived with a haunting assumption that they are "fundamentally defective, unworthy, not fully valid as a human being" (Lewis, 1995, p. 11). Not surprisingly, the life review of these older adults focuses on memories of injuries inflicted and received, missed opportunities, and recycled patterns of dysfunctional behaviors. They obsess that their inferiority was exposed to others who scornfully concurred in their self-assessment. Caught in the circularity of viewing themselves through the distorted lens of their own shame, they thwart the developmental potential of life review. To recover this potential, reminiscing must occur from a different, more gracious lens, a perspective that reframes troublesome memories.

The following section will examine how paradoxes provide more compassionate perspectives from which shame-filled older adults can assess their life review. These perspectives do not raise the basic level of reviewers' self-esteem. They do, however, elicit assessments of memories that are characteristic of higher levels self-esteem and stretch reviewers to embrace a self-acceptance that had been beyond them. Reviewers can measure their progress by discerning how their reminiscences now facilitate their ability to do the following:

- Allow them to make mistakes rather than raising blame-protection as the primary consideration in decision making (Schneider, 1992)

- Base decisions on what is in their best interest rather than bypassing shame and attending, instead, to emotions less acutely distressing (e.g., guilt, anger, and depression) or to the addictions and eating disorders that shame fuels (Nichols, 1991)

- Own their thoughts, statements, and actions rather than projecting onto others the impulses and personality characteristics that elicit shame in themselves (Nathanson, 1992)

- Evaluate themselves realistically rather than depreciating their competitors and fantasizing themselves as superior

- Rely on their own informed conscience and problem-managing capability rather than conforming to others' expectations, continually seeking positive feedback, and withholding their own opinions (California Task Force, 1990)

- Express feelings frequently and directly rather then anxiously monitoring any spontaneous behavior

- Draw upon multiple, benign metaphors that transcend their childish comprehension of God as Judge

GUIDING PARADOXES

Guiding paradoxes are the strategies I use to enable reviewers to stretch their self-esteem. To the reminiscence groups I facilitate, I explain that these paradoxes are seemingly contradictory statements pertaining to shame-inducing themes that recur in life review. The paradoxes alter the frames of reference from which older adults have been evaluating past events and "change the meaning and value of the events without changing the facts" (Bednar, Wells, & Peterson, 1989, p. 20). They stimulate a creative tension by seeking *both-and* answers to *either-or* dilemmas. As contradictions, paradoxes cause a dissonance that frustrates unquestioned acceptance of shame-driven interpretations. At the same time, they draw reviewers to syntheses that transcend the contradictions and offer novel perspectives for reviewing memories. By considering memories from these several viewpoints, reviewers can appreciate the significance of details they had previously overlooked, for example, the tenacity of specific issues over generations, extenuating circumstances surrounding decisions, and ambiguity about the meaning of people's intent and behavior (Magee, 2002).

I use three kinds of guiding paradoxes with life review groups: paradoxical wordplay, dream analysis, and the metaphysical self.

Paradoxical Wordplay

Paradoxical wordplay is an engaging method of discovering alternative meanings that reviewers can attribute to their memories. To prepare a reminiscence group to use the paradoxes, I provide a cache of sources (period music scores, decades-old *New York Times* front pages, anthologies of poems and plays, books of children's rhymes), and ask the participants to look through them and list examples of paradoxical wordplay that they found meaningful.

One kind of wordplay consists of the poetic metaphors older adults choose for themselves. Many people find that poetry is an inexhaustible resource that revives significant memories, captures the emotional tone of scenes from their past, and expresses the meaning that these scenes now hold for them. Those who have few literary associations refer to the lyrics of songs and family jingles in lieu of poems.

Delia, for example, was an 81-year-old caregiver for her diabetic husband. She avoided mentioning her own needs, since her family regarded references to one's needs as weakness. Her received family motto was simply, "You have to dip-to-rise on your own" (i.e., learn how to cope with a new situation until you achieve a higher level of performance). The process never ended, however, as solutions to earlier problems became new problems and accrued knowledge became obsolete. Even harder for Delia, she seemed to "dip" without a corresponding "rise." Her life review revealed that, in the course of a single year, she had added the following to her regular schedule of work in her husband's picture frame shop: babysitting her granddaughter, caring for her terminally ill father, and attending to her mother's clinical despondency.

In reframing her recollections, Delia saw how her exhausting self-denial had been, in fact, a denial that she even had a self. She tempered a mood of depression by peacefully reciting from "The Hound of Heaven," by Francis Thompson:

> Is my gloom, after all,
> Shade of His hand outstretched caressingly?

Delia saw that over the decades she had "risen" repeatedly simply to cope with crises. When a colleague interjected at this point, "But the 'rises' feel slight compared to the severity of the 'dips,'" she replied, "No problem. I know my mood is a caress. I acclaim it so each time I sing our African-American anthem, 'Lift Every Voice and Sing':

> Shadowed beneath Thy hand,
> May we forever stand.

■

Timid 87-year-old Madelyn shared how she zealously conformed throughout her career to supervisors' expectations, too anxious "even once to speak the truth to power." She dignified her earlier self-image with a metaphor from Samuel Taylor Coleridge's "Rime of the Ancient Mariner":

> Fear at my heart, as at a cup,
> My life-blood seemed to sip!

She said, "But now I am intent on visiting my favorite harbors as I continue my nautical journey in my mind." Then, quoting from Alfred Lord Tennyson's "Ulysses," she added, "and I mean to make this other traveler's words my own:"

Old age hath yet his honor and his toil.

Madelyn's "honor" now lay in the courage to replace her openness to others' expectations with a new, unmonitored openness toward her own feelings, motives, and personal experiences.

■

The oldest participant, 93-year-old retired schoolteacher Veronica, used a metaphor that regally epitomized her group's vital task of accomplishing ego integrity. Erik Erikson describes this accomplishment as "the acceptance of one's one and only life cycle as something that had to be and that, by necessity, permitted of no other substitutions (Erikson, 1963, p. 87)." Veronica captured Erikson's challenge with her recitation from Percy Bysshe Shelley's "Ode to the West Wind":

Make me thy lyre, ev'n as the forest is:
What if my leaves are falling as its own?
The tumult of thy mighty harmonies
Will take from both a deep autumnal tone.

She passionately articulated her awareness that a rich quality of life in her own autumnal season involved imperceptible, yet nonetheless heroic, alterations within herself. Not least among them was giving up the notion that her self-acceptance could occur without some "tumult."

■ ■ ■

A second type of wordplay that I introduce is buried in homonyms from the reviewers' own speech. Group members are asked to bring to one another's attention that they are using two or more words that sound alike but differ in meaning. I encourage them to free-associate about the alternative meanings of the soundmate of a homonym that a reviewer uses. This feedback disrupts the problematic mood initially arising from the reminiscence and creates an opportunity for the reviewer to reapply the intended meaning of the homonym as a novel, refreshing viewpoint from which to approach memories.

■

For example, Agatha, a 74-year-old lawyer, was forced to retire because of emphysema. Her life review focused on the compulsivity with which she had approached her career and her painfully meticulous preparations for courtroom presentations. Her colleagues pointed out her repeated use of "read" as a homonym term. She responded that read/reed did have resonance for her. She recited a text she had heard often in church as a young girl: "A bruised reed He will not break; and a smoking flax He will not quench" (Isaiah 42:3). She added, "But that's the trouble. I bruised myself continuously—obsessing over details, concealing the conviction that I was less competent than my colleagues, driven and unable to relax—and all that time succeeded as a lawyer. Excruciatingly, I could always manage both to suffer and read."

Though her forced retirement had stirred feelings of depression, she hoped that her reminiscence group colleagues could accept her as a "bruised reed" that did not have to justify its existence. She recognized that her compulsive preparations had been her way of keeping depression and shame at bay, and at last she was allowing herself to feel them.

■

Constance, age 79, and Nell, age 76, were sisters who lived in separate apartments at a development for older adults. They argued vigorously with each other or exchanged sarcastic swipes, only briefly and intermittently making peace. Whatever the disagreement, the topic invariably included their lifelong grievances. Constance complained that she and her late husband had had to rescue Nell repeatedly from "the sordid relationships and financial ruin" that accompanied her sister's alcoholism. Nell excoriated Constance for her self-righteousness and controlling intrusiveness. However, in doing the "homework" assignment, Nell had read the score from Show Boat and "had a new take" on their relationship. "We've kept at each other all this time because that's how we show we care. It hit me when I caught the paradox in 'We Could Make Believe I Love You.' The song requires that the singer already be in love in order to make believe. So, today, Constance, let's begin by making believe we love each other."

Lennie, a retired landscaper who now kept a critical eye on the residence groundskeepers, gave his opinion: "I'm not worried about you two working out your differences. Your family tree, like a hickory, has an anchoring *taproot* that conducts all the nutrients you need." Constance replied, "The only *tap route* Nell knows is the map to a pub." With gentle humor, Nell broke the tension by adapting a line from the Marquise de Sévigné, "Constance, you lack only a few vices to be perfect."

■

Seventy-eight-year-old Gladys, hemiplegic since her stroke seven years earlier, was not able to speak clearly enough to express herself, so she had made copies of these lines from Christopher Fry's *The Lady's Not for Burning*:

I travel light; as light
That is, as a man can travel who is
Still carrying his body around because
Of its sentimental value.

She added this postscript:

Silence means *assent*, and I hope that my halted voice somehow expresses acceptance of my condition. You are looking at a woman who is graced in her infirmities. Over the past seven years I have had many dips emotionally, but now I am in ascent. The very limits the stroke imposed are vantage points that give the grandest perspective on my life. From Edmund Waller's Old Age, consider:

The soul's dark cottage, battered and decayed,
Lets in new light through chinks that Time hath made.

Dream Analysis

The second kind of guiding paradox is older adults' interpretations of their dreams. In introducing dream analysis, I explain the interplay between reminiscing and dreaming. The long-term memories raised in life review groups are fertile catalysts for evoking thematically similar dreams. Dreams, in turn, raise in metaphorical imagery themes that reviewers may have ignored, weighed too lightly, or failed to use in resolving current problems. When group members understand dreaming as "simply the form our consciousness takes at night to make us aware of our feelings" (Ullman & Zimmerman, 1979, p. 52), they can more readily grasp how dreams can help them discern emotional issues in their life review.

I explain that though metaphors in dreams appear as a variety of persons, objects, colors, sounds, and situations, they generally represent aspects of the dreamers themselves. Thus, reviewers need to identify the associations-any word, mental picture, feeling, or memory—that occur to them as they speculate about the revelation a metaphor is making to them about themselves. Eventually, they will feel drawn to attribute one meaning more than any other to a given metaphor (Johnson, 1986).

■

Eric, for example, had dreamed three nights during the week that he was free-body flying. He was a recently retired corporate executive who had joined the Y's reminiscence group primarily because it was scheduled shortly after he finished his daily racquetball "competition." (The term was his own for an activity that others referred to as a game or exercise.) His life review emphasized two themes: a family history of underachieving men and the character-building quality of "spirited competition" that enabled him to transcend that history. However, he recognized that instead of expressing how he had "soared," his dreams revealed how "sore" his body felt from his racquetball regimen. He shared with the group that he seemed to be resisting the transition to retirement by perpetuating his adversarial attitude.

■

Muriel was a 79-year-old widow who integrated dream interpretation with religious themes in her life review. She had rejected three suitors because their religious affiliation was different from her own. For four decades, she had been a foster parent in her church's child welfare program. She was a lifelong choir member and now a volunteer worker in the church's telephone reassurance program with elderly shut-ins. In the preceding week she had had similar dreams on two consecutive nights.

Although she had not lived away from her parents until she married, in the dreams she appeared as a 12 year old at a summer camp. Each morning the entire camp attended a religious service. In the first dream, she was wearing one shoe and one sneaker. Although campers were expected to wear sneakers, she had lost one when her canoe overturned. She awoke still feeling the dread that her peers would notice and ridicule her. In the second dream, she wore sunglasses in the chapel because her eyes were tearing from the glare of the lights and candles. Again she awoke feeling anxious about the other campers' reactions. In her dream analysis, she attended to many metaphors. She interpreted "being 12" as being in transition and the chapel as the religious identity that tempered each transition in her life. She had married in a chapel and had not "slept away" beforehand. The uncomfortable affect in the dreams, however, led her to revise her perception of her religious identity. Of the many associations she made with footwear and sunglasses, she noticed that her solutions to the problems in both cases drew attention to herself, which she found threatening. The sunglasses suggested that attention to her own needs was equivalent to posing as a starlet. She was showing the ability in her life review to question whether she had loved herself enough while she was trying to love her neighbor.

The Metaphysical Self

The third kind of guiding paradox occurs when older adults review their lives from the perspective of the metaphysical self, which appears in the imagery of many mystical traditions. For mystics, the metaphysical self refers to "the depths of people's hearts where neither sin nor desire nor self-knowledge can reach, the core of their reality, the person that each one is in God's eyes" (Merton, 1966, p. 208). Here God's esteem is the foundation for self-esteem, with each self residing in God's unconditional acceptance. From this perspective, shame-filled older adults can accept themselves because God already has.

The metaphysical self is a paradoxical lens with which to review memories, for it does not enable reviewers to trace how it has healed and sustained them throughout their personal history. They can only approach life review in attentive passivity, awaiting those gifted intimations that may serendipitously reveal the metaphysical self in their reminiscences. One reviewer discerned "how God wrote straight with crooked lines" in her life.

Another recognized a providential design in her life review and applied to it Psalm 139:5: "You have hedged me behind and before, and laid Your hand upon me." A third was able to glimpse in his reminiscences the significance of extenuating circumstances, ambiguities, and nuances of meaning that he had not previously weighed and that now encouraged more compassionate self-acceptance (Magee, 2001).

I assembled from public libraries copies of mystical classics from a variety of religious traditions, highlighted chapters especially relevant to the metaphysical self, and encouraged the participants to read excerpts they found intriguing and exchange them with one another. The culturally idiomatic expression in works from Middle Eastern and Eastern spirituality can be particularly engaging, and typically elicits an expansive exchange of insight, self-disclosure, and continuing feedback. Even residents with no religious beliefs were curious about mysticism and participated in an effort to compare its expression in different traditions.

The following were among the most popular quotations chosen from the sources I distributed:

"The soul is so completely one with God that the one cannot be understood without the other. One can think heat easily enough without fire and the shining without the sun, but God cannot be understood without the soul nor the soul without God, so utterly are they one" (Meister Eckhart, in McGinn, 1986, p. 167).

"One went to the door of the Beloved and knocked. A voice asked, 'Who is there?' He answered, 'It is I.' The voice said, 'There is no room for Me and Thee.' The door was shut. After a year of solitude and deprivation he returned and knocked. A voice from within asked, 'Who is there?' The man said, 'It is Thee.' The door was opened for him" (Kwaja 'Abdullah Ansari, 1978).

"In seeing your true self, He is your mirror and you are His mirror in which He sees nothing other than Himself" (Fakhruddin 'Iraqi, 1982, p. 85).

"Man's essence is only the soul that is within him, which is a portion of God above. Thus, there is nothing in the entire world except the Holy One" (the Maggid of Mezhirech, in Uffenheimer, 1993, p. 74).

"You are my face. No wonder I can't see you" (Rumi, in Breton & Largent, 1998, p. 168).

■

Sarah was an 86-year-old unmarried woman, a retired potter, who had supported herself by selling her fine crockery at fairs along the East Coast. Her compulsive management of time both hid poor self-esteem and ensured prodigious volume. She rigidly scheduled her time and felt agitated whenever she was interrupted or underproductive. This discomfort permeated her life review as well. She repeatedly compared her reputation and productivity to the artistic success of her grandparents and great aunts and uncles in Europe. On a deeper level, she intuited an anger toward her parents for their fervid expectations for her artistic career. She did not actually feel this anger so much as it aggravated a competitiveness that detracted from her ability to delight in her work for its own sake. An indeterminate sense of loss permeated her life review.

She had already perused several of the mystical authors and reported that she had found the metaphysical self to be a theme that evoked a mood of wonder rather than self-criticism. Before, she would have exhumed from her life review incidents of recycled frustration. Now, she appreciated the irony that God's unconditional acceptance of her meant God's embrace of a self in large part prescribed by her family's programming. In fact, she could finally enjoy the paradox that the sources of her personal talents were in her entanglements in family relationships.

Daniel was a retired dentist, 81 years old. He reminisced at length about his lifelong commitment to civil rights. He recalled the challenges in creating dental clinics for migrant workers, mentoring minority interns, and serving Medicaid patients others had turned away. However, he was despondent over his hidden satisfaction in seeing himself as more honorable than those who had not taken the same risks he did. He was fixated on the idea that his work had all been self-serving.

When he finished speaking, group members joined in a spirited discussion about the severe, emotionally loaded words Daniel used to assess himself. A colleague observed that the dentist's concern about the purity of his intentions was preventing him from acknowledging that everyone's behavior is the result of multiple motives. Another commented that he needed to know and love himself with the compassion with which God knows him and loves him. "You're right, of course," Daniel answered. "I recall from the sources we read how God addresses each person, 'As far as my love for you is concerned, it does not matter whether you change or not, for my love for you is unconditional'" (de Mello, 1984, p. 164).

CONCLUSION

Mental health professionals and graduate students in nursing, social work, psychology, pastoral counseling, and gerontology can use the guiding paradoxes to complement their strategies for addressing recalcitrant problems involving older adults' life review. Facilitators conducting groups in senior centers, YMCAs/YWCAs, libraries, parishes, and skilled nursing residences can adopt many of the paradoxes to amplify the benefits of life review. Family members, confidants, clergy, and physicians can use these guidelines for reframing the memories older adults share with them. Older adults who are aware of the benefits of life review can use paradoxes to evoke reminiscences that suffuse their personal history with the conviction that it is good enough. ■

James J. Magee, PhD, is professor emeritus in counseling and gerontology at the Graduate School, College of New Rochelle, where he taught for 30 years. He is the author of A Professional's Guide to Older Adults' Life Review: Releasing the Peace Within *and of 40 journal articles. He is a volunteer in the Pastoral Care Department at Sound Shore Medical Center in New Rochelle.*

REFERENCES

Bednar, R., Wells, M., & Peterson, S. (1989). *Self-esteem: Paradoxes and innovations in clinical theory and practice.* Washington, DC: American Psychological Association.

Branden, N. (1994). *How to raise your self-esteem.* New York: Bantam Books.

Breton, D., & Largent, C. (1998). *Love, soul, and freedom: Dancing with Rumi on the mystical path.* Center City, MN: Hazelton.

California Task Force to Promote Self-esteem and Personal and Social Responsibility. (1990). *Toward a state of esteem.* Sacramento, CA: California State Department of Education.

de Mello, A. (1984). *Wellsprings: A book of spiritual exercises.* New York: Doubleday.

Erikson, E. (1963). *Childhood and society.* New York: W. W. Norton.

Fakhruddin 'Iraqi. (1982). *Divine flashes.* New York: Paulist Press.

Garland, J. (2001). *Life review in health and social care: A practitioner's guide.* Philadelphia: Brunner-Rutledge.

Haight, B., & Webster, J. (2002). *The art and science of reminiscing: Theory, research, methods, and applications.* Bristol, PA: Taylor and Francis.

Johnson, R. (1986). *Inner work: Using dreams and active imagination for personal growth.* San Francisco: Harper and Row.

Kotre, J. (1995). *How we create ourselves through memory.* New York: Free Press.

Kwaja 'Abdullah Ansari. (1978). *Intimate conversations.* New York: Paulist Press.

Lewis, M. (1995). *Shame: The exposed self.* New York: Free Press.

Magee, J. (2001). Mysticism and reframing memories in life review groups. *Journal of Religious Gerontology 13*(1), 69.

_____. (2002). A paradoxical model empowering reminiscence group members to transcend physical impediments to participation. *Activities, Adaptation, and Aging, 27*(2), 75.

_____. (1988). *A professional's guide to older adults' life review: Releasing the peace within.* Lexington, MA: Lexington Books.

McAdams, D. (1993). *The stories we live by.* New York: Morrow.

McGinn, B. (Ed.). (1986). *Meister Eckhart: Teacher and preacher.* New York: Paulist Press.

Merton, T. (1966). *Conjectures of a guilty bystander.* New York: Doubleday.

Nathanson, D. (1992). *Shame and pride.* New York: W.W. Norton.

Nichols, M. (1991). *No place to hide: Facing shame so we can find self-respect.* New York: Simon and Schuster.

Schneider, C. (1992). *Shame, exposure, and privacy.* New York: W. W. Norton.

Uffenheimer, R. (1993). *Hasidism as mysticism.* Princeton, NJ: Princeton University Press.

Ullman, M., & Zimmerman, N. (1979). *Working with dreams.* New York: Delacorte Press.

■ CHAPTER 3 ■

Supporting Families During the Process of Death

Carla J. Sofka

"I'm not afraid of dying,
I just don't want to be there when it happens."
—Woody Allen

"Death is peaceful. It's the transition that's troublesome."
—Isaac Asimov

"Why fear death? It is the most beautiful adventure in life."
—Charles Frohman

These quotes from a comedian, a science fiction writer, and a theater producer represent three different points on the continuum of perceptions of death. As members of a society that has historically been "death denying," many people would prefer to avoid anticipating a loved one's moment of death. However, when a family is expecting the death of a loved one following a terminal illness, anticipation and preparation for that death are normal and necessary. When death is imminent, a complex equation of events is occurring for the patient and family. Hospice team members, hospice volunteers, and other allied health professionals play an important role in assisting families during this stressful time. This chapter identifies common barriers and challenges patients and families face during the final days/hours of life and potential needs of families at the moment of death and immediately thereafter. It also provides practical strategies for supporting family members during this significant event in their shared history.

SUPPORTING FAMILIES IN THE PERIOD BEFORE DEATH

The process of watching a loved one "fade away" and die is a significant transition for families (Davies, Reimer, Brown, & Martens, 1995), and the literature contains numerous articles that describe challenges families face. This section will focus on the final days of life, when death is imminent, and will summarize common situational challenges and barriers to providing effective care and support during that time.

Communication Issues

Communication with the patient and family throughout the diagnostic process and dying trajectory is both the most commonly discussed challenge and perhaps the most important component of effective care for patients and their families (Francke & Williams, 2005; Hanson, Danis, & Garrett, 1997; Kayser-Jones, 2002; Kirchoff, Song, & Kehl, 2004; Norton, Tilden, Tolle, Nelson, & Eggman, 2003). These sources emphasize two basic but crucial suggestions. First and foremost, provide information that is honest and straightforward in terms that a layperson can understand. Information must also be adequate to assist the family in making timely decisions. Choice may be disempowering if people must make decisions based on no information or poor information, if people have no grounds for confidence that choices being offered will meet the patient's needs, or if people feel that they have no influence over the options available to them (Barnes & Prior, 1995). Family members feel frustrated, burdened, and resentful when they must try to "grab somebody" to gain information or when they are "left hanging." Families appreciate information that is up front, frank, and direct. One family member noted the need for professionals not to be afraid to talk about death (Norton et al., 2003). It is also important to inform families about the benefits and limitations of hospice care, since some families have reported unfulfilled expectations about what hospice would provide.

Second, always remember to listen to and act upon information family members offer.

It is not hard to find examples of horrendous situations in which patients received inappropriate interventions or inadequate pain control simply because professionals did not listen (Hanson et al., 1997; Jaffe & Ehrlich, 1997; Norton et al., 2003). Failure to listen leaves family members feeling not only that they may not have honored their loved one's final wishes, but also that professionals simply do not care. Doka (1993) considers active listening one of the most important communication skills and includes the use of silence, restatement of content, reflection of feelings, and summarization of content and feelings as components of active listening.

According to Del Rio (2004), additional strategies to remove barriers to effective communication include the following: (1) clarify who will serve as the primary decision maker should the patient become noncommunicative; (2) inform other family members of the established mechanisms to communicate any concerns they may have; (3) minimize changes in professional caregivers (to ensure consistency); (4) recognize, honor, and respect cultural influences on communication; and (5) use an interpreter if language creates a significant obstacle to effective communication.

Caregiving, Family Conflict, and Decision Making

Family life and interactions with significant others can be complicated by a myriad of factors, including cultural expectations regarding one's relational commitment (a natural caregiving role based on the relationship with the ill person) or expectation (filial piety), geographic mobility, blended and nontraditional families, generational differences in beliefs and traditions, diverse personalities and coping styles that may clash during times of stress and grief, and different relationships and histories with the person who is dying (Beckwith, 2005; Davies et al., 1995). Beckwith (2005) notes that it is not uncommon for family members and significant others to disagree over "virtually any issue associated with the care of a loved one" (p. 146) during the last days or hours of patients' lives as well as over the rituals surrounding their death and how their life is remembered. Hospice workers must remember that ongoing assessment of family dynamics is crucial to provide effective support to all individuals involved in the case.

In a world where contact between the terminally ill and their families is limited by geographic dispersion and conflicting demands on people's time, the absence of shared caregiving responsibilities can result in resentment and hurt feelings. Resolution of family conflict is never easy and sometimes impossible. Members of the hospice team need to work together closely to ensure that team-related issues do not complicate an already complex situation.

Nontraditional Relationships

In a society where describing relationships as "traditional" or "nontraditional" becomes increasingly complex, it is crucial to recognize the potential for added stress in a situation where a patient's family consists of members who are not related biologically or legally. Striving for a system of care wherein caregivers are not at risk of receiving inappropriate or inadequate support or services due to sexual orientation remains an important goal. An individual who has faced a history of intolerance based on sexual orientation may be reluctant to reveal the true nature of his or her relationship with the patient, rendering him or her powerless and potentially invisible during the terminal phase of a partner's life. Thompson and Colon (2004) note that a practitioner can be most helpful to gay and lesbian individuals and their families by bearing witness; validating and supporting them; and providing a safe space for the individual, the couple, and the family to talk.

Distressing Psychosocial Issues, Physical or Psychiatric Symptoms

Werth (2005), in a comprehensive summary of the literature documenting the characteristics of a "good death" as defined by patients, families, and their care providers, notes the importance of addressing psychosocial issues, managing physical symptoms, and assisting the patient in remaining mentally alert. Of particular significance for family members during the final moments of life is the perceived presence of psychological suffering and distressing physical symptoms. Psychological suffering is a significant but potentially surmountable component of the dying process.

Family members may also experience distress during the final days and hours of a loved one's life if they are not aware of and prepared for the physical changes that occur when death is imminent and after death has occurred.

ROLE OF DIVERSITY, CULTURAL COMPETENCE, AND SPIRITUALITY

The influence of diversity and culture must be considered, particularly in terms of the needs and preferences of patients and their families as well as the impact of diversity and the role of culture on the availability and quality of services and access to those services (Capitman, Bhalotra, & Ruwe, 2005).

Several basic strategies should be used when working with every patient and family. Del Rio (2004) recommends the use of a conceptual framework for multicultural end-of-life care that recognizes the intersection between ethnicity, race, and culture with health care, particularly noting the potential role of historical and current discrimination (e.g., social and economic inequalities, language barriers, and disproportionate access to health care). Davies et al. (1995) also note the importance of having an accurate understanding of how the patient and family normally function as a unit, since the transition of fading away is profoundly influenced by the following characteristics: prior experiences with illness, loss, and adversity; ways of dealing with feelings; problem-solving style; use of resources; degree to which each member shows consideration of others; family identity characteristics; how roles and responsibilities are fulfilled within the family; and capacity to tolerate differences.

It is important to allow each patient and family to educate you about their concept of spirituality and to incorporate those concepts into their care. Baggini and Pym (2005) remind us of the importance of remembering that some individuals, particularly humanists, may "share a skepticism toward, and a rejection of, traditional religion and religious ritual, and a positive commitment to living a morally responsible life" (p. 1235). Doing anything that might imply that an individual cannot live a happy, full, and moral life without religion or spirituality would be highly offensive to those with humanistic perspectives about life and death. However, failure to acknowledge openly expressed religious or spiritual strategies for coping can also be offensive to patients and their families (Dalton, 2004).

It is also crucial to recognize that there are common, universal needs among patients and families facing an impending death, while respecting the differences in how they are experienced, communicated, and met across cultures (Blevins & Papadatou, 2006). Each of these needs—which include the need for information; the need to attribute meaning to suffering, life, dying, and death; the need to ensure a "good or appropriate death"; and the need for care and support—must be carefully assessed to facilitate the provision of culturally sensitive care. Doka (1993) recommends that caregivers assume a stance of "enlightened ignorance" (p. 255), simply asking patients and families to provide information about their beliefs, traditions, or behaviors.

While individual care providers have a responsibility to develop cultural competence, it is also important to consider the role of the institutional culture within which care is provided. Opportunities to provide culturally competent care by sensitive and dedicated individuals may be thwarted by the distrust that many minorities, particularly African Americans, may hold toward the health care system as a result of years of exclusion, racism, and discrimination (Turner, Wallace, Anderson, & Bird, 2004; Winston, Leshner, Kramer, & Allen, 2004/2005).

If racism, as defined by Lum (2004), occurs within an institution by individuals (i.e., manifests itself attitudinally through prejudice and behaviorally through discrimination by individual members of the staff) or by the institution itself (i.e., is perpetuated through policies or practices within the organization), patients and families are at risk of receiving inadequate services or inappropriate care. Professionals delivering end-of-life care to populations who have been victims of discrimination or racism within the health care system have a responsibility to reach out to individuals and families in a manner that provides an opportunity for them to develop renewed trust in a system that has previously failed them.

MAINTAINING HOPE

The concept of hope is a complex one (Clark, 2004), and definitions of hope surrounding end-of-life issues are numerous. Fanslow-Brunjes, Schneider, and Kimmel (1997) define hope as "an inner dynamic life force that helps each dying patient live his life until the final moment of death" (p. 54) and have designed The Hope System as a tool to clarify the hopes of dying patients and their families. Veach, Nicholas, and Barton (2002) note that hope may be defined in the final moments of life as hope for a peaceful death without pain or fear, hope that the family will be strengthened by their experiences, hope stemming from religious or spiritual beliefs (and I would recommend adding cultural beliefs to the list), and hope for the patient's continued existence in some form of an afterlife or otherwise. Using information about the role of hope in the process to date (i.e., how hope has changed from the time of diagnosis to the point where an illness was determined to be terminal) provides a useful starting point to facilitate discussion of the family's definition of hope surrounding the final moments of life.

ONGOING ASSESSMENT OF FAMILY NEEDS AND WISHES

The hospice philosophy of care notes the importance of assessing family needs and concerns throughout the patient's illness, impending death, and the bereavement process. The concept of "user involvement," defined by Small and Rhodes (2000) as the degree of involvement and participation in the planning, design, and delivery of services by the people who use them, is relevant throughout this partnership among professionals, patients, and families. Empowering patients and families to remain in a high position on the "ladder of empowerment" (i.e., to have a high degree of active involvement in the decision-making process, as described by Hoyes, Jeffers, Lart, Means, & Taylor, 1993) is beneficial for everyone involved. The following strategies can be used to accomplish this goal.

Ideally, early in the relationship with each patient and family, an assessment of patient wishes regarding the final moments of life and what he or she requests in the immediate aftermath of his or her death will occur, and this information will be shared with family. However, it is important to assess the level of congruence and comfort with these wishes among the patient's family members throughout the process, particularly as death approaches and thoughts about and reactions to the patient's impending death may be changing. It is also important to assess strategies that families use to facilitate as well as to block and shift direct communication and how members of the family are affected by these communication patterns (Lichtentritt & Rettig, 2002). Preparing the family for the patient's final moments and the immediate aftermath as the patient's condition deteriorates is equally important. The literature identifies the following topics for assessment and discussion: addressing unfinished business and providing opportunities for saying goodbye; supporting the desired balance between alertness and pain management; preparing family members for (a) the dying process and the final moments of life, (b) reactions immediately following the death, and (c) activities and rituals immediately following the death; managing unpleasant details; and beginning the journey through grief.

Challenges of Teamwork

It is important to recognize the possibility that barriers to effective care in the final days and hours of life may be independent of the patient and family system. Norton et al. (2003) provided the following advice: "Get together as a team." They described a variety of situations in which clinicians either seemed misinformed or sent mixed messages about the patient.

Barriers to continuity of care can include schedules that involve rotation of caregivers, shifts in assignments, multiple clinicians, turnover of clinicians, poor coordination, and the transfer of patients to other care facilities (Sellick, Charles, Dagsvik, & Kelley, 1996).

Also, it is not uncommon for patients and families to observe and be affected by staff's interpersonal conflicts. Team members and administrators have a responsibility to facilitate effective interdisciplinary teamwork. They can do this by (1) communicating effectively through timely sharing of information and the absence of secrets, (2) establishing common goals, and (3) balancing respect for appropriate "role blending" with acceptance of discipline-specific duties (Corless & Nicholas, 2004).

ADDRESSING UNFINISHED BUSINESS AND SAYING GOODBYE

The phrase "unfinished business" and the idea of "achieving closure" are commonly used in the literature and remind us of the importance of providing an opportunity for patients and families to communicate their thoughts and feelings before death occurs (Byock, 1997; Doka, 1993). Byock (1997) describes five things that must be said if there is to be closure in a significant relationship: "Forgive me. I forgive you. Thank you.

I love you. Goodbye." Ideally, family members will have identified and addressed any unresolved issues prior to the final days of life.

Remember that not everyone will need to or be able to resolve issues involving forgiveness, gratitude, and expression of emotions. Professionals and volunteers must recognize that the ideal resolution of complicated relationships and family histories will not occur in all cases. However, efforts should be made to allow family members to express and process their reactions to the current status of these issues with a member of the team who is properly trained to assist them.

SUPPORTING FAMILIES AT THE MOMENT OF DEATH

There comes a time when the paradox of balancing aspects of "living" with the reality of "dying" (Davies et al., 1995) ceases to exist, and family members must confront the fact that death is imminent. This final period in the terminal phase of life has been referred to as the "deathwatch" (Doka, 1993), the "death vigil" (Pitorak, 2003), or within some spiritual frameworks as the period of "crossing over" (Barnard, Towers, Boston, & Lambrinidou, 2000) or "passing on" (Holloway, 2003).

As signs and symptoms indicate that death is imminent, "this space of time, hiatus, or period of limbo can be experienced as a time of quiet, peaceful closure or be turbulent and unsettling" (Victoria Hospice Society, Cairns, Thompson, & Wainwright, 2003, p. 215). Experienced hospice providers note that the sense of familiarity with the caregiving routine is replaced by the unfamiliar closeness of death, requiring families to shift from *doing* to *being*. Professionals and volunteers can aid the family by addressing and incorporating the following components of care during the final moments of life and immediately after the death occurs.

Balancing Alertness and Pain Management

Remaining alert and pain free are common desires of dying patients (Kuhl, 2002). It is also important to note that the state of mind immediately prior to and at the moment of death has a significant impact on the afterlife within some religious/spiritual perspectives. Balancing these aspects of terminal care during the last days and moments of life can be a challenge.

In a study of 100 terminally ill cancer patients, Morita, Ichiki, Tsunoda, Inoue, and Chihara (1998) noted that 56% were awake one week before the death, 44% were drowsy, and none was comatose. In the final six hours of life, 8% were awake, 42% were drowsy, and 50% were comatose. The researchers concluded that it is essential that providers encourage communication between patients and families before the final hours of life if possible. While it is not clear how receptive comatose or nonresponsive individuals are to external stimuli, anecdotal evidence exists that some people may maintain at least some level of hearing (Doka, 1993).

Families should be encouraged to say what they feel needs to be said, even if the patient is not able to respond verbally. While the patient may not acknowledge the communication, this will prevent, to some degree, regrets over having missed a last chance to communicate important thoughts and feelings. Pitorak (2003) also notes the importance of educating families about the difference between social withdrawal that may be associated with depression during the dying process and transitional withdrawal that frequently occurs during the final hours of life. Changes in levels of alertness and communication with family and friends do not mean that the patient is rejecting them.

Nearing death awareness, as defined by Callanan and Kelley (1992), is "a special knowledge about—and sometimes a control over—the process of dying" (p. 21) by the terminally ill person. These authors recommend keeping an open mind and listening carefully to dying people in order to understand the information they are communicating during their final days or hours. Callanan and Kelly (1992) note that even when disoriented, a dying patient's utterances may be significant and can be symbolic.

Facilitating Last-Minute Communication

It is important to assist family members in thinking about how they can redefine their role in the provision of care as the physical needs of the patient decrease. As previously noted, although the patient may not be able to respond, family members should be encouraged to identify alternate means of communicating (Dane, 2004; Doka, 1993; Pitorak, 2003; Victoria Hospice Society et al., 2003). They might play music, recite poetry, read the patient's favorite book or religious/spiritual passage, say a prayer, or reminisce about shared experiences or favorite memories. Touch can promote a strong sense of connection between people and can counteract any sense of isolation a dying patient may experience (Kuhl, 2002). Freeman (2004) notes the value of silence: "It is possible to have whole conversations about these topics without speaking a word" (p. 14).

Callanan and Kelly (1992) point out that some dying people have a sense of conditions under which they will die more peacefully. Professional caregivers can assist families by noting that a patient may need permission from a loved one to die ("leave taking") and warning families that some patients die as soon as some or all people leave the room (even if for a short time) or wait until they know that loved ones "will be okay" (Callanan & Kelly, 1992; Doka, 1993; Pitorak, 2003). Staff at the Victoria Hospice (2003) encourage family members to take regular breaks from the vigil, realizing that it is normal that some patients die when alone. Discussing this possibility and asking family members how they might respond if it occurs is strongly suggested.

Preparing Family Members

Experienced providers of end-of-life care recognize the importance of reviewing a patient's wishes regarding interventions that are desired and not desired as the patient's condition begins to deteriorate. In addition to medically oriented decisions, the following practical issues should be discussed: (1) where the person would prefer to die—at home, in an institutional setting, or elsewhere (family member or friend's home), and (2) who, if anyone, should be present at the time of death. If the patient has significant relationships with any children and would like to maintain physical contact with them, parents should offer each child informed choices about contact with the dying person and being present at the time of death. Children may not be able to think about all the implications of contact with someone who is ill or dying and may need assistance in processing emotional responses to what they have seen or heard. Giving children an informed choice will prevent them from harboring ill feelings toward adults they perceive to have interfered with their desired level of contact with a dying person. It is advisable to provide options for maintaining contact if children do not wish to be physically present or if their presence is not feasible (through letter writing, phone calls if possible, artwork).

Wilsnack (2003) notes that dying may not be just a quiet change from sleep (and may suddenly become distressing to witness); educating families about things they may fear (such as hearing the "death rattle") or will observe (e.g., color changes, cooling of the extremeties, changes in respiration, possible confusion or restlessness) may assist them in making informed decisions about whether they are comfortable being present. Doyle and Jeffrey (2000) note that family members also need reassurance that the actions of the care team are neither hastening death nor prolonging suffering, but working to maintain the dignity of the dying patient. Providing education and reassurance helps to allow for discussion of any expectations family members have about handling care during this phase of the dying process and to correct any misconceptions they may hold about the biological changes that will occur. It will also assist them in recognizing that death is imminent or has occurred if they are present when the patient nears the final moments of life.

SUPPORTING FAMILIES AFTER THE DEATH

The role of ethnicity, culture, religious/spiritual beliefs, and family tradition will influence what should and should not occur immediately following the moment of death. The following areas are important to assess to prepare for assisting families in dealing with a loved one's death immediately after it occurs.

It is helpful to understand beliefs about appropriate emotional or other type of expression following a death (Dane, 2004; DeSpelder, 1998). Families may need emotional and practical support during this time. It is also possible that conflict may arise if reactions or rituals prescribed by a culture are perceived as disruptive (e.g., keening or screaming, as noted by Freeman, 2004; chanting or singing, as noted by Brokenleg & Middleton, 1993) or are a potential violation of policy (e.g., lighting candles or incense, as observed by the author). If staff are aware of the possibility of these types of behaviors or rituals, they can take appropriate actions to minimize disruption or conflict when the death occurs. Staff should also be prepared to assist anyone experiencing signs of shock (e.g., cool, pale, and clammy skin; weak, rapid pulse; shallow, rapid breathing;, low blood pressure; shaking, nausea, and vomiting; confusion or anxiety; faintness, weakness, dizziness, or loss of consciousness, as noted by Victoria Hospice Society et al., 2003).

Inquiring about beliefs regarding what happens after death is also helpful (DeSpelder, 1998; Merman, 1992). In addition to having an impact on comfort with facing death and potential levels of distress when death occurs (Exline, 2003), these beliefs may affect the types of rituals that may be performed as well as who should be present immediately after the death.

Rituals regarding handling of the body may range from none (families request that staff handle this) to very specific bathing, handling, and dressing of the body as prescribed by cultural or religious beliefs (e.g., Jewish and Muslim traditions, as noted by Murphy, 1999). If none are prescribed by cultural or religious beliefs, Murphy (1999) recommends that family be invited to participate as an opportunity to provide direct care for their loved one for one last time.

It is important to evaluate whether culture or religious/spiritual beliefs dictate a particular time frame during which the body should not be moved. If the final disposition of the body is direct cremation, it is important to remind family members and friends that, unless special arrangements have been made, they may not have another opportunity to view or touch the deceased once removal from the site occurs. Double-checking that everyone who wishes to view the deceased has had time to arrive is important prior to the removal. Children (or others who have chosen not to visit recently) should be asked one last time if they wish to view the body or say goodbye in person (MacPherson, 1999).

Having an opportunity to debrief and process the death may defuse any concern about the deceased's experience of death and relieve any trauma that family and friends may have experienced by witnessing the death (Victoria Hospice Society et al., 2003).

MANAGING "UNPLEASANT DETAILS"

Once rituals have been completed and the family has said its final goodbyes, it can be difficult to transition the family to what MacPherson (1999) refers to as "unpleasant details." MacPherson notes that "no matter how prepared a family is, no matter how thorough a patient is in prearranging the 'unpleasant details,' survivors can be overwhelmed by cold technicalities that can intrude on grief at its rawest" (p. 305). Unpleasant details include waiting for the official pronouncement of death and calling for removal of the deceased if a funeral home has already been selected. If funeral arrangements have not been made prior to the death, deciding about how to handle the practical details can seem overwhelming (e.g., selecting a funeral home, signing documentation, informing other family and friends of the death, writing the obituary). Ideally, advance planning will make some of the "unpleasant details" easier to handle, and staff is encouraged to be proactive with these tasks before death is imminent.

Pitorak (2003) notes that making the call to the funeral home may be difficult for several reasons. First, this task forces the family to confront the reality of the death. Second, natural reactions (e.g., lack of concentration and focus) may make this task difficult. Finally, some family members may not want to see the removal process but may want to remain at the site where the death occurred.

If family and friends plan to remain in the presence of the body for any length of time, Pitorak (2003) notes the importance of preparing them for the natural physical reactions that occur after death. Family and friends may feel embarrassed or unnerved by bodily functions that are commonly perceived as "private" or "disgusting."

CONCLUSION

This chapter has noted the importance of providing culturally competent care and the need to evaluate the possibility that diversity factors may prevent some individuals from receiving appropriate care. In a community where vulnerable and underserved populations are present, readers are encouraged to consider working with the appropriate departments in their facility (e.g., social work, administration, community relations, quality assurance) to develop and conduct a needs assessment. Identifying these populations and involving them in working toward a solution will not only enhance the ability of your program to meet their needs, but will increase access to services that enhance the quality of life of the dying and their families. Conducting town hall meetings in collaboration with respected community leaders and representatives of underserved minorities is one approach. As Byock (1997) notes, "Collectively, as communities, we must take back responsibility for the care of our dying members. Rather than relying on medical professionals and institutions, community members must retain the responsibility to see that the needs of the dying persons are met" (pp. 246-247). All members of the community should be invited to attend to reinforce the message that support, companionship, and recognition of the continued needs of dying persons are a responsibility of all.

Bern-Klug (2002) notes the need to consider how end of life is defined and believes that our current conceptualization may contribute to a health care system that does not provide adequate services at the end of life and serves only a small portion of the population who could benefit. Advocating for changes in policies and practices of concern within your own institution, once they are identified, is another suggestion, as is evaluating the availability of resources within various settings in your community where dying may occur (Mezey, Dubler, Mitty, & Brody, 2002).

A common theme is apparent in case studies and narratives about hospice care: working with patients and their families during the final moments of life and accompanying families through the first moments and hours after death is an honor and a privilege (Barnard et al., 2000; Golubow, 2002; Jaffe & Ehrlich, 1997). There may be times during this intense work when hospice professionals and volunteers feel overwhelmed and unsure of their abilities or uncertain that their efforts have been effective. Many others doing this work have experienced these feelings and have discovered, sometimes long after the events have occurred, that families are eternally appreciative of not only their efforts, but their caring presence during a time that, under most circumstances, will not be forgotten.

It is my hope that this compilation of strategies to prevent or overcome common challenges and barriers to supporting patients and their families will be useful to those for whom this task is new as well as to those for whom this information serves as a gentle reminder to wisely use our prior knowledge and experience to provide effective end-of-life care. ■

Carla J. Sofka, Ph.D., is an associate professor of social work at Siena College in Loudonville, New York. She has clinical experience with medical, psychiatric, and hospice social work and has conducted research on widowhood and grief following public tragedy. She has written about the use of the World Wide Web as a resource for death education and has studied the 9-11 sympathy materials at the New York State Museum, writing about museum exhibits as a "healing space." She has served as an adjunct instructor for thanatology courses at Washington University in St. Louis, the University of Western Ontario, and the Institute for Life and Death Education and Counseling in Tapei, Taiwan and is a fellow at the Alden March Bioethics Institute in Albany, New York. Her favorite task as an associate editor of Death Studies *is writing in the* News and Notes *column about her "Adventures of a Thanatologist" (finding thanatology-related sites during her travels). She currently serves on the board of directors of the Association for Death Education and Counseling.*

REFERENCES

Baggini, J., & Pym, M. (2005). End of life: The humanist view. *Lancet, 366* (9492), 1235-1237.

Barnes, M., & Prior, D. (1995). "Spoilt for choice?" How consumerism can disempower public service users. *Public Money and Management,* July-September, 53-58.

Barnard, D., Towers, A., Boston, P., & Lambrinidou, Y. (2000). *Crossing over: Narratives of palliative care.* New York: Oxford University Press.

Beckwith, S. K. (2005). When families disagree: Family conflict and decisions. In K. J. Doka, B. Jennings, & C. A. Corr (Eds.), *Ethical dilemmas at the end of life* (pp. 143-156). Washington, DC: Hospice Foundation of America.

Bern-Klug, M. (2004). The ambiguous dying syndrome. *Health and Social Work, 29*(1), 55-65.

Blevins, D., & Papadatou, D. (2006). Cultural issues at the end of life. In J. L. Werth, Jr., & D. Blevins (Eds.), *Psychosocial issues near the end of life: A resource for professional care providers* (pp. 27-56). Washington, DC: American Psychological Association.

Brokenleg, M., & Middleton, D. (1993). Native Americans: Adapting, yet retaining. In D.P. Irish, K.F. Lundquist, & V.J. Nelsen, (Eds.), *Ethnic variations in dying, death, and grief: Diversity in universality* (pp. 101-108). Washington, DC: Taylor & Francis.

Byock, I. (1997). *Dying well: The prospect for growth at the end of life.* New York: Riverhead Books.

Callanan, M., & Kelley, P. (1992). *Final gifts: Understanding the special awareness, needs, and communications of the dying.* New York: Poseidon Press.

Capitman, J. A., Bhalotra, S., & Ruwe, M. (2005). *Cancer and elders of color: Opportunities for reducing health disparities.* Burlington, VT: Ashgate Publishing Company.

Clark, E. J. (2004). You have the right to be hopeful. Available through the website of the National Coalition for Cancer Survivorship, http://www.canceradvocacy.org/resources/pubs/pdf/Hopeful.pdf.

Corless, I., & Nicholas, P. K. (2004). The interdisciplinary team: An oxymoron? In J. Berzoff and P. R. Silverman (Eds.), *Living with dying: A handbook for end-of-life healthcare practitioners* (pp. 161-170). New York: Columbia University Press.

Dalton, S. D. (2004). Doc, we need to pray. *Medical economics, 81*(1), 83-84.

Dane, B. (2004). Integrating spirituality and religion. In J. Berzoff & P. Silverman (Eds.), *Living with dying: A handbook for end-of-life health-care practitioners* (pp. 424-438). New York: Columbia University Press.

Davies, B., Reimer, J. C., Brown, P., & Martens, N. (1995). *Fading away: The experience of transition in families with terminal illness.* Amityville, NY: Baywood Publishing Company, Inc.

Del Rio, N. (2004). A framework for multicultural end-of-life care. In J. Berzoff & P. Silverman (Eds.), *Living with dying: A handbook for end-of-life healthcare practitioners* (pp. 439-461). New York: Columbia University Press.

DeSpelder, L. (1998). Developing cultural competence. In K. Doka & J. Davidson (Eds.), *Living with grief: Who we are, how we grieve* (pp. 97-106). Washington, DC: Hospice Foundation of America.

Doka, K. (1993). *Living with life-threatening illness: A guide for patients, their families, and caregivers.* San Francisco: Jossey-Bass Publishers.

Doyle, D., & Jeffrey, D. (2000). *Palliative care in the home.* Oxford, UK: Oxford University Press.

Exline, J. J. (2003). Belief in heaven and hell among Christians in the United States: Denominational differences and clinical implications. *Omega, 47*(2), 155-168.

Fanslow-Brunjes, C., Schneider, P. E., & Kimmel, L. H. (1997). Hope: Offering comfort and support for dying patients. *Nursing, 27*(3), 54-57.

Franke, A. L., & Williams, D. L. (2005). Terminal patients' awareness of impending death: The impact upon requesting adequate care. *Cancer Nursing, 28*(3), 241-247.

Freeman, M. L. (2004). Caring for the dying. *Commonwealth, 131*(2), 11-15.

Golubow, M. (2002). *For the living: Coping, caring, and communicating with the terminally ill.* Amityville, NY: Baywood.

Hanson, L. C., Danis, M., & Garrett, J. (1997). What is wrong with end-of-life care? Opinions of bereaved family members. *Journal of the American Geriatrics Society, 45*, 1339-1344.

Holloway, K. F. C. (2003). *Passed on: African American mourning stories.* Durham, NC: Duke University Press.

Hoyes, L., Jeffers, S., Lart, R., Means, R., & Taylor, M. (1993). *User empowerment and the reform of community care.* Bristol, UK: School for Advanced Urban Studies.

Jaffe, C., & Ehrlich, C. H. (1997). *All kinds of love: Experiencing hospice.* Amityville, NY: Baywood Publishing Co., Inc.

Kayser-Jones, J. (2002). The experience of dying: An ethnographic study. *The Gerontologist, 42* (Special Issue III), 11-19.

Kirchoff, K. T., Song, M-K., & Kehl, K. (2004). Caring for the family of the critically ill patient. *Critical Care Clinics, 20*, 453-466.

Kuhl, D. (2002). *What dying people want.* Cambridge, MA: Public Affairs/Perseus Books Group.

Lichtentritt, R. D., & Rettig, K. D. (2002). Family beliefs about end-of-life decisions: An interpersonal perspective. *Death Studies, 26*(7), 567-594.

Lum, D. (2004). *Social work practice and people of color: A process-stage approach.* Belmont, CA: Brooks/Cole.

MacPherson, M. (1999). *She came to live out loud: An inspiring family journey through illness, loss, and grief.* New York: A Lisa Drew Book/Scribner.

Merman, A. (1992). Spiritual aspects of death and dying. *Yale Journal of Biology and Medicine, 65,* 203-211.

Mezey, M., Dubler, N. N., Mitty, E., & Brody, A. A. (2002). What impact do setting and transitions have on the quality of life and the quality of the dying process? *Gerontologist, 42,* 54-67.

Morita, T., Ichiki, T., Tsunoda, J., Inoue, S., & Chihara, S. (1998). A prospective study on the dying process in terminally ill cancer patients. *American Journal of Hospice and Palliative Care, 15*(4), 217-222.

Murphy, N. M. (1999). *The wisdom of dying: Practices for living.* Boston: Element Books, Inc.

Norton, S. A., Tilden, V. P., Tolle, S. W., Nelson, C. A., & Eggman, S. T. (2003). Life support withdrawal: Communication and conflict. *Journal of Critical Care, 12*(6), 548-555.

Pitorak, E. F. (2003). Care at the time of death. *American Journal of Nursing, 103*(7), 42-53.

Sellick, S. M., Charles, K., Dagsvik, J., & Kelley M. L. (1996). Palliative care providers' perspectives on service and education needs. *Journal of Palliative Care, 12,* 34-38.

Small, N., & Rhodes, P. (2000). *Too ill to talk? User involvement and palliative care.* New York: Routledge.

Thompson, B., & Colon, Y. (2004). Lesbians and gay men at the end of their lives: Psychosocial concerns. In J. Berzoff & P. R. Silverman (Eds.), *Living with dying: A handbook for end-of-life healthcare practitioners* (pp. 482-498). New York: Columbia University Press.

Turner, W. L., Wallace, B. R., Anderson, J. R., & Bird, C. (2004). The last mile of the way: Understanding caregiving in African American Families at the end-of-life. *Journal of Marital and Family Therapy, 30*(4), 427-438.

Veach, T. A., Nicholas, D. R., & Barton, M. A. (2002). *Cancer and the family life cycle: A practitioner's guide.* New York: Brunner-Routledge.

Victoria Hospice Society, Cairns, M., Thompson, M., & Wainwright, W. (2003). *Transitions in dying and bereavement: A psychosocial guide for hospice and palliative care.* Baltimore: Health Professions Press.

Werth, J. L. (2005). Becky's legacy: Personal and professional reflections on loss and hope. *Death Studies, 29*(8), 687-736.

Wilsnack, R. W. (2003). Those who stay behind: When a family member is dying. *Gerontologist, 43*(5), 782.

Winston, C. A., Leshner, P., Kramer, J., & Allen, G. (2004/2005). Overcoming barriers to access and utilization of hospice and palliative care services in African-American communities. *Omega, 50*(2), 151-163.

CHAPTER 4

The Role of the Funeral as Survivors Cope with Death

Paul E. Irion

Death rituals are observable behaviors, usually public, by which individuals and groups mark the death of someone who has been significant in their lives. They involve such things as the preparation of the dead body, a funeral service or an equivalent ritual, various ways of memorializing the one who died, and an opportunity to express a sense of loss. Through repetition over time, the rituals become customs or traditions. They may reflect the belief system of a faith community or the customs of an ethnic group or a family. Although at times they may be highly individualized, they are usually observed in a participatory community setting.

THE UNIVERSALITY OF DEATH RITUALS

Virtually every culture examined by anthropologists has some set of rituals surrounding death. Malinowski (1961) hypothesized that death rituals were a way of coping with, of trying to control, the mysterious, threatening power of death. Mandelbaum (1959) took this a step further:

> Certain things must be done after a death, whether it occurs in a very simple or in a highly complex society. The corpse must be disposed of; those who are bereaved—who are personally shocked and socially disoriented—must be helped to reorient

themselves; the whole group must have a known way of readjustment after the loss of one of its members. These things "must"
be done.... When people find that they have no set pattern for
dealing with death—as may occur in newly coalesced groups—
or when they discover that the former pattern is no longer a
feasible one, they tend quickly to establish some clear plan for
coping with the occasion of death. (p. 189)

This can be seen even in the prehistoric period. In Bøgebakken,
Denmark, 17 burials of Stone Age hunters and their families, dating
from 6,500 years ago, show a pattern of spreading red ochre on the corpses.
A cave in southern Wales, a foremost Ice Age archeological site 20,000 years
older than Bøgebakken, contained a burial where the body was sprinkled
with red ochre and accompanied by beads, necklaces, and other grave
goods (Museum of Antiquities, n.d.). Other very early burials indicate
established regional patterns of arranging the corpse in a sitting position or
curled in a fetal position, of spreading ochre on the body, of arranging
grave goods for a journey or for protection. The repetition of these patterns
suggests that they were ritualized.

So thoughout human history there is evidence of death rituals from
which various purposes can be inferred. These include honoring the
deceased, acknowledging a loss, and communicating some beliefs about
what happens after death (Jupp & Chitting, 1999).

Niyi Awofeso (2003), an Australian physician, offered an intriguing
perspective. "Burial rituals are essentially 'noble lies' that help survivors of
the deceased to live consistently and, eventually, happily with the reality of
death, while at the same time facilitating social cohesion. Noble lies are
fictions that appeal to reality of another kind. For without a consistent
framework for understanding the meaning of death, life itself might
become meaningless for many."

We frequently refer to rites of passage. This concept originated in the
work of Arnold van Gennep (1960), who described common rituals
surrounding birth, adolescence, marriage, and death in many cultures.
These all mark the passage from one state in life to another. Van Gennep
proposed that these rites had three stages: separation from a former state,
transition to a new state, and incorporation into that new state. This is a

helpful model for understanding how death rituals involve these three stages for both the deceased and those who mourn the death.

DEATH RITUALS IN THE PRESENT DAY

Ritual patterns surrounding death change as generations pass. Sometimes changes are gradual, and other times new forms emerge with the rapidity of fads. In our own time we have seen most religious communities make changes in time-honored liturgical forms. Gregorian chants are replaced by jazz masses; somber funerals are replaced by life celebrations. Modern language has replaced Elizabethan English; gender-inclusive language has replaced older patriarchal words. Worship services are much more participative, rather than being a clerical performance before a passive audience. On a secular level, in many communities ethnic assimilation and class mobility bring transitions from long-standing traditions. Multiculturalism has brought contact with death rituals from once unfamiliar religions and societies.

Until recently, in America and truly in the Western world, death rituals have been largely formulated and carried out by religious communities in the Judeo-Christian traditions. Virtually every one of myriad faith communities has developed formal or informal funeral patterns. Some are based on centuries-old liturgies, and others reflect local customs that have appeared much more recently.

A few years ago I undertook a study of new funeral liturgies in Protestant and Roman Catholic churches and in Reform Judaism (Irion, 1990-1991). Six trends appear in recent funeral services.

1. An integrated, more comprehensive understanding of the function of ritual.

Where earlier understandings of the funeral were almost exclusively theological and ecclesiastical, the new liturgies reflect an increased pastoral sensitivity based on the psychology and sociology of grief and mourning. The literature on dying and grief, which has grown in the past several decades, has had an impact on the development of new funeral liturgies.

Ministers, priests, and rabbis are being instructed to consider the psychological, as well as the spiritual, needs of mourners, helping them to deal with the fact that a death has occurred and to express their sense of loss and shared grief. Comfort is seen not just in spiritual assurances of new life after death, but also in the empathic support of others. These services give attention to the value of sharing memories of the deceased. The approach to mourners is holistic, sensitive to the many dimensions of their needs: spiritual, psychological, social.

The instructions that accompany the new funeral services of a number of faith communities suggest that the clergy take into account the diverse backgrounds of grieving families. While the core of the funeral presents the traditional liturgical components of the service, there is encouragement to incorporate the wisdom of customs and traditions that may be held by others.

2. The funeral as a participatory occasion.

Funeral customs do not develop randomly, by accident. They grow as a response to the needs of people who have experienced loss through a death. The funeral has almost always been a public event, because the death of one person diminishes not only a family, but the community. The community has usually responded by attending the funeral service conducted by the clergy.

Emerging customs encourage family and friends to minister to one another. Recognizing the value of community, funeral services have become much more participatory. Many new orders include congregational hymn singing, and where once the funeral service was conducted entirely by the clergy, now lay people participate as readers of portions of the service. Some funeral liturgies invite family members and friends to share personal reflections on the contributions of the life of the deceased or memories of their relationship. All these practices demonstrate that gathered family and friends help one another cope with loss.

3. The importance of facing the reality of death.

Existentialism made an impact on the 20th century by asserting that one can fully affirm life only as one truly affirms death. Following the same quest of authentic living, the field of psychology added insights, making religions aware that death in general must be confronted as a reality. These trends have influenced funerals to become more open to facing death in the particular.

This development was not totally new. In some communities the funeral traditionally has been preceded by a ritual involving the body, variously described as a wake, a vigil, a visitation, a viewing, *shemira* in Judaism. Sometimes this included a religious element: prayers, saying the rosary, a vigil service. There was also social value in the gathering of family and friends who shared their memories and expressed condolences. Such ritual time can be a poignant hour, because the presence of the body, seen now as dead, is a confrontation with the reality of separation. These rituals can undergird the grieving process in its early stages, helping mourners toward spiritual and psychological well-being.

On the other hand, many faith communities in the past wanted to "spiritualize" death by deliberately minimizing any attention to the body: no viewing, immediate disposition, memorial services without the body. Often attention to the body was dubbed "pagan."

Now the instructions accompanying a number of the new services support the presence of the body during the funeral service as a means of mourners' coping with reality. This is a departure from the earlier efforts to deemphasize the dead body.

The funeral liturgies and other death rituals play an important role of bonding the reality of death with life itself, embracing the entire area of caring for the dead and the bereaved. Death rituals that consciously or unintentionally try to cover up the reality of death and the necessity for grieving are a disservice to those who need to cope with their loss.

4. Attention to the context of the mourning process.

Our present knowledge of grief and mourning indicates that normal grief is a process that lasts many months, rather than being something quickly healed, as was formerly supposed. Funerals in the past often tended to assume a "quick fix:" give a strong antidote of hope and comfort and obviate most of future grieving. The new funerals acknowledge an extended process of grieving as natural and normal. All the new orders I have studied have three rites surrounding death. They are rites conducted at the time of the death or in the period of immediate adjustment, the traditional funeral rite in the church or funeral home, and the rite of committal and separation. In addition to these is an explicit concern for extended pastoral care, beginning at the time of the death and extending over some months, as well as a provision for memorialization in rituals over time.

Protestant churches have generally disavowed the need of prayers for the dead. However, some of the new services suggest that it is a valuable practice. In all likelihood this recommendation grew out of psychological understanding rather than new theological insight.

In addition to the ritual shortly following a death, many religious communities have rituals for observing the anniversary of an individual death or holding a service annually to remember all those who have died during the year. The Jewish practice of the *Jahrzeit* or one-year anniversary of the death is another way of surrounding the extended time of grieving with ritual. In other religious traditions, cemetery visits may be ritualized on a personal basis.

5. Responses to the dynamics of pluralism.

Pluralism exists not only between various religious bodies—for example, Protestants, Catholics, and Jews—but within these faith communities, as well. No longer should one assume that all Roman Catholics, or all Methodists, or all Reform Jews believe the same. Likewise, it is not uncommon for families to have members belonging to several faith communities. Rituals have to be responsive to these complexities.

Not every funeral has to be the same: one size fits all. A number of the instructions for the new funeral rituals urge sensitivity to ethnic traditions and local customs. They allow for some flexibility in adapting portions of the structured ritual to reflect the circumstances of a particular family of mourners. For example, in the Roman Catholic Church the traditional recitation of the rosary at the wake is replaced or is often supplemented by a Scriptural Vigil Service. This is explicitly described as an effort to help people from other faith communities who have come to the wake to find more meaning in such a service.

6. Lay ministries.

As pointed out earlier, funerals have more lay participation than they once did. This is a consequence of a growing awareness in many religious communities of the importance of lay ministries. No longer is religious caring and support of the bereaved the sole province of the clergy.

Every believer has the responsibility to provide a ministry of comfort. This may take the form of attending the visitation or the funeral or even taking part in it; making condolence calls or in the Jewish tradition, sitting Shiva; sending caring gifts and memorials; and maintaining social contacts during the extended bereavement period. Some of these caring practices flow not only from religious tradition, but also from ethnic or regional folk customs, all of which derive from primary human affections.

In all these ways, my own study found, many faith communities have revised their death rituals to help people better cope with loss. But the net of change has been cast wider than this.

OTHER WORLD RELIGIONS AND CULTURES

My survey covered only elements of the Judeo-Christian death rituals. In the context of the growing religious pluralism and multiculturalism of our time, we are learning to respect the death rituals of Islam, Buddhism, Hinduism, and other traditions that have throughout centuries developed ways of coping with death. Each way has its own prescribed patterns: its methods of caring for the body of the deceased, its religious services at the time of death, the body's ultimate disposition by burial or cremation or exposure, and—unlike American tradition—an extended structured mourning period.

As people from the Middle East, Asia, and Africa emigrate to the Western world, they bring their communities' death rituals with them. In their homelands, the structure of the whole culture and the lifestyle of the society supported these ritual observances. However, in their new cultural environment, they find it difficult to observe the old practices. Until immigrant religious communities reach a certain size, they usually do not have places of worship or professional religious leaders and ritual specialists. So carrying out traditional rituals depends on the memories and leadership of older family members. Western employment policies do not accommodate ritual observances that extend over many days. Western public health and environmental regulations do not permit certain traditional ritualistic dispositions of the body.

For example, consider the effects of Western society on Hindu death rituals (Hockey, Katz, & Small, 2001, 237-245). Traditionally, a dying person is placed on the floor by family members. Water from the Ganges and a tulsi leaf are placed in the mouth for spiritual purification. These practices, which were quite possible in the homeland, are profoundly affected by the Western practice of removing seriously ill persons to a hospital. In the hospital, extended family presence may be severely limited. Death might take place when no family members are present. Traditional public expressions of grief, such as wailing, might be discouraged.

Hindu tradition calls for ritual preparation of the body by family members before cremation. In the West this custom is inhibited by the practice of assigning care of the dead body to funeral directors.

The Hindu practice of open cremation of the body, ignited by the chief family member, cannot be carried out in its traditional pattern. Rather, the body is taken by the funeral director to the local crematory, where after a brief service the body is cremated by the staff.

The Hindu practice of 12 days of structured public and private mourning in the home does not fit well with employment policies that permit only a few days' paid absence from work following the death of a close relative

In all these ways, family participation in death rituals for immigrant Hindus is limited and marginalized. Hockey et al. (2001) said of Hindu practices, "The purpose of the funeral is shifting toward the consolation of the mourners in this world, rather than the welfare of the dead in the next. The entire family is more involved and delays allow overseas relatives to come. The biggest loss [when Hindus emigrate to the West] is failure to perform the appropriate rituals at the deathbed, which creates guilt, remorse, and anger, complicating normal reactions to loss, adding anxiety about the ghost of the deceased disturbing the family and bringing bad luck" (p. 244).

Faced with these obstacles to their death rituals, Hindu families have had to make many accommodations and compromises. Family members have to carry out the rituals in the hospital or at the mortuary. Symbolic cremations are held at the home before the actual cremation by crematory staff. The extended structured mourning has been shortened and compressed to enable shorter family visits and timely return to work.

Similar adaptations have been necessary in all immigrant religious communities. The justifiable need to maintain traditional death rituals to preserve a measure of religious and cultural identity has to be balanced with patterns imposed by Western legal regulations and socioeconomic realities.

NEW FORMS OF DEATH RITUALS IN AMERICA

Death rituals are not static. They decay over centuries, even with updating changes of style, as new ways of coping with death arise through the creative process of social change. A number of factors are contributing to emergent contemporary death rituals in many communities.

In recent generations families have become increasingly mobile, both geographically and socially. Like international immigrants, people change their lifestyles when they move from one coast to another, from town to city to suburbs, from union hall to country club.

Many families have changed affiliation from one faith community to another. In the context of the religious pluralism of our day, there have been many interfaith marriages. But even more consequential, large numbers of people have become secular, abandoning the religious affiliations of their earlier life. No longer participants in a religious community, they do not find meaning in the traditional religious death rituals. They do not have a clergyperson or ritual expert to call on.

The so-called Baby Boomers and Generation Xers place strong emphasis on managing their own lives and are less inclined toward involvement in structured group affinities. Hockey et al. (2001) identified a "postmodern" lifestyle that heavily emphasizes personal needs and wishes (p. 186). These generations reputedly have a strong need to control their activities. Durkheim's 1965 thesis that people are integrated into society by observance of collective rituals suggests that these generations participate in society by devising new rituals rather than by abandoning rituals altogether.

The interest in death, dying, and grieving in the past several decades has encouraged a new freedom in the expression of emotion by mourners. People are less inclined to follow socially prescribed mourning behaviors, preferring to express their own feelings in their own ways.

America's economy has placed high value on consumers, rather than on producers or investors. This has resulted in "consumerism," in which people exercise their right to decide what they will or will not purchase. For the past century, death rituals in America have been largely given into the hands of clergy and funeral directors, but as postmodern families see themselves in the consumer mode, they want to plan and conduct the death rituals they are buying.

All these factors are contributing to the emergence of new death rituals. In many communities the "standard" funeral service is no longer typical. Evidence of the new trend, often referred to as the personalization of death rituals, is appearing in America and elsewhere. The trade journals of national organizations of funeral directors have recently carried numerous articles in which funeral directors are reporting more family requests for a service of their own design reflecting the individuality of the deceased, quite often without a religious ritual.

Some of these new personalized rituals are simply modifications of standard rituals. In addition to the traditional funeral service, families add such things as personalized remembrances and tributes from friends and family members, displays of personal memorabilia, casket designs that depict the character and personality of the deceased, and inclusion of the favorite music of the deceased.

Other personalized services radically depart from traditional funeral rituals and from the involvement of religious institutions. A number of resources for humanist funerals have been published to assist families that want to plan a funeral in a secular context. Families or ritual experts develop thoughtful new forms that sensitively portray the values typified by the life of the deceased. Opportunities are given for family and friends to express their appreciation for the contributions of the person who died. Videos of the life of the person are sometimes prepared and shown as part of the ritual. Through music or symbolic acts, the feelings of the mourners are expressed. The ritual may take place in a location appropriate to the lifestyle of the deceased: a favorite place such as a golf course, a woods, a lake, a hotel ballroom or dining room. Some funeral homes are replacing or supplementing their chapels with rooms for social gatherings, even providing catering services.

Still other personalized rituals are much more informal and idiosyncratic. Often the prevailing mood is self-consciously "unfunereal," a social atmosphere. These rituals tend to cover the sense of loss, discouraging public sadness and weeping. As one man said, "When I die, I want my friends to have a party to remember me." Like the grave goods unearthed by archeologists, people are buried with golf clubs, costumes, or other artifacts from work or hobbies. A recent issue of *The New York Times* carried an article titled "It's My Funeral and I'll Serve Ice Cream If I Want To" (Leland, 2006). National Public Radio's "All Things Considered" program (NPR, 2006) presented an essay on "Alternative Funerals," describing numerous contemporary death rituals.

Personalized funerals are very often designed according to the wishes of the deceased. There is a possible conflict of interest here. Suppose that the deceased planned a party, but members of the family are devastated by his or her death. A festive social occasion does little to help them deal with their real feelings. If the basic purpose of death rituals is to help the bereaved cope with their loss, the needs of those who are grieving should take precedence. It is advisable that plans and designs of personalized death rituals remain tentative until the deceased's family can assess their needs following the death.

It is interesting to contrast such personalized rituals with another relatively new informal and increasingly common ritual following a tragic death: An accident or violent death may provoke a spontaneous display of flowers, pictures, candles, and often stuffed toys near the site of the death or the residence of the deceased. The massive response to the death of Princess Diana is an exceptional example, but every community has seen such displays on a smaller scale. It is interesting that virtual strangers— often crying or observing a moment of silence to express a real sense of loss—bring many of these tributes to the deceased. Even this "arm's length" kind of grieving seems to need a ritualized channel to express itself.

NEED-DIRECTED DEATH RITUALS

The critical point is this: Although the death ritual changes themselves are noteworthy, even more important is the fact that the innovative rituals and the new understanding of the older rituals make them more responsive to the needs of mourners and, therefore, more effective resources for coping with death and loss. All death rituals are responses to the demise of a person. Unless they are empty social conventions, merely "going through the motions" without any social rapport, they are meeting needs of the participants. I would argue that whether the death ritual is traditional or innovative, it helps a broad cross-section of people (family, friends, even strangers) meet the same psychosocial and/or religious needs that have always been part of the human experience when a death occurs.

The efficacy of funeral rituals for mourning does not depend on whether they are traditional or nontraditional, but how effectively they function to meet all the needs of surviving family and friends. Time-honored rituals have tended to evolve in response to those needs. Nontraditional or idiosyncratic rituals may not be as comprehensive or as integrated in their well-intentioned spontaneity.

Following the death of a family member or friend, mourners have five needs in relation to the normative psychological process of grieving. Meeting those needs defines the purposes of any death ritual.

1. The need to deal with a new reality.

John Donne's (1999) familiar "No man is an island" meditation contains the truism, "Any man's death diminishes me...." The death of an individual profoundly changes the reality of the lives of those who were close to the deceased.

Helpful death rituals will acknowledge this new reality. Mourners will be encouraged to acknowledge that their lives have changed irrevocably. A significant relationship has ended, yet life must go on for them without the presence of their loved one or friend. A mourner is no longer part of a couple, or is now without parents and becomes the rock on which the family depends, or there is an empty desk at the office or a vacancy in the shop. Something has changed. Those who grieve face the complicated and sometimes difficult task of transitioning into their new reality. Their physical and emotional energies will have to focus on living without the one who is gone.

Pretending that there is no significant loss provides little motivation for coping. Rites of passage begin with acting out the separation from the way things were. Denying death and its impact on the mourners is nonproductive, whether that denial is prompted by a religious service that focuses so much on life after death that death becomes a nonevent, or by a secular ritual that self-consciously applies a Band-Aid of apparent normality and does not acknowledge the hurt of grieving. A funeral, unlike any other event, truly marks the end of a life, the ending of a relationship.

This does not mean that funerals need to be maudlin or unbearably gloomy occasions, but they do have to be realistic. At the very least, they need to acknowledge clearly that a death has taken place and that the situation of the living has irrevocably changed. Although we no longer mark a death by wearing black mourning garb, we cannot simply don party clothes as if nothing significant had happened. Someone is missing!

2. The need to remember.

Mourners have a strong need to memorialize the one who has died. The residual dimension of a relationship broken by death is memory. Without memory we would be totally cut off from those who have died. We continue to think about the deceased, to recollect experiences we shared. Stories are told, the person is eulogized, obituaries are published, memorials are erected. Virtually all types of death rituals we have mentioned memorialize the one who has died.

The importance of remembrance as a part of the grieving process has been noted since the early grief studies of Erich Lindemann (1944). He pointed out that although early on, memories of the one who died are painful, in time mourners "learn to live with memories of the deceased" as a crucial part of their grieving experience.

Mourners, moving through the grief process, make a gradual transition from a relationship of living presence with the deceased to a relationship of memory. Death rituals and funerals help to start this process, but are not the entire process. Religious funeral services contain references to the deceased with prayers for the dead, obituaries, and eulogies. Informal, personalized services focus on detailed recollections of the one who died, supported by pictures or videos, stories about the deceased, personal expressions of appreciation, and respect. Reminiscence is a way of expressing that the deceased is truly missed.

3. The need to express emotions.

Death rituals give permission for grievers to express their emotional responses to their loss in a group context, if they are so moved. We know it is important for mental health that profound emotions be expressed rather than denied, repressed, or covered up.

Faith communities, ethnic groups, and families have unwritten expectations of how one is to respond emotionally to death. Some will have effusive responses; others will be tightly controlled. Sometimes individuals feel constrained to respond the way the group expects, even though that is not what they are really feeling. This tension adds to the burden of their grieving. A helpful death ritual does not require mourners to put on a front. Grief studies indicate that if people cannot be their real selves in the context of death rituals, they will have difficulty adapting to the new reality of their lives

4. The need for a community of support.

Someone said, "Grief is too personal to be private." Death rituals most often involve a group, whether it is family, congregation, or community. Mourners are sustained as others express their sense of loss by joining in the ritual. To know that others care is supportive.

The death of a person who was truly significant in one's life leaves a mourner with feelings of absence and loneliness. The loss of a spouse, a parent, a child, or a close friend understandably leaves a void. The groups to which the individual belonged are also deprived of a member and have a need to share their loss. The gathering of people around death rituals is an acting out of the sense of loss felt in many ways, depending on the degree of relationship to the deceased. Even the less formal rituals of sending sympathy cards or flowers or making memorial gifts are expressions of regard for the one who died and caring for those who mourn.

For many there is an added religious dimension. Their death rituals are religious services in which they are strongly reminded of divine support. Sacred scriptures of their faith community are read to affirm their relationship with God, who cares for them in their time of sorrow. Prayers that manifest that relationship are read or recited. The gathering of the faith community communicates support both in a religious and a social context.

5. The need for meaning.

Like much of life, death by its very nature cannot be empirically known. We can only indirectly experience it by observing someone else's death. So when a person dies, we have questions; we try to make sense of the death; we look to find meaning. Part of the function of death rituals is to provide meaning, if only a subjective one.

This is apparent in religious funerals. Based on centuries of tradition, religious funerals convey the teachings of particular faith communities about what death means, what happens to the soul after death. Traditional Christian belief in resurrection conveys a sense that a life has not ended, that it continues in a spiritual form. Other religious groups affirm reincarnation or some other way to achieve perfection.

For those who are not believers in an established religion, death rituals can still convey meaning. Hockey et al. (2001) wrote, "Faced with the unknowable prospect and event of death, it is aspects of the known world that are brought into play…" (p. 206). Mourners may find meaning and value in the fulfilling experiences and accomplishments of the deceased. They may affirm the heritage and contributions left by the one who died. They may express ways in which the deceased will live on in the memories of those who shared in his or her life. All these are ways of saying that this life that has ended has meaning.

CONCLUSION

Across millennia, in the numerous religions of the world, through constant social change, in every corner of the globe, a multitude of death rituals has evolved. Individuals and groups, large or small, will prefer and follow one form or another in this spectrum of rituals, likely regarding other forms as strange, exotic, or even meaningless.

The purpose of death rituals is to meet the needs of mourners— the surviving relatives, friends, coworkers, and acquaintances of the deceased. As our social contexts and institutions change, and as our understanding of the grieving process expands, our death rituals evolve to better meet those needs. ■

Paul E. Irion is professor emeritus of pastoral theology at Lancaster Theological Seminary of the United Church of Christ in Lancaster, Pennsylvania. He was educated at Elmhurst College, Eden Theological Seminary, and the University of Chicago, with additional studies at Oxford and Cambridge Universities. His books and articles in the field of bereavement and grief have focused on the ritual responses to loss, the theological, psychological, and social ways in which communities and individuals deal with death. His most recent books are Hospice and Ministry, published by Abingdon Press in 1988, and Nobody's Child: A Generation Caught in the Middle, published by United Church Press in 1989. He was founding president of Hospice of Lancaster County and was its pastoral care coordinator. He was honored at the convention of the Association for Death Education and Counseling as one of the pioneers in the field of serving the dying and grieving. His first book, The Funeral and the Mourners, was published in 1954.

REFERENCES

Awofeso, N. (2003). Burial rituals as noble lies: An Australian perspective. *Journal of Mundane Medicine, 4*(1). Retrieved August 4, 2006, from http://mundanebehaviour.org/issues/v4n1/awofeso4-1.htm.

Donne, J. (1999). Meditation XVII, from *Devotions upon emergent occasions and death's duel.* New York: Vintage Spiritual Classics.

Durkheim, E. (1965). *The elementary forms of the religious life.* (J. Swain, Trans.). New York: The Free Press. (Original work published 1912.)

Hockey, J., Katz, J., & Small, N. (2001). *Grief, mourning and death ritual.* Buckingham, England & Philadelphia: Open University Press.

Irion, P. E. (1990-1991). Changing patterns of ritual response to death. *Omega, 3*(22), 159-170.

Jupp, P., and Chitting, C. (Eds.). (1999). *Death in England: An illustrated history.* Manchester: Manchester University Press.

Leland, J. (2006, July 20). It's my funeral and I'll serve ice cream if I want to. *The New York Times.*

Lindemann, E. (1944). Symptomatology and management of acute grief. *The American Journal of Psychiatry, CI*, 141-149.

Malinowski, B. (1961). The art of magic and the power of faith. In T. Parsons (Ed.), *Theories of society, II*. New York: The Free Press.

Mandelbaum, D. G. (1959). Social uses of funeral rites. In H. Feifel (Ed.), *The meaning of death*. New York: McGraw-Hill Book Company.

Museum of Antiquities of the University and Society of Antiquities of Newcastle upon Tyne. (n.d.). Flints and stones: real life in prehistory. *Archeology*. Retrieved June 15, 2006, from http://museum.ncl.uk/flint [site no longer available]

NPR. *Morning Edition*, June 10, 1998. Alternative funerals. Rebroadcast on NPR "All Things Considered," March 10, 2006. Retrieved June 16, 2006, from http://www.npr.org/programs/death/980310.death.html

van Gennep, A. (1960). *The rites of passage*. (M. Vizedom and G. Caffee, Trans.). Chicago: University of Chicago Press. (Originally published in French in 1908.)

Grief: New Insights and Developments

Over the past two decades, understandings of the grief process have changed in a number of significant ways:

- From universal stages to a recognition of personal pathways

- From relinquishing ties to revising and renewing relationships

- From viewing grief as affect to recognizing the multiple and multifaceted reactions that persons have toward loss and the ways that responses to grief are influenced by culture, gender, and spirituality

- From passively coping with loss to seeing the possibilities of transformation and growth in grief

- From seeing grief as an individual problem to viewing it as a relational issue

In the chapter that begins this section, Kenneth J. Doka offers an overview of the significant transitions that have emerged in the ways theorists understand the process of grief. He blends theory and practice. Doka emphasizes the importance of incorporating these new insights not only into grief counseling, but also into grief support groups and other programs for the bereaved.

Dennis Ryan's *Voices* piece illustrates one of these themes. Ryan's moving account of his son's death points to his instrumental way of coping with the loss. While his wife finds solace in her tears, Ryan is able to find comfort in doing—in his case, sculpturing the perfect memorial stone for his child. Ryan's account emphasizes the many ways individuals experience, express, and adapt to loss.

Richard G. Tedeschi and Lawrence G. Calhoun remind us that persons not only cope with or adapt to loss; they are transformed by loss. Sometimes these transformations are negative, as grieving persons are diminished by a significant death or even succumb to disease as a result of depression or a lack of will to live, an impaired immune system, or now unhealthy lifestyles or self-destructive behaviors. Yet others, Tedeschi and Calhoun affirm, find new meaning and purpose in life, develop new insights and skills, and new ways of relating and connecting to those near them. Their chapter also emphasizes the practice of grief counseling. The promise of positive transformations or "posttraumatic growth" reminds counselors that the goal of therapy should not only be to cope with loss but also to examine the ways and possibilities for personal change mandated or possible because of this loss. In significant loss, one can grow up or down. For although there are no choices about loss or grief, there are choices within grief.

Culture influences responses to loss as well. In fact, at a very basic level, culture not only determines how grief is experienced and expressed but even influences the relationships one forms and manner in which one attaches to others. Paul Rosenblatt offers his research and insights on the grieving process. To Rosenblatt, there are no cultural universals in grief other than the fact that loss is difficult for everyone. Grief is "socially constructed," that is, every society creates norms of what relationships engender grief, the ways grief is to be expressed, and the appropriate manner to mourn. As thanatology becomes more aware of these cultural distinctions, it is likely to become more appreciative of the multiplicity of ways that individuals grieve, more cognizant of other ways to help, and even more reflective of the lessons learned.

One of those lessons already learned involves the renewed emphasis on "continuing bonds" (see Klass, Silverman, & Nickman, 1996). This work challenged the Freudian notion of detachment, emphasizing instead the ways that individuals maintain a relationship with the deceased. Clearly this work reflected Klass et al.'s interest in Asian spirituality, in which ancestors are remembered and revered. It is a reminder to grief counselors to reaffirm that the goal of counseling is not necessarily to detach from the deceased, and to reiterate close to termination the times in the future when bereaved individuals may experience surges of grief. Jane Yolen's *Voices* piece, a brief poem entitled "Two Months Later," reinforces both issues. Although the pain of grief is still very present, she still asks those around her "to help me to remember"—a sentiment that will still be shared years later.

The final chapter in this section is written by one of the pioneers in the study of grief, Colin Murray Parkes. Parkes writes on the most current controversy in the field—should the *Diagnostic and Statistical Manual* include a diagnosis for complicated grief? This diagnosis of complicated grief disorder (or possibly now to be termed prolonged grief disorder) is distinct from depression and anxiety reactions. As this diagnosis cannot be determined for at least six months after the loss, it is critical not to overly interpret or pathologize grief. The discussion and controversy over whether grief disorder should be a distinct diagnosis continues, and the criteria and debate will evolve as well.

The reactions that are found in complicated or prolonged grief should be distinguished from factors that complicate loss, such as multiple losses; highly ambivalent relationships; normal situational or developmental factors where individuals can experience surges of grief, such as at holidays or special events; or different life stages where individuals review earlier losses. However, certain "red flag" behaviors or reactions such as dependency on alcohol or drugs, self-destructive behaviors, behaviors destructive to others, deteriorating sleep patterns, or physical problems should be immediately referred to a qualified specialist.

This section beckons to the many ways that understandings of grief have changed. The next section reinforces the critical issue of how these types of changes inform the process of grief counseling. ■

REFERENCE

Klass, D., Silverman, P., & Nickman, S. (1996). *Continuing bonds: New understandings of grief.* Washington, DC: Taylor and Frances.

■ CHAPTER 5 ■

Challenging the Paradigm: New Understandings of Grief

Kenneth J. Doka

In 1989, Wortman and Silver published a controversial yet influential article entitled "The Myths of Coping With Loss," in which they identified five "myths" that were widely accepted by professionals treating bereavement:

- Depression and distress are inevitable in grief.

- Distress is necessary, and its absence is problematic.

- Survivors must "work through" a loss.

- Survivors can expect to recover from a loss.

- Survivors can reach a state of resolution.

The research, in Wortman and Silver's evaluation, did not support the widespread acceptance of these propositions.

Wortman and Silver's article crystallized a challenge to what might be called the *grief work hypothesis*. This hypothesis was really a conceptual belief that one must work through powerful feelings in order to detach from the deceased, reinvest in life, and recover from and resolve the loss.

Originally derived from Freud's seminal 1917 article "Mourning and Melancholia," (Freud, 1917) the concept is pervasive in self-help books. Staudacher (1991), for example, expresses this notion:

> Simply put, *there is only one way to grieve* [emphasis in original]. That way is to go through the core of grief. Only by experiencing the necessary emotional effects of your loved one's death is it possible for you to eventually resolve the loss. (p. 3)

Although the grief work hypothesis was evident in much work in the field, especially in trade and self-help literature, it was not universally accepted. In the professional literature, the hypothesis was continually challenged in one way or another and coexisted with other ideas and approaches. In many ways, Wortman and Silver had oversimplified some very subtle and nuanced approaches to the understanding of grief and loss, but their article had great heuristic value, bringing forth many modifications and challenges to these early and popular understandings of grief.

The past 15 years have seen an increasing number of challenges to the early paradigms. In this chapter, I will describe five significant ways in which earlier understandings or paradigms of grief have been challenged. I will also discuss three current challenges to the field and two others that are likely to occur in the not-too-distant future.

FIVE NEW UNDERSTANDINGS OF GRIEF

1. Extending the definition of grief.

One of the basic questions in the field relates to the definition of grief. Is grief a reaction to the death of a significant person, or can it be more broadly understood as a reaction to loss? Freud's illustration of grief in "Mourning and Melancholia" is a bride left standing at the altar. Most contemporary work emphasizes grief as a reaction to death. Yet confusion over the issue still remains. The major death-related professional organization founded in the United States (though international in membership) was called the Association for Death Education and Counseling (ADEC). The Australian counterpart is called NALAG, the National Association for Loss and Grief. Yet, it remains unclear if the differences between these organizations, in terms of focus or mission, are, in fact, significant.

However, recent work has begun to emphasize grief as a more widespread reaction to loss. Some of this loss is certainly related to dying or death. For example, there has been long-standing recognition that people grieve *secondary losses*; that is, losses that follow a primary loss and engender additional grief. For example, a parent who has experienced the death of a child may mourn not only the loss of the child but also the absence of the child's friends, who were often present in the home. Rando's (1986, 2000) work on anticipatory mourning further develops the idea that losses other than death can generate grief. The original concept of anticipatory grief was that at the onset of a life-limiting disease, a person anticipated a future death and mourned that expected loss. Rando considerably expanded the concept to include anticipatory mourning, which she defined as a response to all the losses encountered—past, present, and future—in the course of an illness. For example, both patient and family may mourn the progressive disabilities and role losses that accompany the disease, as well as the loss of dreams, such as for an idyllic retirement, that now seem unlikely to be fulfilled. Rando's sensitivity to the myriad forms of loss is illustrated in *The Treatment of Complicated Mourning* (1993), in which she discusses tangible losses, such as an object that is stolen or a fire that destroys one's home, and intangible or symbolic losses, such as a divorce.

My work on disenfranchised grief (Doka, 1989, 2002) also addresses the wide range of losses that engender grief, stressing that the very lack of recognition of the grief experienced in such losses complicates grief. Some of these losses involved deaths that were unacknowledged by others—such as the deaths of former spouses, lovers, friends, and even animal companions. The work also emphasized the effects of other types of losses—such as incarceration, divorce, or infertility—that can generate significant grief. The concept of disenfranchised grief emphasizes that every society has "grieving rules" that determine a socially conferred "right to grieve." Generally, for example, these rules give family members the right to grieve the deaths of other family members. But in many situations—including non–death-related losses—a person might experience a significant loss but be deprived of the opportunity to publicly acknowledge the loss, openly mourn, and receive social support. This is disenfranchised grieving.

Harvey (1998) also notes the pervasiveness of loss and suggests the need for a larger psychology of loss that would complement and move beyond the study of dying and death. This shift is a critical one, as it allows the application of the study of grief to areas such as divorce and job loss, and allows the study to draw from the considerable literature around stress, coping, and adaptation (i.e., seeing grief as a type of stress reaction and mourning as a form of coping or adaptation).

However, the danger exists that grief will be trivialized. If every loss evokes "grief," the word becomes less important and signifies little. The antidote is to support research that clarifies the grief reactions and outcomes in a wide array of losses, allowing comparisons between grief reactions and outcomes from a death with those from other losses.

2. The application of new models.

Most of the early models of grief were drawn from the work of Kubler-Ross (1969) and emphasized that people were likely to experience grief by going through a series of predictable reactions, or stages. Kubler-Ross originally studied the ways adults with life-threatening illness coped with impending death, but her work quickly was applied to the process of grief, in which a person was expected to experience a relatively linear movement through denial, bargaining, anger, and depression to reach a state of acceptance. This understanding of grief has become widespread.

Despite the popular embrace of these stages, most of the newer models have avoided the language and assumptions of stage theories. Worden (1982) broke new ground in his book *Grief Counseling and Grief Therapy* by conceptualizing mourning as a series of four tasks:

1. To accept the reality of the loss

2. To work through the pain of grief

3. To adjust to an environment where the deceased is missing

4. To withdraw emotional energy and invest it in another relationship (In the second and third editions (1991, 2002), this task was revised to read "To emotionally relocate the deceased and move on with life," a modification that is discussed later in this chapter.)

While Worden's tasks clearly identified grief and mourning with death, they represented a significant paradigm shift from the predominant stage theories. Worden's task model was not linear; people worked on whatever issues arose in the process of mourning. The model stressed individuality (different survivors completed the tasks differently) and autonomy (survivors could choose when they were ready to tackle any task).

I recognized the value of Worden's approach and suggested a fifth task: *to rebuild spiritual systems challenged by the loss* (Doka, 1993). This task recognizes that some losses challenge personal spiritual belief systems, causing individuals to question and possibly redefine their faith.

After Worden, other models appeared. Rando (1993), for example, proposed the "R" processes of mourning: recognizing the loss; reacting to the separation; recollecting and reexperiencing the deceased and the relationship; relinquishing the old attachments to the deceased and the old assumptive world; readjusting to move adaptively into the new world without forgetting the old; and reinvesting. Stroebe and Schut (1999) offered a dual-process model, suggesting that successful coping in bereavement means oscillating between loss-oriented and restoration-oriented processes.

Both these models, along with Worden's task model, reaffirmed that mourning was more than simply a series of affective responses to loss. In addition, the new models asserted that mourning involved not only a response to the loss of another but also an effort to manage life in a world altered by significant loss.

All these new models offer value to counselors in assisting bereaved persons. Stage models suggested a limited role for counselors: interpreting the reactions of bereaved persons and helping them move through the stages. The newer models allow a more significant role, in which the counselor helps the bereaved person understand what factors are complicating the completion of certain tasks or processes and develops interventions that can help the person adapt to loss.

The models also have implications for group programs. One way to evaluate a program is to determine the underlying model. Programs based on newer models should do more than simply allow participants to express affect. They should reflect the variety of tasks and processes that are part of the experience of grief and mourning.

3. Beyond affect.

While research from Lindemann (1944) on has emphasized that grief is manifested in many ways—including cognitive, physical, emotional, behavioral, and spiritual reactions—much attention has been placed on affect, to the exclusion of other responses. This focus reflects a general Western preoccupation with affect in counseling and therapy (see Sue & Sue, 2003). A number of writers have stressed reactions to loss other than affect; two will serve as examples.

Neimeyer (2001) emphasizes that the reconstruction of meaning is a critical issue—if *not* the critical issue—in grief, adding strong cognitive and spiritual components to the study of grief. Neimeyer's "narrative" approach to therapy helps people "reweave" the narrative of their lives, which has been torn apart by significant loss.

Martin and Doka (2000) suggest a continuum of grieving styles ranging from the intuitive to the instrumental. Intuitive grievers experience, express, and adapt to grief in strongly affective ways. Instrumental grievers, on the other hand, are likely to experience muted affective reactions. Their experience is more likely to be cognitive and behavioral, and they will favor such strategies for expression and adaptation to loss. Martin and Doka's work strongly challenges the notion that expressing feelings is the most effective way to adapt to loss. The work began as an attempt to understand the grieving patterns of males; the authors now see these patterns as related to, but not determined by, gender.

Other researchers have strongly challenged the idea that expression of feelings and emotions in grief should be encouraged and that a lack of open affect suggests difficulty. In his social-functioning approach, Bonanno (2004) suggests that adaptation to loss is facilitated when grief-related distress is minimized and positive affect is accentuated. Similarly, Nolen-Hoeksema, McBride, and Larson (1997) suggest that excessive rumination might not be helpful and, in fact, is associated with poor outcomes. The excessive processing of loss can exacerbate distress. Resilient individuals minimize rumination by distraction—shifting their attention in a positive direction. However, Nolen-Hoeksema and her associates also found that deliberate avoidance and suppression of grief were maladaptive.

These insights have important implications for grief counselors, grief groups, and grief curricula. The ideas reflected in the newer models reaffirm that grief is more than emotion. They suggest that leaders should try to move their groups beyond shared anguish to discussions of effective ways to cope with grief and should encourage the recognition of positive memories and experiences, even within a state of grief. These concepts reaffirm the individuality of the grief experience and discourage dogmatic, one-size-fits-all strategies.

4. Beyond coping.

Early work in the field tended to emphasize the difficulty of coping with loss and focused on restoring a sense of equilibrium while slowly and painfully withdrawing emotional energy from the deceased. The perception of the survivor was primarily passive, besieged to cope with changes out of his or her control.

This concept was strongly challenged in the work of Catherine Sanders (1989). In her phase model of grief, Sanders suggested that the process of grieving involves a series of phases, and most people follow a common sequence. The first phase is *shock*, as the person begins to feel the impact of the death. In each phase, Sanders related the psychological, cognitive, and physical sequelae of grief. For example, in the shock phase, physical symptoms may include weeping, tremors, and loss of appetite. Bereaved persons may experience psychological distancing, egocentric phenomena, or preoccupation with thoughts of the deceased. Cognitive manifestations at this phase may include disbelief, restlessness, and a heightened state of alarm or a sense of unreality or helplessness. In each of the phases, Sanders recognized both the individuality and the multiplicity of grief reactions— a significant advance over the stage theory (Kubler-Ross, 1969).

The second phase, Sanders said, is *awareness of loss*. Here the funeral rituals are over and support has ebbed. Until now, shock and support have acted as a buffer. Now, as the shock recedes and family and friends withdraw, the primary grievers experience the full force of their loss. This is a period of high emotional and cognitive arousal; separation anxiety is intense and stress is prolonged. Grief is both raw and deeply painful. The bereaved person becomes exhausted and needs to withdraw from others to conserve limited energy.

Sanders proposed *conservation-withdrawal* as the third phase of bereavement. This is a long (possibly endless) phase of grief. The grieving person seems to be functioning, and pain is more chronic than acute. But the person feels physically weak and helpless—going through the motions rather than actively living life. Bereaved persons in this phase often express a belief that they are in state of hibernation, a sort of holding pattern as they struggle to adapt to the loss.

Sanders said that in the first and second phases, people are motivated largely by unconscious or biological factors. In this phase, she suggested that people have three choices. In the face of extreme physical and psychological stress, some may consciously or unconsciously seek their own death rather than live without the person who died. Others may assume that the necessary major life adjustments require more strength and power than they possess. They may choose the status quo, living the rest of their lives in a diminished state of chronic grief. Still others may decide to move forward and adjust to their loss.

According to Sanders, bereaved persons who choose to move forward often experience a fourth phase: *healing/the turning point.* In her research, many persons could point to a moment when they consciously decided that their lives needed to change. In one vignette, a widow recalled hearing her young granddaughter ask her mother, "Why does Grandma always cry?" The widow resolved then and there that she would not be remembered as "the grandma who always cried." In this phase, people reconstruct their identities and lives, and enjoy restored physical health, increased energy, and psychological vigor.

Finally, those who experience the turning point move to a fifth phase that Sanders called *renewal.* While they still experience occasional bad days and episodic moments of grief, they experience a new level of functioning characterized by enhanced self-awareness, increased levels of energy, personal revitalization, and the renewal of social ties. At this phase, the bereaved person has learned to live without the physical presence of the loved one, while retaining an internal sense of the deceased person's presence. Sanders noted that in this phase, people could often process and even enjoy memories of the deceased without the high emotional arousal experienced earlier in the grieving process.

Later, Sanders began to develop the notion of a sixth phase: *fulfillment.* In this phase, the grieving person can look back on his or her own life in a way that integrates the loss into the fabric of that life. While the loss was neither expected nor welcomed, the person can no longer imagine what life would be like without the loss (Doka, 2006).

Sanders was one of the first theorists to affirm that people had choices in the mourning process. Her writing emphasized that bereaved persons were active participants in the mourning process rather than passive copers with little control. Her renewal phase presaged such trends in contemporary bereavement theory as grief as a transformative experience (Neimeyer, 2001; Prend, 1997; Schneider, 1994), in which loss can lead to significant personal growth as the bereaved person struggles to adapt to life without the deceased. These concepts are supported in the research of Calhoun and Tedeschi (2004), which emphasizes the human capacity for resilience and notes that loss may trigger growth and change.

This work emphasizes that the point of therapy is not to "recover" from the loss. Rather, it suggests therapists can pose a larger question: "How will this loss change you?" The question implies an active response. Grieving persons are not passive: While they might have no choice about grief, they do have choices about what they will do with their loss.

5. Continuing bonds.

The Freudian notion that the work of grief is to detach from the deceased and reinvest in other relationships has been strongly challenged. In 1987, Attig compared "letting go" in grief to letting go of an adult child. By that Attig meant that even though there may be less physical presence, the connective bonds and sense of presence remain strong. Synthesizing other work, I suggested in the *Encyclopedia of Death* (Doka, 1984) that rather than emotionally withdraw, survivors might find ways to creatively retain their attachments to the loss object. Using his own research, Worden (1991) revised the wording of his fourth task from the Freudian concept of withdrawing emotional energy from the deceased to relocating the deceased, emphasizing that the bond between the deceased and the survivor continues, albeit in a different form.

In other work, LaGrand (1999) described a connection he labeled "extraordinary experiences," in which bereaved persons recounted dreams, sense experiences, and other phenomena after the death of someone they loved. Often these experiences were therapeutic—reaffirming a bond and offering comfort. Such experiences are so common that I suggest counselors routinely ask bereaved persons about them—they may be comforted by the experiences but reluctant to bring them up.

The challenge to the idea of withdrawal received its fullest treatment in the groundbreaking book *Continuing Bonds: New Understandings of Grief,* edited by Klass, Silverman, and Nickman (1996). The editors emphasize that throughout history and across cultures, bereaved persons have maintained bonds with their deceased. The research in this book deeply challenges the idea that emotional withdrawal is essential or even desirable.

Counselors should assure clients that the goal of grief therapy is not to abolish memories of the deceased. The amelioration of grief means that over time the intensity of the grief experience lessens and the bereaved person functions as well as (or perhaps even better than) before the loss, although surges of grief may occur even years later, brought on by significant transitions or other experiences. The point is that relationships continue even beyond death, and the grief process has no final end point.

However, not all bonds with the deceased are helpful. Some persons may retain connections to a loved one who has died that impair relationships with others or adaptation to the loss. Recent research described by Stroebe (2006) suggests that bonds may be supportive for some persons but maladaptive for others. The therapeutic challenge is to recognize that not all attachments are positive.

CURRENT CHALLENGES

These new understandings have received considerable attention and widespread acceptance. Three current challenges may further modify the way we understand grief.

1. Increasing diversity: The challenge of culture.

The United States and many other nations are becoming increasingly racially and ethnically diverse. Much of the research has been based on white, middle-class samples, so it may not be possible to generalize our understanding of grief. A more diverse society will cause us to rethink basic questions. For example, what does loss actually mean? Different societies, with different patterns of attachment and different expectations about life and death, may respond to a loss quite differently. What, for example, is the impact of a child's death in a society with high levels of infant and child mortality?

A more diverse society may challenge what we believe we know about grief. Different cultures may have distinct ways of describing the experience of grief, as well as their own modes of expressing grief and adapting to loss. It may be that the only thing all cultures share is that each one responds and adapts to loss. We may be able to learn from other cultures—their rituals and methods of expression and adaptation may teach us effective strategies and offer insights on different approaches to dealing with loss.

The issue of diversity also has programmatic implications for hospices and bereavement programs. How sensitive are programs to ethnic and cultural differences? Are there significant differences in participation or withdrawal from grief programs or bereavement groups? Do other programs such as memorial services and other forms of community outreach reflect sensitivity to diversity? Do "interfaith services" truly reflect religious and cultural diversity? As Islam and other nonwestern faiths grow in the United States and many other western nations, is this growth reflected in the religious affiliations of chaplains and the nature of spiritual care? Are resources on grief—such as books or brochures—available in all the languages spoken in our communities?

Social class is another aspect of diversity, and strategies and programs need to acknowledge the differences. Are fees for services based on a sliding scale? Social class also encompasses differences in life style. For example, for many lower income families, photographs are a luxury. A common activity in children's groups involves creating photographic montages and picture boxes. Such exercises may isolate lower income children or expend a precious and not easily replaced resource.

Sexual orientation is yet another source of diversity. How inclusive are groups and materials? Are bereavement groups solely for widows and widowers or also for partners? Would bereaved unmarried partners— either gay or straight—be comfortable in the grief groups offered, or is it clear that the groups are meant to serve heterosexual widowed spouses?

Sue and Sue (2003) remind us that counseling is a culture itself, with its own distinct values. How well do these values match the values and approaches of the cultures being served?

2. The challenge of research and evidence-based practice.

As Neimeyer (2000) notes, little research has been done on the actual methods of grief counseling and grief therapy. In the past, we simply assumed that these methods worked. Grief counseling requires the integration of theory, practice, and research. Interventions need to be theoretically grounded and empirically assessed. Evidence-based practice is becoming the standard.

This standard has implications for practitioners, including the need for constant evaluation of grief programs. How can we be sure that the programs we offer are effective? On what evidence do we base programs? More integration is needed between clinical practice and research. This integration is facilitated when researchers and theoreticians explore the practice applications of their work and when clinicians take an empirical approach to therapy—constantly assessing how well their therapy is helping the client adapt to loss. Research on the link between theory and practice will likely cause us to reassess and reevaluate the concepts and models that underlie the study of grief and grief therapy.

3. The challenge of technology.

The challenge to research and evaluate is especially clear with regard to the many resources offered through the Internet. Online resources include grief information, grief groups, chat rooms, counseling, and opportunities for memorialization. Yet there has been little evaluation of these resources and little study of their efficacy.

The Internet may offer support for bereaved persons, but it may itself be a source of grief. The exponential increase in cyberspace relationships raises questions for the study of attachment and loss. If close relationships can form online, will these people constitute a future class of disenfranchised grievers? Will these relationships raise new questions regarding the processes of death notification?

ON THE HORIZON

Two additional issues are likely to affect future understanding of grief. The first one is the move to add a "grief" category to the forthcoming DSM-V. One of the proposals before the American Psychiatric Association is on *complicated grief* (formerly called *traumatic grief*). Jacobs and Prigerson and others (see Jacobs & Prigerson, 2000; Prigerson & Maciejewski, 2006) suggest that certain symptoms evident early in the process of grieving predict problematic outcomes, and they recommend early intervention. For years, the field has eschewed a medical model of grief and avoided using terms like "symptoms." Grief, it is argued, is a normal part of the life cycle, not an illness. These proposals challenge that notion, asserting that at least some experiences of grief show evidence of psychiatric illness. The proposals are a sign of increasing recognition that there is a need for correction, that the emphasis on the normalcy of loss and grief has led to the neglect of problematic variants. Receptiveness to these proposals is probably also fueled by the growth of managed care in the United States and the need to have a clear grief-related diagnostic code. Regardless of the motivation, adding a diagnostic category for grief will constitute a paradigm shift.

The second issue is the demographic change as the Baby Boomers age. Many of them are experiencing the loss of their parents; in a few decades, they will face their own deaths. Also, each generation develops unique forms of attachment; many boomers have developed extremely close attachments to their children, so their deaths may create different problems for their offspring than in previous generations. This is a generation that has challenged and changed every institution it has experienced in its collective journey through the life cycle. Boomers demand choices in programs and avoid programs that ignore individual differences. They tend to trust individuals rather than institutions. They want to be active participants in programs rather than passive recipients. The Baby Boomers will surely change the ways we encounter loss, death, and grief.

Over the past 15 years, our understanding of grief has experienced major modifications. Changes and challenges are likely to continue to affect how we think about and respond to loss. As a popular baby boom song, Dylan's *"The World It Is a Changin"* put it "the wheel is still in spin." ■

Kenneth J. Doka, Ph.D., M.Div., is a Professor of Gerontology at the Graduate School of The College of New Rochelle. He is also a senior consultant to Hospice Foundation of America and helps direct the annual Living with Grief teleconference. Dr. Doka has written or edited 17 books, including HFA's Living with Grief ® series, and has published 60 articles and book chapters. He is editor of Omega, a professional journal, and Journeys, HFA's monthly bereavement newsletter. Dr. Doka was elected president of the Association for Death Education and Counseling (ADEC) in 1993, and in 1998, ADEC presented him with an Award for Outstanding Contributions in the Field of Death Education. He was elected to the Board of the International Work Group on Dying, Death and Bereavement in 1995, and served as chair from 1997 to 1999. His alma mater, Concordia College, presented him with its first Distinguished Alumnus Award. In 2006, Dr. Doka was recognized as a mental health counselor under New York State's first licensure of counselors. Dr. Doka is an ordained Lutheran minister.

REFERENCES

Attig, T. (1987). Grief, love and separation. In C. Corr and R. Pacholski (Eds.), *Death: Completion and discovery.* Lakewood, OH: Association for Death Education and Counseling.

Bonnano, G. (2004). Loss, trauma and human resilience: Have we underestimated the human capacity to thrive after extremely aversive events? *American Psychologist, 59,* 20-28.

Calhoun, L. G., & Tedeschi, R. G. (2004). The foundations of posttraumatic growth: New considerations. *Psychological Inquiry, 15,* 93-102.

Doka, K. J. (1984). Grief. In R. Kastenbaum and B. Kastenbaum (Eds.), *Encyclopedia of death.* Phoenix, AZ: Oryx Press.

Doka, K. J. (1989). *Disenfranchised grief: Recognizing hidden sorrow.* Lexington, MA: Lexington Press.

Doka, K. J. (1993). The spiritual crises of bereavement. In K. J. Doka (with J. Morgan) (Ed.), *Death and spirituality* (pp. 185-195). Amityville, NY: Baywood Publishing Co.

Doka, K. J. (2002). *Disenfranchised grief: New directions, challenges, and strategies for practice.* Champaign, IL: Research Press.

Doka, K. (2006). Fulfillment as Sanders' sixth phase of bereavement: The unfinished work of Catherine Sanders. *Omega: The Journal of Death and Dying, 52,*141-149.

Freud, S. (1957). Mourning and melancholia. In *Standard Edition,* Vol XIV. London: Hogarth.

Harvey, J. (1998). *Perspectives on loss: A sourcebook.* Philadelphia: Brunner/Mazel.

Jacobs, S., & Prigerson, H. (2000). Psychotherapy of traumatic grief: A review of evidence for psychotherapeutic treatments. *Death Studies, 21,* 471-498.

Klass, D., Silverman, P., & Nickman, S. (Eds.). (1996). *Continuing bonds: New understandings of grief.* Washington, DC: Taylor & Frances.

Kubler-Ross, E. (1969). *On death and dying.* New York: Macmillan.

LaGrand, L. (1999). *Messages and miracles: Extraordinary experiences of the bereaved.* St. Paul, MN: Llewellyn Publications.

Lindemann, E. (1944). Symptomatology and management of acute grief. *American Journal of Psychiatry, 101,* 141-148.

Martin, T., & Doka, K. J. (2000). *Men don't cry, women do: Transcending gender stereotypes of grief.* Philadelphia: Brunner/Mazel.

Neimeyer, R. A. (2000). Grief therapy and research as essential tensions: Prescriptions for a progressive partnership. *Death Studies, 24,* 603-610.

Neimeyer, R. A. (2001). *Meaning reconstruction and the meaning of loss.* Washington, DC: American Psychological Association.

Nolen-Hoeksema, S., McBride, A., & Larson, J. (1997) Rumination and psychological distress among bereaved partners. *Journal of Personality and Social Psychology, 72,* 855-862.

Prend, A. (1997). *Transcending loss.* New York: Berkley Books.

Prigerson, H., & Maciejewski, P. (2006). A call for sound empirical testing and evaluation for complicated grief proposed for DSM-V. *Omega, The Journal of Death and Dying, 52,* 9-20.

Rando, T. A. (1986). *Loss and anticipatory grief.* Lexington, MA: Lexington Books.

Rando, T. A. (1993). *The treatment of complicated mourning.* Champaign, IL: Research Press.

Rando, T. A. (2000). *Clinical dimensions of anticipatory mourning: Theory and practice in working with the dying, their loved ones, and their caregivers.* Champaign, IL: Research Press.

Sanders, C. (1989). *Grief: The mourning after—Dealing with adult bereavement.* New York: Wiley.

Staudacher, C. (1991). *Men and grief.* Oakland, CA: New Harbinger Publications.

Schneider, J. (1994) *Finding my Way: Healing and Transformation Through Loss and Grief.* Colfax, WI: Seasons Press.

Stroebe, M., & Schut, H. (1999). The dual process model of coping with bereavement: Rationale and description. *Death Studies, 23,* 197-224.

Stroebe, M. (2006, April). *Continuing bonds in bereavement: Toward theoretical understanding.* Keynote presentation to the Association of Death Education and Counseling, Albuquerque, NM.

Sue, D. W., & Sue, D. (2003). *Counseling the culturally diverse: Theory and practice.* New York: John Wiley and Sons.

Worden, J. W. (1982, 1991, 2002). *Grief counseling and grief therapy: A handbook for the mental health practitioner* (eds. 1-3). New York: Springer.

Wortman, C., & Silver, R. C. (1989). The myths of coping with loss. *Journal of Clinical Counseling, 57,* 349-357.

Expressing Grief for an Infant Son

Dennis Ryan

My son, Raymond, died suddenly after two short weeks of life. I was numb, in a daze, awake and aware, yet not really present to what was going on. My mind raced with things I had to do, funeral arrangements, notifications. My emotions raced too, but they were in the background somewhere.

Even if I had wanted to express these feelings, I didn't have the habit, the skills, or the words. I didn't have any male models for this. No one had ever taught me that I needed to find a way to express my feelings of grief.

One element of my grief was sorrow over what might have been. I remember holding my son in my arms and singing the song from Carousel, "My Boy, Bill." As I sang, I imagined myself teaching him football and how to go camping. I wanted him to be proud of me. When he died, I lost that. It hurt, but I kept it back in the shadows of my consciousness.

My wife, Judy, was deeply grieved. I tried to support her as best I could, but at that point in my life I knew very little about

Continued

how to support the bereaved. I wasn't a good listener, nor was I comfortable when she cried. I used to try to get her to stop, rather than letting her express her sorrow.

Judy would talk about Raymond's death to her mother, to my mother, to my sisters, and to her friends. I would overhear the conversations on the phone and even encouraged Judy to call them when she was sad. When they got together, I would see the intense expressions on their faces as they sat close together holding each other's hands. I saw and heard the tears, but I was mute.

There are many ways people express grief; doing something was the way that worked for me. I didn't realize this until a year and a half later when my older sister died suddenly because of a massive cerebral hemorrhage. In shock, something inside me drove me to go up into my parents' attic and find boxes of old family pictures. I started making an album with pictures of my sister and me. They started with pictures of us when I was a baby and she was three, and it ended with a picture of us together six days before she died. I didn't make the album to show to others. I did it because I needed to. It was my way to express my grief. After I went through the finished album, I knew I had moved closer toward acceptance of her death.

I couldn't create an album like that for Raymond. There were only six or seven pictures of him and only a very short time together. Rituals are something we do to express grief, but because we were poor, we couldn't afford a big funeral. We found a funeral director who was compassionate and generous. The service at the funeral home was simple. There was no wake.

On the morning of the burial, we arrived at the funeral home. A priest friend said some prayers. The funeral director had dressed Raymond in the baptismal robe and cap that Judy had knitted during her pregnancy. Raymond's body was on a table, in a small white casket. He looked so peaceful. My wife and I held each other and cried. When we finished, I felt lighter, freed from the horrible image of his dead body in the hospital after losing his fight with infection.

We buried Raymond in the plot of his great-grandparents who died so long ago that we were able to reuse their plot. This grave provided me with more opportunities to express my grief. Judy and I went back many times to his grave where, in private, the two of us could express our shared sorrow in tears and prayers and manual labor. We would fix the plot, planting grass and flowers that would bloom during the different seasons of the year.

After Raymond's death I started to read about grief. I learned about the importance of personalizing grief. In one book, I read about a couple who had made their own tombstone for their child's grave. As soon as I read this, I knew that this was something I needed to do for my son, even though I had never carved anything before. I recognized that I had the same need as the couple in the book. I told Judy and she suggested I talk to her friend who taught college sculpting. The teacher was very encouraging and helpful. She suggested I make a pillow stone to lay in front of the tombstone that was already there.

First I needed to find a piece of granite. Three months after Raymond's death, my wife and I drove down to the western shores of the Chesapeake to visit her aunt. I took a walk along the Bay where the town had erected a wall to protect the land from erosion during storms. To shore up the wall against the waves, they had dumped large chunks of rock. I couldn't believe my eyes. It was granite! I spent hours searching for just the right-size piece. Even though I hadn't taken any measurements, I knew the piece that would fit when I first laid eyes on it.

Continued

Once I got it home, we decided on the engraving. I had a hammer, chisel, and safety glasses. I spent many hours carefully chipping away at the granite, stopping periodically to wipe tears from my eyes. I didn't understand that I had to do this to express my grief; I just knew it was the right thing for me to do.

Judy and I took the completed stone to the cemetery on one of the first mild days in March. The ground had thawed and seemed to welcome the rock to its new home. That Saturday, when I placed the pillow stone before the old, larger tombstone, I felt I had done something that my son would have liked.

Dennis Ryan is associate professor of Religious Studies at the College of New Rochelle. He received his Ph.D. in theology from Fordham University. He is the author of numerous journal articles and The Religious Elements of Life *from the University Press of America. He is also the author of* Dreams about the Dead, *published by University Press of America, which presents edited interviews and the interviewees' descriptions of the dreams' meanings in an attempt to show the importance of dreams in the grieving process.*

CHAPTER 6

Grief as a Transformative Struggle

Richard G. Tedeschi and Lawrence G. Calhoun

Although the loss of a loved one is difficult under any circumstances, it may be most difficult when there is no sense of meaning to the loss. People who take the perspective that their loved one died in vain or that the death was senseless may have a more difficult path than those who see some redeeming aspect to the loss. Some of these redemptive aspects might be that the loved one died for an important cause or doing what he or she loved, or that the death was part of God's plan.

Another possible outcome in grief is positive transformation in the aftermath of the struggle with the loss (Calhoun & Tedeschi, 1989-1990). There has been a growing recognition of this possibility among professionals who serve the bereaved (Hogan & Schmidt, 2002; Kessler, 1987; Nerken, 1993; Tedeschi & Calhoun, 2004b; Znoj, 2006). We coined the term "posttraumatic growth" (Tedeschi & Calhoun, 1996) to describe positive transformations that people can experience as they cope with grief and other highly stressful life circumstances (Calhoun & Tedeschi, 1999). As we have elsewhere, we use the words *traumatic* and *posttraumatic* to mean something broader than the very restricted meanings in the current *Diagnostic and Statistical Manual of Mental Disorders* (American Psychiatric Association, 2000). The words are used here interchangeably with the terms *life crisis, major stressor, highly stressful event,* and the like to mean life circumstances that severely challenge people's resources, particularly their general ways of understanding the world and their place in it. Our focus in this chapter is on the answer to this question: In what ways can people be transformed by their struggle with grief, and how does this happen?

When a child dies, for example, parents typically face intense suffering and anguish, the possibility of significant impairment in major social roles, and a grieving process that may be protracted and distressing (Hazzard, Weston, & Gutteres, 1992; Oliver, 1999; Romanoff, 1993). Almost paradoxically, however, some persons who experience the death of a loved one report significant psychological growth emerging from their struggle with major loss (Calhoun & Tedeschi, 1989-1990; Lehman et al., 1993; Talbot, 1998-1999; Tedeschi & Calhoun, 2004b).

DOMAINS OF POSITIVE TRANSFORMATION

Consider the words of some bereaved parents with whom we have worked and who were participants in our research. These statements reflect the five dimensions of posttraumatic growth that we have uncovered empirically (Tedeschi & Calhoun, 1996).

> With my husband, it has not affected [our relationship] at all adversely. I'd say that it has probably made it even stronger because he's been so supportive.

> We realize that life is precious and that we don't take each other for granted. In fact, my daughter in Raleigh, I talk to her almost every day on the phone, and I've found I've become much more protective than I've been before. And I'm also very much more generous with her than I have been with her previously.

These statements refer to positive changes in ways of relating to others. Very difficult situations can strain and sometimes break relationships, but sometimes people develop deeper emotional connections with others as a result of having to deal with trauma and loss. It appears that relationships can be strengthened for a number of reasons. People are often compelled after traumatic losses to seek out others who will listen to their story. The experience of intimacy that comes from disclosure of such emotional experiences can produce an appreciation for relationships and a comfort with intimacy that was not previously felt. The greater sense of connectedness may go beyond connections to significant others to include an enhanced sense of connectedness to other human beings in general and especially to those who suffer, especially persons who have undergone or are undergoing a similar kind of suffering. It is not yet clear whether this increased feeling of being connected and wanting to comfort others who have experienced a similar loss results in a general tendency toward greater altruism. But certainly the sense of increased psychological connectedness to other human beings appears to be present.

Grieving persons may also experience positive transformation in the form of a new understanding of themselves as stronger or more capable (Janoff-Bulman, 2006).

> The main thing is the strength. The understanding that God is going to get you through anything that happens to you. And that gives you a different outlook on life. That gives you a different view of how to handle things. That takes away a lot of the fear and trepidation that most of us walk through life with. That doesn't mean I don't have any fear or that I don't think about the future or any of that stuff. I do, just like normal people. But I'm not constantly worried about it.

> I've been through the absolute worst that I know. And no matter what happens, I'll be able to deal with it.

Dealing with a crisis can produce a new recognition of one's personal strength. After a highly stressful event, it may be hard to imagine that anything worse could happen, and people may conclude that no other event can overtax their coping abilities. This may be true; however, a person can encounter a terrible "pileup" of traumas that overwhelms his or her resources and makes growth less likely (Harvey, Barnett, & Rupe, 2006).

> I think that you become conscious of the fact that every day is a new day; a beginning or a possible ending.... I have always appreciated what I have, but I just think you have a greater appreciation for things that are there that maybe you have experienced and shared with that child that you lost.

These statements reflect the increased appreciation of life that can come with severe losses. Losing something precious can demonstrate that one should appreciate what one has. Strikingly, many people who report this type of posttraumatic growth mention their newfound appreciation for rather ordinary, everyday living. This suggests a shift in the perception of what is truly valuable, a shift in priorities regarding how one should spend time and effort.

> I've become very empathic toward anybody in pain or in any kind of grief. I think that's one reason I went into oncology nursing—because I felt so comfortable around grief. And I felt very comfortable around death and dying because I've learned so much about it and love talking about it.

Some people strike out on new life ventures or pathways in the aftermath of loss. This may be related to the other dimensions of posttraumatic growth. For example, finding the value in relationships may move a person toward service to others and appreciating life more profoundly may produce a shift toward activities that embrace experiences that seem simple but are now more vividly felt.

> I have had to work out my relationship with God. For a while, I wasn't sure I had one anymore. But in the end, I think I have a deeper understanding of things like grace, and I think I have had to really figure out how to be forgiving, too.

Another domain in which bereaved persons can experience growth is in spiritual, religious, and existential matters. The trajectories and content of change vary greatly, but the central theme is a change in one's general philosophy of life that leads to a philosophy with which one is more satisfied. Persons who struggle with significant loss do not necessarily become more religious or spiritual. For some, this is the case; for others, the change is to a more satisfying but perhaps less orthodox stance. The death of a loved one raises existential questions for some bereaved persons, and growth may be reflected in a greater satisfaction with one's religious or spiritual views but not necessarily a greater adherence to particular beliefs or practices.

HOW DO TRANSFORMATIONS OCCUR?

A substantial body of literature exists describing the transformations people report in the aftermath of loss. But exactly how are people transformed by their grief? (See Calhoun & Tedeschi, 2004, 2006, and Tedeschi & Calhoun, 1995, 2004a for fuller descriptions of the hypothesized process.) To understand this transformation, it may be useful to see the loss of a loved one as a major life crisis.

For many people, a major life crisis triggers a series of difficult cognitive and emotional adjustments that are necessary to make sense of the loss. These attempts to adjust produce growth. In our description of this process (Calhoun & Tedeschi, 2006), we draw on the work of Janoff-Bulman (1992, 2006), who in turn uses Parkes's (1971) conception of the role of assumptive worlds and Epstein's (1990) ideas about the individual's "world-theory" to guide expectations about the life course.

Significant losses can challenge—and perhaps shatter—these expectations or assumptions, and require people to rethink them. The assumptions tend to be basic beliefs (such as views on the nature of human beings, good and evil, and the workings of the universe) and specific assumptions (such as predictions about how vulnerable one is to tragedy, how benevolent the world is, and what the future holds). Losses that are particularly unexpected or that go against the "normal" course of events, such as the death of a child, are most likely to set in motion the questioning and reconsideration that may eventually allow the person once again to think of the world as understandable or predictable. This process can take years. Losses that seem unbelievable long after they have occurred are particular challenges to the assumptive world.

Another way to consider this process of transformation is to consider it from the standpoint of narrative psychology (Neimeyer, 2006). If we think of people as semi-deliberately engaged in a process of creating their own autobiographies, losses can be seen as discontinuities in their life stories. These surprising and unwanted intrusions demand a change in the story. If a loss is going to be transformative, it will be highly disruptive to the ongoing story, which has a planned and assumed structure. People often describe these losses later in terms of "before" and "after"—

they are the turning points in their lives. Life has been transformed by the intrusion of death. It cannot proceed as it was; the person's life story has been permanently changed.

The transformations that occur as a result of the struggle with loss are sometimes for the better and sometimes for the worse, although they are not usually an either/or proposition. Both positive and negative consequences are part of the story, as disruption sets into motion the questioning of the assumptive world—the predictions made about how life will go and what kind of person one will be. Posttraumatic growth may not necessarily produce an abatement of distress; however, it may allow the loss to be somewhat better tolerated, because the loss and the suffering have not been in vain. If the loss produces something useful, it can be honored and not merely endured.

Another factor that may be important in the process of transforming grief is the kind and quality of the social responses grieving persons receive, especially from those closest to them (Calhoun & Tedeschi, 2006). In response to trauma, some people want to tell the story of what happened—the events and their aftermath. It may be necessary for some people to retell the story of their loss, perhaps many times, before they are able to accept the outcomes. Friends and family may need to have patience with the grieving person. If they are unwilling or uncomfortable listening and, therefore, put constraints on the person who is attempting to describe his or her grief and bereavement, that person may have even more difficulty coming to terms with the loss. It appears that the cognitive processing often necessary in the aftermath of a major loss can be helped or hindered by the responses of others. Therefore, we can expect that positive transformations hinge on the extent to which the grieving person receives support or suffers from social constraints against talking about the loss generally and the experience of transformation in particular.

What does social constraint look like? How is it experienced by the grieving person? Constraints on disclosure and negative responses of others to disclosure can lead to feelings that the process is taking too long, that the emotions need to be cut short or put away, or that the person or the story is to be avoided. This response is hurtful to bereaved persons, who may tend to adopt the view of those who impose the constraints. Grieving persons in such social contexts may come to question the appropriateness of their thoughts, feelings, and behavior, and may worry that they are not grieving in "healthy" ways. An antidote to this situation that can enable more adaptive processing of the loss is what we call "expert companionship" (Calhoun & Tedeschi, 2006; Tedeschi & Calhoun, 2004b, 2006). Cognitive processing of loss into growth experiences can occur when listeners are sensitive, courageous, and patient, and respect the bereaved person's ways of coming to terms with the loss.

HOW TO ASSIST

Although it is currently enjoying great interest and popularity (justifiably so), the idea that clinicians need to understand their clients in the context of specific cultural contexts is not new at all (e.g., Kanfer & Saslow, 1969). We have addressed this issue in more detail elsewhere (Calhoun & Tedeschi, 2004, 2006; Tedeschi & Calhoun, 2004a), but it may be useful to make some recommendations here about the grieving person's sociocultural context.

All of us are members of social and cultural groups that range from geographically and interpersonally close, usually small, communities (a gang, a team, a family), to much larger and somewhat more abstract social entities (a nationality, an ethnic group). The groups to which we belong provide cues on how we should behave and sometimes provide feedback on the desirability or undesirability of our behavior. The most important feedback comes from the groups of people with whom we regularly interact. This is clearly the case for grief and bereavement: Different social groups have different rules about how, when, and where mourning rituals should unfold; appropriate and inappropriate ways to experience loss; and how people should express their experience to others. What follows must be considered in light of the wide array of social and cultural prisms through which individuals experience bereavement.

The clinician who wishes to assist bereaved persons should be a companion and equal first but also must have expertise (Tedeschi & Calhoun, 2004b, 2006). Bereaved persons who seek professional help may need *expert companions* to help them manage significant emotional distress, reconsider and perhaps disengage from goals that are no longer attainable, and rework their life narratives. This process can be a lengthy one. Expert companions can tolerate the sometimes slow process of reconsidering the assumptive world, constructing a new version that accommodates the loss, and dealing with subsequent difficulties.

It is important to note that although our focus here is on helping bereaved persons who have sought professional help with their grief or who appear to be having significant difficulties adapting to their loss, most people who lose a loved one do not require or seek professional help (Bonanno, 2005; Tedeschi & Calhoun, 2004b; Wortman & Silver, 1989). We believe that most grieving persons appreciate and are probably helped by the socially intelligent support provided by the various communities and social groups to which they belong—extended families, friends, and members of social communities—but most people neither want nor need professional mental health interventions designed to address "grief issues."

Although our audience here consists primarily of professionals whose work puts them in regular contact with dying or bereaved persons, the following recommendations can also provide a useful framework for those who offer informal support for grieving friends and relatives. The following suggestions can be used to help grieving persons survive a loss and to acknowledge any posttraumatic growth they may have experienced.

Throughout the process, it is important to recognize that the transformations of grief are essentially paradoxical. The fundamental paradox is that loss can produce gain. There are other paradoxes as well: Grieving involves oscillation between attempts to restore life and engagement in the emotional tasks of mourning the loss (Stroebe & Schut, 1999); grieving involves taking action and tolerating inaction; and support from others is important, even though the loss is a painfully personal and sometimes lonely situation. The more substantial the grieving person's coping abilities, the more successful he or she will be at engaging in these processes. Znoj (2006) describes how adaptive coping—especially good emotional regulation, the ability to accept tragic situations, and the use of (rather than abuse of) available supports—is crucial to this process. The expert companion may be able to use these approaches to help people, even those who do not have the best coping abilities, find their way through grief to personal transformation.

In a form of support that is based primarily on companionship, several elements can facilitate posttraumatic growth. The message given by the expert companion is that grieving persons can be trusted to find their way through the grief. Grieving is an individual journey; it does not follow one set of steps or involve certain universal responses. The message that the client can be trusted with the process of grief honors the personal strength of clients, even when they may doubt it themselves. This is an important building block for the development of an enhanced sense of personal strength that many people report as an aspect of posttraumatic growth.

The expert companion can model and nurture closer relationships with others. This kind of companionship is based on a type of listening that allows the listener—that is, the expert companion—also to be changed, rather than focusing on changing the client. This open attitude toward listening can encourage a deeper exploration of feelings and a level of trust in a relationship that may never have been possible before. The devastation of grief can leave people emotionally raw and much less able to manage their impressions and contain their tears. Responding to this raw emotion with expert companionship can produce a new depth of relating.

Among the many issues that may concern grieving persons who seek help are spiritual and existential questions, and dilemmas about the life course. Expert companions must be comfortable discussing questions with spiritual and existential content that touch on, for example, the extent to which God controls events and whether comfort can be found in the spiritual life. The loss of a close relationship can also alter the life course, bringing new roles and new responsibilities.

Many people in grief are reluctant to see their struggle with loss as contributing to positive transformation. Clients who are desperately missing a loved one might mistake recognition of growth for a suggestion that the death was in some way fortunate. The expert companion takes the view that it is not the loss itself that has value, but the struggle with that loss that can lead to change. Losses can be mourned even as positive changes become evident. At the appropriate time and in the appropriate context, the expert companion judiciously helps the client acknowledge and accept the positive transformations that have occurred.

While some people are reluctant to acknowledge growth in the aftermath of grief, others embrace it as a way of honoring the loved one who has died. They may take responsibility for carrying on the person's work or keeping his or her memory alive, which may take them to places in life that they never anticipated. The bereaved parent quoted above who became an oncology nurse did so in part to honor the memory of the child she lost to cancer. These new possibilities are one of the domains of posttraumatic growth and may be the most unambiguous indications of growth.

The expert companion can encourage clients as they begin to move into new territory. For example, a widow was faced with a decision about what to do with her husband's business. She had always been a homemaker, but she had discussed the business with her husband for years and knew most of the employees. She decided to run it herself and was surprised at her ability and the joy she found in the work. At first, she felt that she was preserving what he had built rather than letting it die with him, but over time she expanded and improved the business, putting her own stamp on the endeavor. She could take pride in her accomplishments and honor her husband as well. This path also allowed her to channel her grief into productive activity.

CONCLUSION

Although it is clear that grief can be a transformative event, those who work with grieving persons should be careful not to judge outcomes by the presence or absence of such transformations. Grief can take a longer course than was assumed in the past, and transformations may take longer as well. Where a client is at one point in time may not indicate the reactions he or she will be showing later in the process. It is also important to recognize the complicated relationship between resolution of grief and posttraumatic growth. Bereaved parents may experience ongoing distress related to posttraumatic growth, and parents who say they have resolved their grief may be less likely to see anything good as having come out of their struggle with the loss of a child (Znoj, 2006).

The view that growth and suffering, positive transformation and distress coexist, or that ongoing distress may serve as the impetus for growth, tends not to fit well with the general assumptions of many North American clinicians. A pervasive way of thinking about growth seems to go like this: Growth is positive and positive psychological outcomes mean the person is happy and not distressed; therefore, growth should be correlated with more positive psychological outcomes and fewer negative outcomes. The findings that growth and distress tend to be independent do not easily fit into the general framework of clinicians.

We are not suggesting that a therapeutic goal of enhanced client happiness is undesirable. We are suggesting, however, that the almost intuitive assumption that growth must be correlated with more happiness and less sadness is incorrect. This concept is particularly important for clinicians who work with people who are grieving an upcoming loss (as in hospice care) or the death of a loved one.

The available data do not permit a definite conclusion about the relationships among posttraumatic growth, well-being, and distress. But the data are quite clear that growth and psychological distress tend not be related in the way we might assume. Our own view, based on our clinical work (and we are fully aware of the danger of relying on such limited and subjective data), is that some degree of ongoing psychological discomfort may ensure the maintenance of the positive transformations that can arise from the struggle with grief.

Whether continued discomfort is necessary for continued growth, it is clear that even in the midst of great suffering, a person can, at the same time, experience significant growth. Clinicians who work with grieving persons should not assume that themes of growth in the client's narrative mean that the pain of grief has been commensurately abated. But the presence of growth may be an indicator that the client is experiencing positive transformations that may make the suffering more bearable, even if it is not diminished. Both expert companions and those they are trying to serve may need to remember the words of the old Protestant hymn: *Shun not the struggle—'tis God's gift.* ■

Lawrence G. Calhoun is professor of psychology at University of North Carolina at Charlotte and a licensed clinical psychologist. Dr. Calhoun is co-author/co-editor of the books Dealing with Crisis *(1976),* Psychology and Human Reproduction *(1980),* Trauma and Transformation *(1995),* Posttraumatic Growth *(1998),* Facilitating Posttraumatic Growth *(1999),* Helping Bereaved Parents *(2004), and* The Handbook of Posttraumatic Growth *(2006), and of more than 80 articles published in professional journals. His scholarly activities are focused on the responses of persons encountering major life crises (e.g., major illness, traumatic loss), particularly posttraumatic growth. He is a recipient of the Bank of America Award for Teaching Excellence and of the University of North Carolina Board of Governors Award for Excellence in Teaching. He has taught undergraduate and graduate courses in a variety of clinical areas and his professional practice has been focused on individuals and couples coping with highly challenging life circumstances.*

Richard Tedeschi, Ph.D., received his B.A. in psychology from Syracuse University, his Ph.D. in clinical psychology from Ohio University, and completed his Clinical Psychology Internship at The University of North Carolina School of Medicine. Dr. Tedeschi is currently professor of psychology at the University of North Carolina at Charlotte, where he conducts research on trauma and posttraumatic growth, teaches personality and psychotherapy, and supervises graduate practice. He is a Licensed Psychologist specializing in bereavement and trauma, and leads support groups for bereaved parents for a non-profit organization in Charlotte, where he also maintains his private practice. He has published, together with his colleague, Lawrence Calhoun, several books on parental bereavement and on posttraumatic growth including most recently, Helping Bereaved Parents, *and the* Handbook of Posttraumatic Growth. *He has served as a consultant to the American Psychological Association in developing materials on trauma and resilience for use by psychologists and the public, and appeared in the APA/Discovery Channel documentary on coping with the terrorist attacks of September 11, 2001. He has provided workshops on trauma and posttraumatic growth for groups such as police and the military and various universities and professional organizations in psychology.*

REFERENCES

American Psychiatric Association. (2000). *Diagnostic and statistical manual of mental disorders.* Text revision (4th Ed.). Washington, DC: Author.

Bonanno, G. (2005). Clarifying and extending the concept of adult resilience. *American Psychologist, 60,* 265-267.

Calhoun, L. G., & Tedeschi, R. G. (1989-1990). Positive aspects of critical life problems: Recollections of grief. *Omega, 29,* 265-272.

Calhoun, L. G., & Tedeschi, R. G. (1999). *Facilitating posttraumatic growth: A clinician's guide.* Mahwah, NJ: Lawrence Erlbaum Associates.

Calhoun, L. G., & Tedeschi, R. G. (2004). The foundations of posttraumatic growth: New considerations. *Psychological Inquiry, 15,* 93-102.

Calhoun, L. G., & Tedeschi, R. G. (2006). The foundations of posttraumatic growth: An expanded framework. In L. G. Calhoun & R. G. Tedeschi (Eds.), *Handbook of posttraumatic growth: Research and practice* (pp. 1-23). Mahwah, NJ: Lawrence Erlbaum Associates.

Epstein, S. (1990). The self-concept, the traumatic neurosis, and the structure of personality. In D. J. Ozer, J. M. Healy, and A. J. Stewart (Eds.), *Perspectives in personality: Vol 3* (pp. 63-98). London: Jessica Kingsley.

Harvey, J., Barnett, K., & Rupe, S. (2006). Posttraumatic growth and other outcomes of major loss in the context of complex family lives. In L. G. Calhoun & R. G. Tedeschi (Eds.), *Handbook of posttraumatic growth: Research and practice* (pp. 100-117). Mahwah, NJ: Lawrence Erlbaum Associates.

Hazzard, A., Weston, J., & Guterres, C. (1992). After a child's death: Factors related to parental bereavement. *Journal of Developmental and Behavioral Pediatrics, 13,* 24-30.

Hogan, N. S., & Schmidt, L. A. (2002). Testing the grief to personal growth model using structural equation modeling. *Death Studies, 26,* 615-634.

Janoff-Bulman, R. (1992). *Shattered assumptions: Toward a new psychology of trauma.* New York: Free Press.

Janoff-Bulman, R. (2006). Schema-change perspectives on posttraumatic growth. In L. G. Calhoun & R. G. Tedeschi (Eds.), *Handbook of posttraumatic growth: Research and practice* (pp. 81-99). Mahwah, NJ: Lawrence Erlbaum Associates.

Kanfer, F. H., & Saslow, G. (1969). Behavioral diagnosis. In C. M. Franks (Ed.), *Behavior therapy—Appraisal and status* (pp. 417-444). New York: McGraw-Hill Book Co.

Kessler, B. G. (1987). Bereavement and personal growth. *Journal of Humanistic Psychology, 27,* 228-247.

Lehman, D. R., Davis, C. G., DeLongis, A., Wortman, C. B., Bluck, S., Mandel, D., Ellard, J. H. (1993). Positive and negative life changes following bereavement and their relations to adjustment. *Journal of Personality and Social Psychology, 12,* 90-112.

Neimeyer, R. (2006). Re-storying loss: Fostering growth in the posttraumatic narrative. In L. G. Calhoun & R. G. Tedeschi (Eds.), *Handbook of posttraumatic growth: Research and practice* (pp. 68-80). Mahwah, NJ: Lawrence Erlbaum Associates.

Nerken, I. R. (1993). Grief and the reflective self: Toward a clearer model of loss resolution and growth. *Death Studies, 17,* 1-26.

Oliver, L. E. (1999). Effects of a child's death on the marital relationship. *Omega, 39,* 197-227.

Parkes, C. M. (1971). Psycho-social transitions: A field study. *Social Science and Medicine, 5,* 101-115.

Romanoff, B. D. (1993). When a child dies: Special considerations for providing mental health counseling for bereaved parents. *Journal of Mental Health Counseling, 15,* 384-393.

Stroebe, M. S., & Schut, H. A. (1999). The dual process model of coping with bereavement: Rationale and description. *Death Studies, 23,* 197-224.

Talbot, K. (1998-1999). Mothers now childless: Personal transformation after the death of an only child. *Omega, 38,* 167-186.

Tedeschi, R. G., & Calhoun, L. G. (1995). *Trauma and transformation: Growing in the aftermath of suffering.* Thousand Oaks, CA: Sage Publications.

Tedeschi, R. G., & Calhoun, L. G. (1996). The Posttraumatic Growth Inventory: Measuring the positive legacy of trauma. *Journal of Traumatic Stress, 9,* 455-471.

Tedeschi, R. G., & Calhoun, L. G. (2004a). Posttraumatic growth: Conceptual foundations and empirical evidence. *Psychological Inquiry, 15,* 1-18.

Tedeschi, R. G., & Calhoun, L. G. (2004b). *Helping bereaved parents: A clinician's guide.* New York: Brunner-Routledge.

Tedeschi, R. G., & Calhoun, L. G. (2006). Expert companions: Posttraumatic growth in clinical practice. In L. G. Calhoun & R. G. Tedeschi (Eds.), *Handbook of posttraumatic growth: Research and practice* (pp. 291-310). Mahwah, NJ: Lawrence Erlbaum Associates.

Wortman, C. B., & Silver, R. C. (1989). The myths of coping with loss. *Journal of Consulting and Clinical Psychology, 57,* 349-357.

Znoj, H. (2006). Bereavement and posttraumatic growth. In L. G. Calhoun & R. G. Tedeschi (Eds.), *Handbook of posttraumatic growth: Research and practice* (pp. 176-196). Mahwah, NJ: Lawrence Erlbaum Associates.

CHAPTER 7

Grief:
What We Have
Learned from
Cross-Cultural Studies

Paul C. Rosenblatt

Cross-cultural studies of grief have taught us that if we want to understand or help a grieving person, that person's cultural background matters enormously (e.g., Klass, 1999; Rosenblatt, 1993, 1997, 2001; Stroebe & Schut, 1998). In the past, most literature about grief seemed to assume a basic human pattern to grieving: No matter what our culture, we were all essentially the same. The classic sources on bereavement—for example, Freud (1959) and Lindemann (1944)—were written and read as though culture were irrelevant. Research traditions developed, practice studies were carried out, theoretical analyses were developed, a case study literature grew, and textbooks were written that offered a view of grieving in which culture did not matter. At the same time, however, a very substantial literature had developed, particularly in anthropology, that showed that culture *does* matter in trying to understand grief. Studies were conducted to explore similarities, differences, and patterns of grief across cultures (e.g., Rosenblatt, Walsh, & Jackson, 1976). Now we have reached the point where every volume of the major thanatology journals includes articles exploring how culture shapes grieving. Many practitioners understand how important it is to attend to culture, and they work at being culturally knowledgeable about the people they hope to help.

We have learned two major lessons from cross-cultural studies. First, we have learned that knowledge and perspectives derived from one culture (including the sociological and psychological sciences of that culture) do not necessarily apply to other cultures. Second, we have learned basic ideas about how to become culturally sensitive helpers of grieving people.

CULTURAL PATTERNING OF GRIEF

The cross-cultural literature has challenged us to back away from general statements about bereavement. Some aspects of how people grieve may be common across cultures, but it is a mistake to say that all humans do this or that. It is even more of a mistake to take the next step and assume that all grieving people *should* do this or that, or that something is wrong with a bereaved person who does not do this or that. Take any aspect of grieving that at one time was said to apply to all humans—it may still fit some people but may not apply to many people or many cultures. Crying, expressing sadness or depression, developing narratives about the death and the deceased, grieving over a defined time course, grieving in stages, attaching certain meanings to the death and the bereavement—any generalization misses the diversity across cultures and is probably wrong for billions of people. So we have been forced to move from claims about what is human to claims about what is possible or what fits specific people in specific cultures. Our knowledge (of the literature and of practice) is a knowledge of possibility, not certainty.

There is a cultural basis to what we think is true. In the writings from which we have learned, in our own language about grief, in our practice experience, powerful cultural forces are at work that shape and limit our sense of what grief is. We may think we have learned about human nature, but we have only learned one culture's way of classifying, framing, and making sense of things. These culturally rooted views can have an aura of truth because of the rhetoric in which they are couched, because we function in a community of people who think along the same lines, and perhaps because we do not know alternatives. Scholarly writings may have been vetted by grants agencies and editorial boards, which also gives them an aura of truth. However, seeing the thanatology we have learned as socioculturally constructed rather than as truth that transcends culture and time encourages a critical, analytic perspective that can provide rich new insights (see, e.g., Walter, 2005-2006). Knowing that our own foundation for understanding grief is socially constructed opens us to the possibility that the realities of others—including the people we are trying to help—may be quite different (see, e.g., Lopez, 2006).

For example, in some cultures, for some deaths of close family members, people apparently grieve little or not at all (Scheper-Hughes, 1985, writing about child deaths among impoverished people in north-eastern Brazil). In some cultures, people who have experienced major losses try to appear upbeat and undistressed and are strongly supported in that effort by the people around them (e.g., Wikan, 1988). In other cultures, people try not to cry over a major loss, conceal feelings of distress, and try to get over the loss quickly (e.g., Whittaker, Hardy, Lewis, & Buchan, 2005, writing about Somalis). On the other hand, it would be normal for an Egyptian woman in Cairo who has experienced the death of a child to grieve through years of muted depression, withdrawal, inactivity, self-absorption, and palpable suffering (Wikan, 1988).

Nor is grief necessarily expressed through emotional channels, as is common in the United States. It may be somatized (Abu-Lughod, 1985, writing about Egyptian Bedouins; Fabrega & Nutini, 1994, writing about Mexican Tlaxcalans). If we do not understand a person's cultural code, we might not connect severe headaches or chest pain with grief. Grief is also expressed in some cultures through rage and violence, which is outside the experience of many people who work with the bereaved in North America, Europe, or East Asia (Robarchek & Robarchek, 2005, writing about the Waorani of Ecuador; Schiefflin, 1985, writing about the Kaluli of New Guinea).

In opening up to realities that are outside our personal experience, we will learn that our language and concepts are not sufficient to understand core concepts of grief in some cultures. Some terms in the grief vocabulary have no equivalent in English. For example, the Ifaluk, a Pacific island society, use the terms *lalomweiu* and *fago* (Lutz, 1985). Lalomweiu can be translated as loneliness combined with sadness, as in "I lalomweiu my uncle who died." *Fago* can be translated as compassion combined with love and sadness; it is used primarily to talk about people one misses, as in

"I fago my relatives who are away." The Ojibwe term *gashkendam* combines grief with loneliness, affliction, dejection, homesickness, and melancholy (McNally, 2000). Even language that seems to be very straightforward—for example, "I feel sad"—may have underlying cultural meanings and complexities that are outside the experience of most English speakers. Thus, "I feel sad" might include fear, indignation, shame, or feelings of inadequacy.

There also is considerable diversity among cultures in what is grieved. We cannot assume that a person in another culture is weeping for the same reasons people in our own culture weep. For example, a widow might be weeping about the extreme poverty in which she now finds herself (Rosenblatt & Nkosi, in press, writing about Zulu widows of South Africa). A Bumbita Arapesh man grieving the death of his father might be focused on his loss of a mentor and of help in obtaining a wife (Leavitt, 1995). Part of a bereaved African-American's sorrow about the death of a loved one might be related to the racism that limited what the loved one could do (educationally, occupationally, and in other ways) and made life more difficult for the loved one (Rosenblatt & Wallace, 2005). In Latin American societies in which military dictatorships and assassination squads have killed or "disappeared" many, grief over a death or disappearance may be entangled with feelings about the injustice of the violence, rage at those who instigated the violence, and fear that one could also be a victim (Hollander, 1997; Zur, 1998).

Some cultures have notions of what grieving should be like and what forms of grieving are not good, something like indigenous notions of grief pathology. For example, the Ifaluk worry about any newly bereaved person who does not quickly get back to ordinary daily life after a good cry (Lutz, 1985). The Balinese worry about a grieving person who does not present a façade of happiness (Wikan, 1990). On the other hand, the Toraja of Indonesia are greatly concerned about a bereaved person who does not adequately express feelings of grief (Hollan, 1992; Wellenkamp, 1988).

MOURNING

Cultural practices in dealing with death and bereavement are key to the patterning of grief across cultures and inseparable from cultural diversity in the psychology of grieving. These practices may be focused on the deceased, the ancestors, trying to figure out the cause of death, protecting the bereaved, dealing with property, or protecting the community from spirits who are or who might become dangerous. To understand a grieving person from another culture, we must understand the cultural requirements that shape what that person may or may not do. For example, many cultures have a mourning period (often a year) during which bereaved people are limited in what they may do, where they may go, what they wear, their demeanor, and much more (Rosenblatt, Walsh, & Jackson, 1976). At the end of this period, there is almost always a ceremony that ends the mourning and deals with the spirit, and perhaps the remains, of the deceased. It may seem to an outsider that the grieving person is artificially limited and that his or her feelings, thoughts, and inclinations might be inconsistent with the requirements of ritual. But often grieving people are comfortable with or adapt to whatever their culture's mourning rituals require of them.

During mourning periods, bereaved people may be isolated from most or all others and may be marked in special ways by what they wear and changes in appearance (Rosenblatt, Walsh, & Jackson, 1976). These ritual practices give them time to grieve—in contrast, say, with the demands most U.S. employers put on bereaved people to get back to work almost immediately after a significant death (Rosenblatt, 2000). Cultural practices may also organize and recruit help for a bereaved person, so the person is not alone in his or her grieving. For example, a bereaved person who is isolated may be helped by a few others in the community with drawing water and acquiring food. The help may seem to be material, but it may be experienced as emotional support.

In many cultures, the mourning period includes relating to the spirit of the deceased. That spirit may be loved or feared; may be helped, supported, and appeased in various ways; or may be ignored. In some cultures, one must guard against harm from the spirit by, for example, never mentioning the name of the deceased (Shepard, 2002, writing about the Matsigenka of Peru) or by fleeing the grave site as soon as burial is complete. The Jivaro, an Amazonian people, actively work at forgetting the deceased (Taylor, 1993), and the Haya of Tanzania work at forgetting some of the meanings attached to objects that had belonged to the deceased as a way of acknowledging that the deceased no longer had the connection he or she had to the objects and to the living (Weis, 1997). Often, the spirits of the deceased are considered more likely to be in contact with the living immediately after the death and possibly to be more troublesome than they will be later (e.g., Dernbach, 2005, writing about the Chuuk of Micronesia; Rosenblatt, Walsh, & Jackson, 1976, pp. 63-65).

The meanings of terms related to dying and death vary across cultures. Take, for example, the word "dead." In Oman, a person whose breathing has stopped is not necessarily considered dead (Al-Adawi, Burjorjee, & Al-Issa, 1997), even after considerable time has passed. In contrast, among the Matsigenka of Peru (Shepard, 2002), some people are considered dead before they stop breathing, and those around them see no point in providing palliative medication. The cause of death is a sense-making matter in which cultures differ widely. The reasons Americans give for the death of a loved one and the causes that appear on U.S. death certificates are as much a reflection of our culture as, say, cultural accounts that focus on sorcery or witchcraft as the cause of death (e.g., Brison, 1992, writing about a cultural group in New Guinea; Mentore, 2005, writing about the Waiwai of Guyana; Rosenblatt & Nkosi, in press, writing about the Zulu of South Africa).

Grieving has meaning in a culture. Everything a grieving person does can be seen as meaning-making activity directed at creating—through narrative, chanting, rituals, expressions of emotion, treatment of the possessions of the deceased, and in other ways—meaning for the deceased, the death, the grieving, and much else. Cultures differ markedly in the meanings that are created and applied. For example, a key bereavement practice for the New Guinea cultural group studied by Brison (1992) is community discussion about who killed the person, and how and why. This discussion is held for all deaths, whatever the cause might be by U.S. cultural standards.

COLLECTIVE GRIEF

Much of the bereavement literature takes the individual as the unit of analysis. It is the individual who has the feelings and beliefs, and perhaps seeks help. But in many cultures, the death is considered a loss to the community, clan, or family, and grieving is collective. In these cultures, activities express the collective loss and deal with the problems the loss creates for the collective. To someone from an individually focused culture, some of the grieving people may seem to be rather far removed from the deceased; for example, a person who wails for a distant relative by marriage. But, in that culture, the deceased might be considered a close and important relative. Alternatively, one person might be, in a sense, the designated mourner (Francis, Kellaher, & Neophytou, 2005, p. 145)—the person among all those who are collectively grieving who carries the greatest responsibility for dealing in culturally appropriate and visible ways with the death (Rosenblatt & Nkosi, in press, writing about Zulu widows as designated mourners). In a related matter, relationship terms can differ from one language to another. For example, a father's brother might be called "father" in the grieving person's language, and a stepsister might be called "sister." If one is trying to help someone from a culture in which kinship terms have different meanings than they do in English and realizes that the "father" isn't actually a father, that is no cause for invalidating the person's grief or statements about closeness to the deceased

THE CULTURALLY SENSITIVE HELPER

It is easy to make the mistake of relying on our own culture and professional literature and thus missing crucial aspects of grieving in the culture of the person we are trying to help. In fact, it is easy not to even recognize this as a mistake. In my early cross-cultural work on bereavement (Rosenblatt, Walsh, & Jackson, 1976), I was sure that our theories would fit people everywhere. I fit the available information from various cultures to the theories of that time, but in the process I dismissed or ignored information that did not fit those theories. I also interpreted information about grieving in cultures different from my own in ways that took me far from the true meanings, understandings, and experiences of people in those cultures.

I realize now that I was missing important cultural differences. I have not come to distrust theory as a result, but I am skeptical of "totalizing theory," theory that applies understanding, classification, and insight to all people everywhere. I have learned that cultural differences are enormous and very important. Trying to provide support to a widow from a culture different from my own, I cannot assume that widowhood—or death, grief, or support—mean to her what they mean in my culture. Even the etiquette of my relationship with her may be far from what I know about etiquette in my own culture. Her responses to my questions and my offers of support may not mean what I think they mean. The very source of her grief might not be what I assume; for example, she may be grieving the fact that, as a widow in an alien cultural setting, she has to deal with me! Even if I understand many things about her culture, I might not understand if she is resisting that culture. She might, for example, be trying to continue her grieving beyond the normal and accepted time in her culture and resisting angry pressure from others in her culture to conform to those standards (e.g., Maschio, 1992, writing about a widow on the Pacific island of New Britain). Even if she is doing the same things a widow in my culture might do, the meaning may be very different—for example, a bereaved person in Taiwan (Hsu & Kahn, 1998-1999) might keep busy for very different reasons than one in the United States (Rosenblatt, 2000, pp. 56-57).

To complicate matters further, the aspects of culture that deal with death and grief are not static. People can be quite creative in dealing with losses in ways that may change their culture for themselves and others (Oushankine, 2006, writing about Russian mothers who organized to deal with the deaths of their soldier sons in ways that were new, though connected to preexisting aspects of their culture). Cultures are also changed through contact with other cultures (e.g., Lohmann, 2005, writing about the influence of Christian missionaries on a culture of Papua New Guinea). And because no culture is monolithic, totally clear in its demands and standards, and able to deal with every situation, intense conflict may arise among people in a culture over matters relating to loss (e.g., Stewart & Strathern, 2005, writing about conflict over who has the right to bury a corpse in a Papua New Guinea cultural group).

Learning specifics about grief in various cultures can make us more humble, respectful, and competent in working with bereaved people from those cultures. This kind of knowledge can also illustrate the danger of a totalizing perspective. But it is easy to slide back to what we know (Krause, 1998, p. 2), especially when the gap between us and a person from a different culture seems immense, but we think we should do *something*. Even with considerable cultural knowledge, we may not be able to help. But the more knowledge we have, the more open we are to possibilities. We can do good with a knowledge of possibility rather than a certainty of truth.

In working with a community, a family, a client, or a patient from a particular culture, we can read about grief in that culture and consult with cultural insiders who have relevant life experience and information or with outsiders who have studied the culture. We could, for example, acquire through reading or conversation a set of ideas about how the Hmong might deal with a death. However, we must treat that knowledge as something less than truth. No matter what we read and what the experts say, the people we work with might be different. Their subculture, their religious identity, or the cultural changes they have experienced might make our knowledge partially or completely irrelevant. Similarly, our understanding of what we have read or heard might involve simplifications or interpretations that render what we think we know inaccurate. Further, some people are not open about aspects of grief in their culture (e.g., Whittaker, Hardy, Lewis, & Buchan, 2005, writing about Somalis), so even the "expert sources" of information may be limited. Also, many people are bicultural or multicultural and thus blend grieving practices and traditions from more than one culture (Adams, 1993). It is necessary in working with people from any culture—even one we think we know—to learn from them what they can and are willing to teach us about what they want, believe, understand, feel, and struggle with.

One cost of cultural ignorance is to see as pathology in a grieving person what is sane, normal, expected, meaningful, respected, and appropriate by the standards of that person's culture. Freud, in his influential 1917 essay "Mourning and Melancholia," did not consider grieving, even in its extreme forms, to be pathological. But contemporary writers in the field have moved toward disciplining and narrowing the sense of what is acceptable grief by defining certain forms of grieving as pathology (Foote & Frank, 1999). Ong (2003, pp. 106-108), for example, writes about Cambodian refugees in the United States who struggled to deal with a mental health clinic that was asking for words they were unwilling to say and offering them medications they feared would block their thoughts and feelings about their terrible losses in the "killing fields" of Cambodia. What seems pathological in one culture may be normal in another. It might be most helpful to respect the grieving we witness rather than labeling it as pathological or not and to respond to it in ways appropriate to the culture of the person we wish to help. For example, we would allow the Zulu widow (Rosenblatt & Nkosi, in press) to avoid eye contact with us, to sit behind us, and to claim to know nothing about the relevance of witchcraft to her situation (although in her culture witchcraft is central). If a person needs help, perhaps that might be help with food, help with ceremonial expenses, and patient listening, rather than antidepressants, a forced conversation with us, or trying to make the person's grief fit into our own cultural framework. ■

Paul C. Rosenblatt has a Ph.D. in psychology and is Morse-Alumni Distinguished Teaching Professor of Family Social Science at the University of Minnesota. His teaching focuses on global and diverse families and qualitative research methods. His recent writing includes the book Two in a Bed: The Social System of Couple Bed-Sharing *(State University of New York Press, 2006), an interview study with John Barner of the effects of a parent's death on a couple's relationship, and an essay with Sungeun Yang on why a couple relationship can become difficult when one of the partners is dying. He is currently working on a book on obliviousness in families.*

REFERENCES

Abu-Lughod, L. (1985). Honor and sentiments of loss in a Bedouin society. *American Ethnologist, 12,* 245-261.

Adams, K. M. (1993). The discourse of souls in Tana Toraja (Indonesia): Indigenous notions and Christian conceptions. *Ethnology, 32,* 55-68.

Al-Adawi, S., Burjorjee, R., & Al-Issa, I. (1997). Mu-ghayeb: A culture-specific response to bereavement in Oman. *International Journal of Social Psychiatry, 43,* 144-151.

Brison, K. J. (1992). *Just talk: Gossip, meetings, and power in a Papua New Guinea village.* Berkeley: University of California Press.

Dernbach, K. B. (2005). Spirits of the hereafter: Death, funerary possession, and the afterlife in Chuuk, Micronesia. *Ethnology, 44,* 99-123.

Fabrega, H., Jr., & Nutini, H. (1994). Tlaxcalan constructions of acute grief. *Culture, Medicine and Psychiatry, 18,* 405-431.

Foote, C. E., & Frank, A. W. (1999). Foucault and therapy: The disciplining of grief. In A. S. Chambon, A. Irving, & L. Epstein (Eds.), *Reading Foucault for social work* (pp. 157-187). New York: Columbia University Press.

Francis, D., Kellaher, L., & Neophytou, G. (2005). *The secret cemetery.* Oxford, England: Berg.

Freud, S. (1959). Mourning and melancholia. In Joane Riviere (Ed.), *Collected papers of Sigmund Freud, vol. 4, Papers on metapsychology, Papers on applied psychoanalysis* (pp. 152-170). New York: Basic Books. (Original work published 1917.)

Hollan, D. W. (1992). Emotion, work and value of emotional equanimity among the Toraja. *Ethnology, 31,* 45-56.

Hollander, N. C. (1997). *Love in a time of hate: Liberation psychology in Latin America.* New Brunswick, NJ: Rutgers University Press.

Hsu, M.-T., & Kahn, D. L. (1998-1999). Coping strategies of Taiwanese widows adapting to loss. *Omega, 38,* 269-288.

Klass, D. (1999). Developing a cross-cultural model of grief: The state of the field. *Omega, 39,* 153-176.

Krause, I.-B. (1998). *Therapy across culture.* Thousand Oaks, CA: Sage.

Leavitt, S. C. (1995). Seeking gifts from the dead: Long-term mourning in Bumbita Arapesh cargo narrative. *Ethos, 23,* 53-73.

Lindemann, E. (1944). Symptomatology and management of acute grief. *American Journal of Psychiatry, 101*, 141-148.

Lohmann, R. I. (2005). The afterlife of Asabano corpses: Relationships with the deceased in Papua New Guinea. *Ethnology, 44*, 189-206.

Lopez, S. A. (2006). The influence of culture and ethnicity on end-of-life care. In R. S. Katz & T. A. Johnson (Eds.), *When professionals weep: Emotional and countertransference responses in end-of-life care* (pp. 91-103). New York: Routledge.

Lutz, C. (1985). Depression and the translation of emotional worlds. In A. Kleinman & B. Good (Eds.), *Culture and depression* (pp. 63-100). Berkeley: University of California Press.

Maschio, T. (1992). To remember the faces of the dead: Mourning and the full sadness of memory in southwestern New Britain. *Ethos, 20*, 387-420.

McNally, M. D. (2000). *Ojibwe singers: Hymns, grief, and a native culture in motion.* New York: Oxford University Press.

Mentore, G. (2005). *Of passionate curves and desirable cadences: Themes on Waiwai social being.* Lincoln, NE: University of Nebraska Press.

Ong, A. (2003). *Buddha is hiding: Refugees, citizenship, the new America.* Berkeley: University of California Press.

Oushankine, S. A. (2006). The politics of pity: Domesticating loss in a Russian province. *American Anthropologist, 108*, 297-311.

Robarchek, C., & Robarchek, C. (2005). Waorani grief and the witch-killer's rage: Worldview, emotion, and anthropological explanation. *Ethos, 33*, 205-230.

Rosenblatt, P. C. (1993). Cross-cultural variation in the experience, expression, and understanding of grief. In D. P. Irish, K. F. Lundy, & V. J. Nelsen (Eds.), *Ethnic variations in dying, death, and grief: Diversity in universality* (pp. 13-19). Washington, DC: Taylor & Francis.

Rosenblatt, P. C. (1997). Grief in small-scale societies. In C. M. Parkes, P. Laungani, & B. Young (Eds.), *Death and bereavement across cultures* (pp. 27-51). London: Routledge.

Rosenblatt, P. C. (2000). *Help your marriage survive the death of a child.* Philadelphia: Temple University Press.

Rosenblatt, P. C. (2001). A social constructionist perspective on cultural differences in grief. In M. S. Stroebe, R. O. Hansson, W. Stroebe, & H. Schut (Eds.), *Handbook of bereavement research: Consequences, coping, and care* (pp. 285-300). Washington, DC: American Psychological Association.

Rosenblatt, P. C., & Nkosi, B. C. (in press). South African Zulu widows in a time of poverty and social change. *Death Studies*, volume unknown at press time.

Rosenblatt, P. C., & Wallace, B. R. (2005). Narratives of grieving African-Americans about racism in the lives of deceased family members. *Death Studies, 29*, 217-235.

Rosenblatt, P. C., Walsh, R. P., & Jackson, D. A. (1976). *Grief and mourning in cross cultural perspective.* New Haven, CT: Human Relations Area Files Press.

Scheper-Hughes, N. (1985). Culture, scarcity and maternal thinking: Maternal detachment and infant survival in a Brazilian shantytown. *Ethos, 13*, 291-317.

Schiefflin, E. L. (1985). The cultural analysis of depressive affect: An example from New Guinea. In A. Kleinman & B. J. Good (Eds.), *Culture and depression* (pp. 101-133). Berkeley: University of California Press.

Shepard, G. H., Jr. (2002). Three days for weeping: Dreams, emotions, and death in the Peruvian Amazon. *Medical Anthropology Quarterly, 16*, 200-229.

Stewart, P. J., & Strathern, A. (2005). Cosmology, resources, and landscape: Agencies of the dead and the living in Duna, Papua New Guinea. *Ethnology, 44*, 35-47.

Stroebe, M., & Schut, H. (1998). Culture and grief. *Bereavement Care, 17*(1), 7-11.

Taylor, A. C. (1993). Remembering to forget: Identity, mourning and memory among the Jivaro. *Man, 28*, 653-678.

Walter, T. (2005-2006). What is complicated grief? A social constructionist perspective. *Omega, 52*, 71-79.

Weis, B. (1997). Forgetting your dead: Alienable and inalienable objects in northwest Tanzania. *Anthropological Quarterly, 70*, 164-172.

Wellenkamp, J. C. (1988). Notions of grief and catharsis among the Toraja. *American Ethnologist, 15*, 486-500.

Whittaker, S., Hardy, G., Lewis, K., & Buchan, L. (2005). An exploration of psychological well-being with young Somali refugee and asylum-seeker women. *Clinical Child Psychology and Psychiatry, 10*, 177-196.

Wikan, U. (1988). Bereavement and loss in two Muslim communities: Egypt and Bali compared. *Social Science and Medicine, 27*, 451-460.

Wikan, U. (1990). *Managing turbulent hearts: A Balinese formula for living.* Chicago: University of Chicago Press.

Zur, J. N. (1998). *Violent memories: Mayan war widows in Guatemala.* Boulder, CO: Westview.

Two Months Later

Jane Yolen

My friends expect me to be over
the worst of the grief;
that writing, dinners, the occasional lunch,
meetings, a movie or two,
work on our daughter's house,
two conferences in states far away
will scab over the deep cut
below my breastbone
where your death removed my heart.

The heart, like a phantom limb,
still hurts, throbs, aches, agonizes
over familiar things. Your shirts
hanging still in the closet,
the dozen or so hats you loved,
shoes two sizes big for me,
three sizes small for our sons.
I cannot yet bear to give them away
to the homeless, the shelters,
the needy, when my need
for you is still so great.

Do not help me to forget.
Help me to remember.

Continued

Jane Yolen is the distinguished author of over 200 books including Owl Moon, Devil's Arithmetic, *and* How do Dinosaurs Say Goodnight? *Her writings have won numerous awards including the Caldecott Medal. A graduate of Smith College and the University of Massachusetts, she was raised in New York City and now lives in Hatfield, Massachusetts.*

CHAPTER 8

Complicated Grief: The Debate Over a New DSM-V Diagnostic Category

Colin Murray Parkes

Much research has shown that bereavement, the loss of a loved person, can cause lasting distress and problems in physical and mental health (see Jacobs, 1993, for a review). It can also lead to improvements in maturity and psychological strength (Neimeyer, 2001). Much is now known about the risk factors that decide what kind of outcome we can expect (Stroebe & Schut, 2002). Those who care for families before and after bereavement are in a position to identify the risks and to steer people toward needed help. Well-conducted studies have shown that "the more complicated the grief process appears to be or to become, the better the chances of interventions leading to positive results" (Schut, Stroebe, van den Bout, & Terheggen, 2001).

Anxiety states and clinical depression are the most frequent psychological problems to follow major bereavements (Jacobs, 1993). These problems are frequent in psychiatric patients; their precursors, diagnosis, and treatment are well known and do not differ from reactions to other types of stress. Less frequent is posttraumatic stress disorder (PTSD), which can occur when a person has "experienced, witnessed, or been confronted with an event or events that involved actual or threatened death or serious injury, or a threat to the physical integrity of self or others" and the person's response involved "intense fear, helplessness, or horror" (American Psychiatric Association, 1994). Indeed, bereavement can act as a trigger for almost any mental disorder to which an individual is vulnerable.

These problems differ from complicated grief (CG), which, as we will see, is peculiar to bereavement, takes a unique course, and responds to different treatments from those prescribed for other conditions. This disorder was first described by Eric Lindemann in 1944, yet it has never been included in the influential *Diagnostic and Statistical Manual of Mental Disorders (DSM)* of the American Psychiatric Association. CG lacks an agreed-on set of diagnostic criteria, and its status remains debatable. If Lindemann was right, this uncertain status has given rise to a great deal of unnecessary suffering.

In recent years, much research has been carried out in this field with the aim of establishing rigorous diagnostic criteria and improving the care of those who suffer from CG. Two main schools of thought have emerged, one from Mardi Horowitz and his colleagues at the Langley Porter Psychiatric Institute at the University of California, and another from Holly Prigerson and her colleagues at the Department of Epidemiology and Psychiatry of Yale University. Both have used sophisticated methods of data collection and analysis to derive their own diagnostic criteria, which differ more in detail than in substance. A recent edition of *Omega* enabled the leading contenders to engage in a "symposium" to clarify the issues involved (Parkes, 2006a). Their conclusions will be summarized here. The debate continues, and it now seems likely that agreement has been reached on most important matters. The contributors to the *Omega* edition were asked three questions:

- Is there a type of grief that can justifiably be regarded as a mental disorder?

- If so, how should the disorder be classified in relation to other disorders?

- What criteria for diagnosis are best supported by systematic research?

This chapter summarizes the answers to these questions.

Is there a type of grief that can justifiably be regarded as a mental disorder?

Horowitz's research followed his own major contribution to the development of diagnostic criteria for PTSD, for which he had developed the Impact of Events Scale (Horowitz, Wilner, & Alvarez, 1979). Although a subscale of this instrument has been used as a measure of severe grief, Holly Prigerson and her colleagues (1995a) developed a more useful diagnostic instrument, the Index of Complicated Grief (ICG), aimed specifically at CG. Neither of these instruments is intended as a substitute for clinical judgment. Rather, they are standardized substitutes, approximations, that are suitable for research purposes but insufficiently precise for individual diagnosis.

Using the ICG, Prigerson's group has confirmed beyond reasonable doubt that for a minority of bereaved people, grief, instead of declining in intensity over time, remains chronic and severe, giving rise to protracted misery and inability to function effectively in the roles that make life worthwhile (Prigerson et al., 1995a, 1995b, 1996a). Indeed, bereaved people with persistent high scores on the ICG are at substantial risk for serious outcomes, ranging from hospital admissions and high blood pressure to suicide (Prigerson et al, 1997). These findings confirm and give powerful credence to much other work; however, some doubt the wisdom of designating CG as a mental disorder. The main objections are a reluctance to label grief as "abnormal," the stigma attached to psychiatric diagnoses, and the danger that family and friends will withdraw their support (Stroebe & Schut, 2006).

Prigerson's group has responded to these objections. The group's research demonstrates that CG is distinct from "normal" grief not only in terms of its persistence and severity but also because of the other symptoms and disabilities associated with it. The researchers do not doubt that stigmatization can take place, even when no psychiatric diagnosis has been made. In fact, it is not uncommon for bereaved people to imagine that they are going mad. However, a formal psychiatric diagnosis of CG, far from confirming such fears, enables the psychiatrist to reassure people that they are not psychotic. In a study of 135 bereaved persons (Prigerson & Maciejewski, 2006), 96% stated that if they were told they met the criteria for CG, "they would be relieved to know that they were not going crazy, that they had a recognizable condition and that the diagnosis would help their family members to understand better what they were experiencing"(p. 16). Likewise, in a recent nationwide study of a Norwegian population of parents who had lost a child, 74% of whom met Prigerson's criteria for complicated grief, Dyregrov concluded, "by claiming to protect the individual from being powerless and dependent on professionals, the demedicalization strategy prevents people in psychosocial crisis [from obtaining] access to professional help" (Dyregrov, 2005, p. 9).

Overall, there seems to be good reason to accept a psychiatric disorder of grieving but also to ensure that, as with all mental illness, diagnosis is reserved for those for whom the benefits outweigh any potential harm. Such people are entitled to the care, compassion, and the privileges accorded to the sick by society: sanction to withdraw from occupational and other demands they are unable to fulfill, the right to receive treatment, and the right to be compensated for any secondary losses resulting from the illness. In addition, when the bereavement is someone's fault, the bereaved have a right to legal compensation for suffering, loss of earnings, and cost of treatment.

How should the disorder be classified in relation to other disorders?

While Prigerson's group has shown that CG is distinct from clinical depression, PTSD, and normal grief (Prigerson et al., 1996a, 1996b), a dispute has arisen between her contention that it is a disorder of attachment and Horowitz's claim that it is a stress response syndrome. Horowitz (2006) finds several points of similarity between CG and PTSD, including preoccupation with intrusive memories and avoidance of painful reminders. Prigerson and Vanderwerker (2006) point out that, whereas the intrusive memories of PTSD are painful, those of CG are usually positive memories of a loved person. Furthermore, CG is frequently associated with a history of insecure attachments that may go back to childhood. That said, Prigerson and Vanderwerker continue to include "symptoms of traumatization" among their criteria for diagnosis.

Since the main function of the attachments we make throughout life is to provide security and support in times of trouble, it is no surprise to find that those with insecure attachments are more vulnerable than others to traumas of all kinds, including bereavement (Parkes, 2006b, p. 70). In that sense, both Prigerson and Horowitz are right. Like a pathological fracture of a bone, CG is both a disorder and a traumatic reaction. However, the essential element of CG is intense pining and yearning for a lost person, which seems to place it firmly in the category of attachment disorders. Another attachment disorder that has been included in the *DSM* is "childhood separation anxiety disorder" (a common cause of school refusal); this disorder is often reported in the history of people with CG (Vanderwerker, Jacobs, Parkes, & Prigerson, 2006).

What criteria for diagnosis are best supported by systematic research?

Thus far, we have been considering complicated grief as if it were one disorder, but several complications of grief have been described. These include chronic grief, delayed or inhibited grief, and identification syndromes (in which the bereaved person develops hypochondriacal symptoms resembling the illness or injury suffered by the person now dead). Chronic grief—the persistence of intense grief over long periods of time—is the most common and has become the focus of Prigerson's research. An alternative term for this syndrome, that is currently under consideration, is "Prolonged Grief Disorder."

Inhibited grief remains contentious. It is difficult, if not impossible, to measure grief that is not expressed. Researchers such as Keltner and Bonanno (1997) have demonstrated that, overall, people who show positive rather than negative emotions after bereavement have less distress later than do overt grievers. Without controlling for the strength of the attachment, it is hard to know whether lack of grieving results from repression of grief or paucity of attachment. Currently, the onus is on the proponents of repression theory to show that the inhibition of grief is a cause of subsequent problems. One possible outcome of inhibition of grief is delay in its onset. This delayed grief is allowed for in Prigerson's CG, provided that the grief that then appears is severe and protracted, and fulfills her other criteria.

Many criteria for diagnosing CG have been proposed at one time or another. Currently, the researchers who have contributed most to the refinement of these criteria agree on the following: (1) persistent pining for a lost person is an essential criterion; (2) a period of 6 months or more should have elapsed since the bereavement; and (3) the syndrome should seriously impair the sufferer's ability to function in occupational or domestic roles and responsibilities.

While the precise wording of the remaining criteria remains under discussion, symptoms of traumatization are also required—thus, feelings of emotional numbness may persist along with inability to accept the reality of the loss and to move forward. People with CG find that their assumptive world—the world they have always taken for granted—has been shattered (Janoff-Bulman, 1992); life seems to have lost its meaning and direction.

Taken together, these criteria provide us with a firm basis for diagnosing the principal form of complicated grief. The inclusion of the diagnosis in the DSM will stimulate future research, and other forms of CG may then be added.

CAN COMPLICATED GRIEF BE PREVENTED?

While many systematic random-allocation studies have been carried out on the effectiveness of bereavement services in improving outcome after bereavement, few have focused on their influence on CG. Even so, lack of clear benefits from such services, when offered to unselected or self-selected samples of bereaved people, gives little cause for optimism.

In their review of these studies, Schut, Stroebe, van den Bout, and Terheggen, (2001) note, "In several of these studies, participants were screened for risk level before being offered intervention. This coincides almost completely with whether or not positive results were found, suggesting that selecting participants raises the chances of intervention leading to positive results."(p. 725) Many palliative care units now use some method of risk assessment to focus bereavement support where it is most needed and, at the same time, identify problems that will need attention. These methods include assessment of the circumstances of the loss (e.g., the extent to which it was unexpected, untimely, or otherwise traumatic); assessment of the vulnerability of the bereaved person (e.g., previous psychiatric history, suicidal threats, attachment problems, current distressing symptoms); and social circumstances (e.g., isolation, dysfunctional family, or lack of future meaningful life). See Stroebe and Schut (2002) and Parkes (2006b) for further details.

Of particular relevance to the prevention of CG is Kissane and Bloch's family focused grief therapy model (2002). This model is intended for use in palliative care units and aims to prevent problems before they arise by increasing cohesiveness, opening communication channels, and enhancing problem solving in dysfunctional families, which are at special risk for CG. A recent random-allocation study indicates that the model reduces bereavement risk in families low on cohesiveness and expressiveness, but not if they are also highly conflicted or hostile.

TREATMENT OF COMPLICATED GRIEF

The most persuasive argument for including CG as a psychiatric disorder would be to demonstrate that it can be cured. While we have some way to go to achieve this aim, evidence exists of substantial benefits from treatment.

Therapies for CG reflect the theoretical assumptions of their proponents, and few have been subjected to adequate scientific evaluation. In the period after World War II, when Lindemann was carrying out his research, delayed and inhibited reactions may have been more common than they are today. He emphasized the danger of repressing grief and developed a method of treatment aimed at facilitating its expression. Random-allocation studies by Mawson, Marks, Ramm, and Stern (1981) and by Sireling, Cohen, and Marks (1988) gave limited support to the value of Ramsay's adaptation of this "guided mourning" therapy (1979), but in most cases the results were disappointing.

More recently the recognition of the importance of coping strategies in bereavement has led to the development of cognitive therapies. Both cognitive (problem-focused) and Lindemann's affective (emotion-focused) therapies have shown benefits in random-allocation studies. One study indicated that women benefit most from cognitive and men from affective interventions (Schut, Stroebe, van den Bout & de Keijser 1997a). The combination of cognitive with affective therapy seems ideal; in one study, it was shown to produce more benefit than cognitive therapy alone (Schut, de Keijser, van den Bout, & Stroebe, 1997b).

None of the above studies focused exclusively on the problem of complicated grief, but a recent evaluation by Shear, Frank, Houck, and Reynolds (2005) of a new method of CG treatment has done so. This method uses Stroebe and Schut's dual process model (1999), which suggests that for healthy grieving to take place, it is necessary to alternate between pining for the lost person (loss orientation) and putting one's grief aside and beginning the painful process of rethinking and revising one's view of the world and future plans (restoration orientation). Consequently, Shear and colleagues' therapy includes both affective and cognitive components.

They randomly assigned bereaved people with high scores on Prigerson's ICG to two groups. One group received 16 sessions of interpersonal psychotherapy, the other received the same number of sessions of complicated grief treatment.

The therapy included an introductory phase during which the therapist provided information about normal and complicated grief and described the dual process model. In the middle phase, both orientations were examined and exercises were undertaken, including "revisiting exercises" in which the patient told the story of the death of the lost person and related it to the level of distress. These exercises were tape recorded and played between sessions. The loss orientation was also addressed during these sessions, in the form of imaginary conversations with the dead person, the aim being to evoke positive emotions. The restoration orientation was addressed by encouraging the patient to set goals and identify ways of working toward them. In the final phase, progress was reviewed, achievements acknowledged, and further targets agreed on.

By 24 weeks after the start of therapy, 60% of those receiving complicated grief therapy and 25% of those receiving interpersonal therapy showed a decrease in the ICG score of 20 points or more; similar, statistically significant differences were observed by independent assessors. While these results are very encouraging, it would be a mistake to assume that complicated grief therapy provides the answer to complicated grief: About a quarter of patients dropped out from both groups in the course of therapy and nearly half showed little or no improvement.

Another promising intervention that is under development is Wagner, Knaevelsrud, and Maercker's Internet-based therapy for complicated grief

(2005). This therapy is of particular interest for its low cost and potential value in developing countries. It includes guided writing of letters to the dead and to a mythical friend who has symptoms of CG similar to those of the patient. A random-allocation study is in training.

The breakdown of the pattern of life that results from CG presents both a challenge and an opportunity. Most therapists believe that, out of the ruins of the assumptive world, a new world can arise—not, as some think, by forgetting the dead, but by recovering the memories, meanings, and messages that continue to enrich us (Klass, Silverman, & Nickman, 1996). Both cognitive and affective strategies have their place. Our future can only be built on the past.

CONCLUSION

The inclusion of complicated grief in the *DSM* will not be the end of the story. If PTSD is a precedent, CG's inclusion will stimulate research that will lead to further modifications and developments. One development may well be the recognition that CG is not confined to bereavement by death. Many other life events give rise to lasting grief and loss of the assumptive world (Kauffman, 2002). Other complications of grief may also need to be included, either as separate categories or subcategories of CG (or "Prolonged Grief Disorder," if this term is adopted).

Psychiatry has lagged behind the rest of medicine in relying on diagnoses based on descriptive phenomenology rather than etiology. Now that PTSD and CG have broken the mold, we can expect further changes in nosology and, with them, more effective methods of prevention and treatment.

As resistance fades to diagnosing CG as pathology, we may become more understanding of those who suffer from it. Few people today would accept that doctors should withhold treatment because "suffering is good for the soul;" indeed, those who work in palliative care and bereavement continue to discover more evidence of the extent to which the alleviation of physical and mental pain leaves people more secure and better able to face their own mortality and that of those they love. Therapy will never remove the pain of complicated grief, but it may make it more bearable and help people find new hope and meaning in their lives. ■

Colin Murray Parkes has been a consultant psychiatrist to St. Christopher's Hospice in Sydenham, England, since its inception in 1966. At St. Christopher's, Dr. Parkes set up the first hospice-based bereavement service and carried out some of the earliest systematic evaluations of hospice care. He worked for 13 years with John Bowlby at the Tavistock Institute of Human Relations and edited books on the nature of human attachments and cross-cultural aspects of death and bereavement. Dr. Parkes is also a consultant psychiatrist to Life President of Cruse: Bereavement Care.

In addition, Dr. Parkes is the author of Bereavement: Studies of Grief in Adult Life; *and most recently,* Love and Loss: the Roots of Grief and its Complications, *published by Routledge. He is also the author of numerous publications on psychological aspects of bereavement, amputation of a limb, terminal cancer care, and other life crises.*

Dr. Parkes has served as scientific editor of Bereavement Care, *the international journal for bereavement counselors, and advisory editor for several journals concerned with hospice, palliative care and bereavement.*

He has also acted as consultant and adviser following several disasters including Aberfan and after the 9-11 terrorist attacks in New York. Dr. Parkes helped set up a trauma recovery program in Rwanda in 1995. In April 2005 he was sent by Help-the-Hospices, with Ann Dent, to India to assess the psychological needs of people bereaved by the tsunami.

Recently Dr. Parkes's work has focused on traumatic bereavements (with special reference to violent deaths and the cycle of violence) and on the roots in the attachments of childhood of the psychiatric problems that can follow the loss of attachments in adult life.

He was awarded an OBE by Her Majesty The Queen (of England) for his services to bereaved people in June 1996.

REFERENCES

American Psychiatric Association. (1994). *Diagnostic and statistical manual of mental disorders.* (4th Ed.). Washington, DC: Author.

Dyregrov, K. (2005). Do professionals disempower bereaved people? Grief and social intervention. *Bereavement Care, 24*(1), 7-10.

Horowitz, M., Wilner, N., & Alvarez, W. (1979). Impact of event scale: A measure of subjective stress. *Psychosomatic Medicine, 41,* 209-218.

Horowitz, M. (2006). Meditating on complicated grief disorder as a diagnosis. Symposium on Complicated Grief. *Omega, 52*(1), 88.

Jacobs, S. (1993). *Pathologic grief: Maladaptation to loss.* Washington, DC, and London: American Psychiatric Association Press.

Janoff-Bulman, R. (1992). *Shattered assumptions: Towards a new psychology of trauma.* New York: The Free Press.

Kauffman, J. (Ed.). (2002). *Loss of the assumptive world: A theory of traumatic loss.* New York and London: Brunner-Routledge.

Keltner, D., & Bonanno, G. (1997). A study of laughter and dissociation: Distinct correlates of laughter and smiling after bereavement. *Journal of Personal and Social Psychology, 73*(4), 687-702

Kissane, D., & Bloch, S. (2002). *Family focused grief therapy: A model of family-centred care during palliative care and bereavement.* Buckingham, England, and Philadelphia: Open University Press.

Klass, D., Silverman, P. R., & Nickman, S. (Eds.). (1996). *Continuing bonds: New understandings of grief.* Washington, DC, and London: Taylor and Francis.

Lindemann, E. (1944). The symptomatology and management of acute grief. *American Journal of Psychiatry, 101,* 141-148.

Mawson, D., Marks, I. M., Ramm, L., & Stern, L. S. (1981). Guided mourning for morbid grief: A controlled study. *British Journal of Psychiatry, 138,* 185-193.

Neimeyer, R. (Ed.). (2001). *Meaning reconstruction and the experience of loss.* Washington, DC: American Psychological Association Press.

Parkes, C. M. (Guest Ed.). (2006a). Introduction and conclusions. Symposium on Complicated Grief. *Omega, 52*(1), 1-112.

Parkes, C. M. (2006b). *Love and loss: The roots of grief and its complications.* London and New York: Routledge.

Prigerson, H. G., Maciejewski, P. K., Newsom, J., Reynolds, C. F., III, Frank, E., Bierhals, E. J., et al. (1995a). The Inventory of Complicated Grief: a scale to measure maladaptive symptoms of loss. *Psychiatry Research, 59,* 65-79.

Prigerson, H. G., Frank, E., Kasl, S. V., Reynolds, C. F., III, Anderson, B., Zubenko, G. S., et al. (1995b). Complicated grief and bereavement-related depression as distinct disorders: Preliminary evaluation in elderly bereaved spouses. *American Journal of Psychiatry, 152*(1), 22-30.

Prigerson, H. G., Bierhals, A. J., Kasl, S. V., Reynolds, C. F., III, Shear, M. K., Newsom, J. T., et al. (1996a). Complicated grief as a distinct disorder from bereavement-related depression and anxiety: A replication study. *American Journal of Psychiatry, 153*, 84-86.

Prigerson, H. G., Shear, M. K., Newsom, I., Frank, E., Reynolds, C.F., III, Houck, P.R. et al. 1996b). Anxiety among widowed elders: Is it distinct from depression and grief? *Anxiety, 2*, 1-12.

Prigerson, H. G., Bierhals, A. J., Kasl, S. V., Reynolds, C.F., III, Shear, M.K., Day, N., et al. (1997). Traumatic grief as a risk factor for mental and physical morbidity. *American Journal of Psychiatry, 154*, 617-623.

Prigerson, H. G., & Maciejewski, P. K. (2006). A call for sound empirical testing and evaluation of criteria for complicated grief proposed for DSM-V. Symposium on Complicated Grief. *Omega, 52*(1), 16.

Prigerson, H. G., & Vanderwerker, L. C. (2006). Final remarks. Symposium on Complicated Grief. *Omega, 52*(1), 92.

Ramsay, R. W. (1979). Bereavement: A behavioural treatment for pathological grief. In P. O. Sjoden, S. Bayes, & W. S. Dorkens (Eds.), *Trends in behaviour therapy* (pp. 217-248). New York: Academic Press.

Schut, H. A. W., Stroebe, M., van den Bout, J., & de Keijser, J. (1997a). Intervention for the bereaved: Gender differences in the efficacy of two counseling programs. *British Journal of Clinical Psychology, 36*, 63-72.

Schut, H., de Keijser, J., van den Bout, J., & Stroebe, M.S. (1997b). Cross-modality grief therapy: Description and assessment of a new program. *Journal of Clinical Psychology, 52*(3), 357-365.

Schut, H., Stroebe, M.S., van den Bout, J. & Terheggen, M. (2001). The efficacy of bereavement interventions: Determining who benefits. In *Handbook of bereavement research: Consequences, coping and care.* M. S. Stroebe, R. O. Hansson, W. Stroebe, & H. Schut (Eds.), American Psychological Association: Washington, DC (pp. 705-737).

Shear, K., Frank, E., Houck, P. R., & Reynolds, C. F. (2005). Treatment of complicated grief: A randomized controlled trial. *Journal of the American Medical Association, 293*(21), 2601-2607.

Sireling, L., Cohen, D., & Marks, I. (1988). Guided mourning for morbid grief: A controlled replication. *Behavior Therapy, 19*, 121-132.

Stroebe, M. S., & Schut, H. (1999). The dual process model of coping with bereavement: Rationale and description. *Death Studies, 23*, 197-224.

Stroebe, M., & Schut, H. (2002). Risk factors in bereavement outcome: A methodological and empirical review. In M. S. Stroebe, R. O. Hansson, W. Stroebe, & H. Schut (Eds.), *Handbook of bereavement research: Consequences, coping and care* (pp. 349-371). Washington, DC: American Psychological Association.

Stroebe, M. & Schut, H. (2006). Complicated grief: A conceptual analysis of the field. Symposium on Complicated Grief. *Omega, 52*(1), 53-70.

Vanderwerker, L. C., Jacobs, S. C., Parkes, C. M., & Prigerson, H. G. (2006). An exploration of associations between separation anxiety in childhood and complicated grief in later life. *Journal of Nervous and Mental Disease, 194*(2), 121-123.

Wagner, B., Knaevelsrud, C., & Maercker, A. (2005). Internet-based treatment for complicated grief: Concepts and case study. *Journal of Loss and Trauma, 10,* 409-432.

Implications for Practice

The new insights about the grieving process need to inform and be integrated within bereavement support. These theoretical advances emphasize that no one program can meet the needs of all grieving individuals. Some will benefit from counseling. Others will find solace in groups. Still others will find value in psychoeducational approaches, perhaps offered in informational seminars of bibliotherapy.

Dale Larson and William Hoyt reaffirm the value of multiple approaches in the first chapter in this section. Larson and Hoyt attempt to answer current critics who have questioned the results of counseling. Their analysis reemphasizes that grief counseling that uses multiple models and approaches and sees grief as a multifaceted process can be effective. They point out that a key factor in grief counseling—and in all counseling—is self-referral. Grief support services, they caution, should "reach but not grab." Larson and Hoyt also reaffirm the importance of psychoeducational approaches and the value of strengthening natural support systems.

Phyllis Silverman's chapter builds on the idea of developing natural support systems. Widow-to-widow programs pioneered the idea of using other widows to offer meaningful support. Support groups can validate loss, offer meaningful respite and activity, explore adaptations as one deals with loss, and engender hope.

One of the significant understandings that has emerged in the past 20 years is the importance of seeing grief as more than affect. Grief counseling and support need to do more than offer opportunities to ventilate emotions. Robert A. Neimeyer's work has emphasized that some losses can cause bereaved individuals to reconstruct their sense of meaning, which is now challenged by loss. Neimeyer's chapter stresses ways to understand and to facilitate grieving clients struggling with the issue of reconstructing meaning.

The next chapters focus on losses throughout the life cycle. David Balk begins by exploring the ways that children and adolescents grieve. Balk makes a basic point: Although developmental processes may influence how children and adolescents experience loss, it is important to acknowledge and validate grief and to offer support in developmentally appropriate ways.

This is underlined by Keith Whitehead's *Voices* piece. Although Whitehead's father died some 17 years earlier and his childhood was rich with supportive others, Whitehead clearly feels the absence of his dad. His essay offers a reaffirmation of the reality that one lives with loss rather than overcomes or outgrows grief.

This reality is also reflected in Dennis Klass's chapter. As Klass explores the worlds of bereaved parents, he notes that many bereaved parents maintain an inner representation of their dead child—an image of the child at the age he or she would be had the child survived. Klass's work in this area, as well as his work with Asian religions, played a significant role in the concept of continuing bonds (Klass, Silverman, & Nickman, 1996).

Miriam and Sidney Moss conclude this section on life-cycle issues with a chapter that focuses on how the death of an older parent affects the adult child. The Mosses note a basic paradox: Even though this is one of the most common loss experiences, it is little researched. Their work brings to fruition many of the themes reflected throughout this book, including the ways one continues connections with deceased parents and the potential of loss to transform—in both positive and negative ways—the lives of survivors.

These chapters underlie another issue: Grief is not simply an individual experience; it affects all within the intimate network. Kathleen Gilbert's chapter stresses how the process of meaning making continues throughout the illness and after death. Gilbert notes that families make meaning both as individuals and as members of a system. The family's attribution of meaning can therefore both complicate and facilitate individual attempts to make meaning of the loss. Gilbert's chapter reminds counselors to explore not only the ways death affects individuals but also the ways family members react to one another.

In her chapter, Kathleen Gilbert uses an inclusive definition of the family, emphasizing that family is more than simply a biological or legal entity. In a very real way, families, or intimate networks, are those people who care about one another. Dana Cable and Terry Martin's chapter focuses on disenfranchised grievers—those whose loss might not be acknowledged by others, who may not have a socially validated right to mourn that loss. Their chapter offers three contributions. First, they sensitize counselors to the many situations that may engender the disenfranchisement of grief. Second, they offer a valuable discussion of counseling techniques. Finally, they reaffirm that one of the major ways that our paradigm of grief has shifted is to a larger recognition of how a variety of different losses can engender grief. ■

REFERENCE

Klass, D., Silverman, P., & Nickman, S. (1996). *Continuing bonds: New understandings of grief.* Washington, DC: Taylor and Frances.

CHAPTER 9

The Bright Side of Grief Counseling: Deconstructing the New Pessimism

Dale G. Larson and William T. Hoyt

In 2000, an alarming research finding shook the bereavement field. A meta-analysis of grief interventions (Neimeyer, 2000) found that more than one third of grief counseling clients were worse off at the end of treatment than they would have been with no treatment. The analysis also found that nearly one in two clients who were "normal" grievers (as opposed to those who were "traumatically bereaved") "suffered as a result of treatment" (p. 546).

Now accepted as scientific fact, the findings of treatment-induced deterioration effects (TIDE) have been widely cited in the bereavement literature and beyond, contributing to a newly pessimistic view of grief counseling that is prevalent in research reports, conference presentations, and the popular press (Larson & Hoyt, in press). This pessimism is reflected in the conclusion by the Center for the Advancement of Health (CFAH, 2003) that

> the evidence from well-conducted studies of interventions . . .
> challenges the efficacy and effectiveness of grief interventions for
> those experiencing uncomplicated bereavement. This evidence
> also indicates that concerns are warranted about the potential
> of interventions to cause harm to some individuals (p. 72).

Such conclusions are, and should be, disturbing. If they are valid, the effectiveness and even the ethicality of much of what grief counselors do is called into question. Given these concerns, the perceived seriousness and far-reaching impact of the TIDE findings are quite understandable.

The TIDE findings have had different impacts on different stakeholders. For practitioners who consider the findings to be valid, they have had a trauma-like impact. These practitioners have had to revise cherished core beliefs about the value of their interventions ("I have confidence in the positive effects of my helping interventions") and to consider the deeply disquieting view "What I am doing might not be helping, and may even be harming, the people I care for." These doubts have only deepened in response to the wave of cautionary, often openly critical comments directed at grief work in the wake of the TIDE data (Wortman, 2006).

Even practitioners who do not accept the findings as valid feel the strain of working in a field that is the target of considerable skepticism, both internally and, increasingly, in the eyes of the public.

For researchers, as we shall see, the striking and unexpected TIDE findings prompted a reworking of some basic beliefs about grief counseling. Bereavement theorists have frequently cited the findings in support of alternatives to traditional grief counseling approaches and the grief work hypothesis.

In this chapter, we shall first summarize the results of recent evaluations of the empirical foundations of the TIDE findings and the new pessimism (Larson & Hoyt, 2006, in press). Those evaluations led to two startling discoveries: (1) The claims of iatrogenic effects for grief counseling have no empirical or statistical basis, and (2) the generally pessimistic portrait of outcomes that pervades the literature rests on misinterpretations of meta-analytic findings, and correcting for these misinterpretations reveals a relatively optimistic picture. The implications of these two discoveries for bereavement research, theory, and practice will be the central focus of this chapter. We argue that these pivotal discoveries provide the rationale and impetus for a deconstruction of the new pessimism in the bereavement field and a corresponding reconstruction of our views of grief and grief counseling. We end with a discussion of some key lessons these developments contain for researchers and clinicians.

EVIDENTIARY BASIS FOR THE NEW PESSIMISM

Recent pessimism about the effectiveness of grief counseling is based on two related claims. First is that grief counseling often harms clients, leaving them worse off than if they had not participated. It is claimed that outcome studies show that an average of 38% of clients deteriorated as a result of treatment. Second, meta-analyses are said to show that grief counseling is almost completely ineffective. It is claimed that treated clients improve little or not at all relative to those in control (no treatment) conditions on measures of such variables as grief, depression, and anxiety.

A third claim, representing a subsidiary finding, has also been influential in defining the scope and clinical relevance of grief counseling. Reviews of the grief literature often assert that outcomes of grief counseling are somewhat stronger for clients who are experiencing complicated grief but near zero for those experiencing "normal" (i.e., noncomplicated) bereavement. Proponents of this view contend that clients who are experiencing normal grief are especially likely to be harmed by counseling. Nearly 50% of these clients are worse off as a result of counseling, according to Neimeyer (2000).

These claims, singly and in combination, have achieved a consensual status bordering on unanimity among bereavement scholars (Larson & Hoyt, in press). Research articles often accept one or more of these notions as a premise. Past findings and theories have been reinterpreted in light of these claims, and these widely cited beliefs have influenced views of the grieving process and of grief counseling in other fields, in the nonscientific press, and in popular books on psychology.

EVALUATION OF CLAIMS OF INEFFECTIVENESS AND HARM

As we have tried to show (Larson & Hoyt, in press), although these claims are cited as research-based findings, none of them has a strong empirical foundation. First, to our knowledge, there is no valid statistical technique to quantify treatment deterioration in psychotherapy outcome studies. The TIDE findings for grief counseling, usually attributed to Neimeyer (2000), are actually derived from a dissertation written by Fortner (1999). Neither Fortner's findings nor the statistical technique on which he relied has been published in a peer-reviewed journal. Reviewers appointed by Gary

VandenBos (American Psychological Association publisher and managing editor of *American Psychologist*) agreed that there is no valid basis for the TIDE claims. In a forthcoming article (Larson & Hoyt, in press), we describe Fortner's method in detail and show that it cannot provide a valid TIDE estimate.

Second, in a thorough meta-analysis published in the *Journal of Counseling Psychology*, Allumbaugh and Hoyt (1999) painted a relatively optimistic portrait of grief counseling outcomes, although they criticized the ecological validity of many of the studies available at that time. (Most available outcome studies used recruited clients rather than clients who sought counseling on their own.) In recent reviews of the literature on grief therapy outcomes, Allumbaugh and Hoyt's findings have often been misrepresented or even ignored by authors who base their conclusions about the effectiveness of grief therapy primarily or exclusively on Fortner's (1999) unpublished study.

Third, the contention that "normal" grief is unresponsive to grief counseling is based on Neimeyer's (2000) summary of a subsidiary analysis in Fortner's dissertation. The validity of this conclusion is difficult to gauge. Fortner did not report on the procedures involved in his analysis, such as how studies of "complicated" bereavement were identified and whether two or more coders were able to agree on which studies belonged in this category (Larson & Hoyt, in press). Allumbaugh and Hoyt (1999), who coded a similar study characteristic (normal versus high-risk grievers), found no evidence of a difference in effectiveness for these two groups.

The related claim (Neimeyer, 2000) that normally bereaved clients are most likely to be harmed is, of course, an application of the TIDE statistic. Because this statistical technique has been shown not to yield valid deterioration estimates (Larson & Hoyt, in press), assertions about greater risk of harm for normal grievers are without empirical grounding.

RECONSTRUCTING OUR VIEWS OF GRIEF AND GRIEF COUNSELING

Our discovery of the erroneous nature of the TIDE findings and of the failure to adequately evaluate and interpret previous meta-analytic findings presents a distinct opportunity for the field. The deconstruction of the new pessimism in the bereavement field permits a corresponding reconstruction of views of grief and grief counseling. These reconstructed views can be shaped by answers to the following question: How would our views be different if the TIDE findings had not entered the scientific literature and if meta-analytic findings had been more accurately interpreted?

This reconstructive process has parallels to the kinds of adjustments we find in coping with loss (Neimeyer, 2000). The TIDE findings had disequilibrating, trauma-like effects because they were so extreme and because they pertained to counseling's key dimension: its efficacy. Some in the field found their strongly held beliefs shaken by the findings, others saw an opportunity to challenge conventional wisdom; however, all needed to adjust in some way to the new empirical realities. The discoveries described here call for a second readjustment or reconstruction and—as recent thinking about coping with loss suggests (Currier, Holland, & Neimeyer, 2006)—present opportunities for discovering new meanings and finding benefits in the midst of change. We turn now to an exploration of what these new meanings and benefits might be.

Professionals' Views of Grief Counseling

A major implication of the new perspective is that bereavement professionals can enjoy a more realistic and positive view of their helping efforts. For the past 6 years, the possibility of harming clients has troubled counselors who accepted the TIDE findings. If 38% of grief-counseling clients and nearly 50% of normally bereaved clients are worse off at the end of treatment than they would have been without treatment, grief counseling is ethically problematic. The perspective offered here should provide relief for these counselors.

Hospice administrators and other nonclinicians who assist the bereaved can also approach their work with greater confidence. Many of these professionals were strongly influenced by the new pessimism. Patti Homan, the Bereavement Professional Section leader for the National Council of Hospice and Palliative Professionals of the National Hospice and Palliative Care Organization, received inquiries from hospice bereavement coordinators in different parts of the country who were concerned because their administrators, as a result of the publicity that attended the CFAH report, were questioning the value of their bereavement programs (personal communication, March 1, 2006).

Correcting these negative views of grief counseling and bereavement services will be difficult; replacing them with the cautious optimism that seems warranted in light of research findings to date will require systematic efforts.

Timing of Interventions and Motivation for Counseling

The view of grief counseling informed by the current analysis brings fresh perspectives on several key clinical issues, including the role of client motivation and the timing of interventions. With regard to client motivation, Allumbaugh and Hoyt (1999) noted that the effect sizes for studies involving self-referred clients were quite large. Schut, Stroebe, van den Bout, and Terheggen (2001), in a review of studies of grief interventions, also observed that self-referral was a key variable affecting counseling outcomes. They concluded, "Almost without exception the studies with less favorable results are those that use [such] an 'outreach procedure'" (p. 731) (i.e., participants were recruited for intervention).

It makes sense that persons who seek treatment on their own (and are not recruited for a study) would have greater improvement. We can speculate that self-referred clients are probably more intrinsically motivated for treatment (Miller, 1985), have more positive outcome expectations (Glass, Arnkoff, & Shapiro, 2001), and are more open to change (Principe, Marci, Glick, & Ablon, 2006). When people acknowledge that they need help and ask for it, helping efforts would seem more likely to have sizable positive effects. Because clients typically come to grief counselors of their own volition, and because there is evidence that these clients have substantially better outcomes than clients who are recruited into treatment studies, we recommend that researchers studying grief interventions design their studies to include self-referred clients, so that their findings will be relevant to practice.

The clinical recommendation that issues from these findings might be summarized as "Reach, but don't grab." Helping works best when people see a problem and take a positive step toward receiving help. All levels of services should be made available to bereaved clients, but there should not be a strong recruitment component.

The picture emerging from the current analysis also shifts our thinking about the timing of interventions. Although findings in the literature are mixed (Schut et al., 2001), Allumbaugh and Hoyt (1999) found that earlier interventions may be associated with highly positive outcomes. In studies involving clients who began treatment within 3 or 4 months of their loss, the effects were approximately the same as the (strong and) typical effects observed in outcome studies with other presenting problems.

The exact optimal timing for bereavement interventions cannot be deduced from existing research. However, it appears to make good clinical sense that interventions offered earlier than is typical in the research studies examined here might show better results. We would argue that in the first days and probably months of bereavement, the optimal helping strategy is to enhance the client's natural support systems. The optimal goal might be to reach out and make a variety of levels of service available, but not to "grab" clients into treatment. What is most important is that clients can easily avail themselves of the support they need if their natural supports prove inadequate, they recognize personal distress, and they opt to seek help.

An unfortunate additional element contributing to the new pessimism has been the conflation of evidence on the ineffectiveness of early inter-vention for trauma with evidence on the effectiveness of grief counseling. Although both kinds of interventions address coping with changed life circumstances and the task of integrating strong emotions following a precipitating event, we do not believe that research on trauma debriefing can be generalized to the effectiveness of grief counseling as typically practiced. However, the findings for trauma debriefing (McNally, Bryant, & Ehlers, 2003) are highly relevant to the issues of recruitment, client motivation, and the timing of interventions. Many crisis interventions are initiated by concerned employers or other organizations, not by the recipients, and are often initiated quite soon after the traumatic event.

These recruitment and timing issues may play a significant role in determining outcomes for trauma debriefing as well as for grief counseling.

Differential Effectiveness for Complicated Versus Uncomplicated Grief

The assumption that effectiveness differs between interventions with complicated and uncomplicated grief has become a strongly held view in the bereavement field (Schut et al., 2001). Fortner's (1999) findings, as reported by Neimeyer (2000), supported the ascendancy of this view, and the purported findings of iatrogenic effects for normally bereaved clients helped coalesce the widely held belief that only complicated grief is the appropriate focus of formal grief therapy interventions. However, Allumbaugh and Hoyt (1999), as noted earlier, found no differences between interventions with these two groups. At this point, one might conclude tentatively that some normal grievers may benefit from counseling and that not all normal grievers will. Our reconstructed view suggests that counseling can and should be offered to all bereaved persons who seek it.

This new perspective suggests that some of the recent promising developments in the treatment of more distressed grieving persons could also guide interventions with normally bereaved persons. For example, Shear and her colleagues (Shear, Frank, Houck, & Reynolds, 2005) report a successful randomized controlled clinical trial using a complicated grief treatment that includes a treatment focus on discussion of the loss, retelling the story of the death, imaginal conversations with the deceased, defining personal goals, and reengaging in meaningful relationships. Consistent with Stroebe and Schut's (1999) dual process model of coping with loss, this treatment model focuses on the twin processes of loss and restoration. Boelen (2006) presents a cognitive-behavioral understanding of complicated grief and treatment procedures that could be adapted for work with a larger segment of the bereaved population. The treatments for complicated mourning developed by Shear and Boelen are welcome additions to the field. They reflect some of the specificity and theoretical grounding, called for by critics of traditional approaches to grief counseling. These refinements in intervention could have much more widespread applicability than is currently conceived.

Also bearing on these issues is research seeking to establish traumatic or complicated grief as a distinct disorder. The work of Prigerson and her colleagues (Prigerson & Jacobs, 2001) has been key in this area, and new assessment tools for grief and complicated grief developed by Prigerson and others are appearing. However, other researchers (Hogan, Worden, & Schmidt, 2004) have questioned the psychometric validity of these distinctions. As research in this area continues, our hope is that it will not result in limiting more focused and theory-driven interventions to persons identified as having a disorder. Our view is that normally bereaved people can have great distress, that they can benefit from focused counseling efforts, and that these services should be available to them if they seek help.

One of the most unfortunate consequences of the TIDE findings and the new pessimism in general has been their publication in the popular media (e.g., "Grieving," 2003; Sommers & Satel, 2005) and the effect this might have on the help-seeking decisions of bereaved persons. We need to reframe grief counseling as a positive and supportive resource that is available to all bereaved persons.

Criticism of the Grief Work Hypothesis

This reconstruction or reconsideration of grief counseling intersects with other developments in the bereavement field. One key development has been the emergence of new research findings on patterns of coping with loss. Extensive investigations have shown that the trajectories for the grief reactions of many bereaved people do not match stereotypical notions of the grieving process (Bonanno et al., 2002; Bonanno, 2004; Wortman & Silver, 1989, 2001). For example, it appears that many people are doing much better earlier in the process than we thought, and more are doing less well much later than we thought. The data also reveal that a large subset of bereaved persons do not show high levels of distress at any point in the grief trajectory, do not report actively engaging in "grief work," and do not later suffer because their grieving process was delayed, inhibited, masked, or in any other way insufficiently worked through. These resilient copers, according to Bonanno (2004), may constitute nearly half of all bereaved persons.

Documentation of these differing grief trajectories has raised serious questions about the value and appropriateness of traditional approaches to grief counseling. If emotionally working through the loss does not seem to be a necessary step in the grief process for many bereaved persons, what is the rationale for grief counseling with the normally bereaved, many of whom fit into the "resilient" category? These considerations have spurred criticism of traditional approaches to grief counseling, with its focus on emotional processing, and of the grief work hypothesis in general (Bonanno, 2004; Wortman & Silver, 2001). The critics conclude that grief work—variously understood as including working through, intensive processing, or emotional processing—has little role in healthy, self-regulated coping with loss. The TIDE findings, in particular, have served as a linchpin for challenges (see Bonanno, 2004, and Wortman & Silver, 2001, for examples) such as this one:

> The lack of support in the present study for the conditional grief work hypothesis suggests the more encompassing conclusion that it may be inadvisable under any circumstances, even those in which a bereaved person appears to be suffering greatly, to encourage intensive processing of a loss. In this same vein, and somewhat surprisingly, individuals who had lost loved ones to relatively sudden death (e.g., accident or homicide-suicide) did not engage in grief processes to any greater extent than other bereaved individuals; thus, even these individuals may not have a greater need for grief work. (Bonanno, Papa, Lalande, Zhang, & Noll, 2005, p. 96)

This bold statement challenges the basic assumptions and everyday clinical experiences of most grief counselors. For example, in the past year, two clients who had earlier completed counseling contacted the first author for assistance in coping with suicides by close family members. Both clients intensively processed the losses (i.e., explored their feelings, expressed their feelings, and engaged in profound struggles to make sense of the loss events and find meaning in them) in fewer than 10 sessions, and both expressed great satisfaction with the outcomes of the sessions at their conclusions and in later follow-up contacts. Their counselor did not then and will probably not in the future heed warnings about the inadvisability of intensive emotional processing by the bereaved in these circumstances. At the same time, strong intuitions grounded in clinical experience can be subject to self-serving and self-confirmatory biases (Meehl, 1997), and should not cause clinicians to disregard or dismiss more systematically collected data on patterns of bereavement. They must instead step back from their immediate clinical experience and let the big picture of evolving research and theory also guide their interventions.

If we step back and look at the big picture, we can see the radical critique of the grief work hypothesis as a corrective reaction to the often unquestioned early belief that to grieve effectively, one must feel and process the loss deeply. The first author recalls health professionals informally charting the number of hours bereaved family members had cried as an index of progress in their grieving process and hearing admonitions to grievers that they must "empty their pool of pain." In contrast, researchers who are critical of the grief work hypothesis test the grief work as rumination hypothesis (Bonanno et al., 2005), and models of resilience in which repressive coping, laughter, and positive affect are seen to play important roles (Bonanno, 2004; Keltner & Bonanno, 1997). Their viewpoint also leads them to consider quite different bereavement interventions:

> It is also important to determine whether the salutary influence of positive emotions, such as laughter, on bereavement can be induced deliberately with intentional strategies such as attending humorous movies or receiving encouragement from friends to share in amusing moments. (Bonanno & Kaltman, 1999, p. 771).

The polarization of views could not be much greater, but their basic outlines are not new in psychology. More than 20 years ago, stress and coping pioneer Richard Lazarus became concerned when his widely read *Psychology Today* article on the positive aspects of denial (Lazarus, 1979) seemed to generate a rash of interventions that he saw as trivializing the distress of people who were facing life-threatening illness and other loss experiences (personal communication, February 1989). He thought that the humor groups and other interventions designed to maximize positive emotions and lessen the focus on difficult experiences trivialized the distress of patients and was inspired to write an article (Lazarus, 1984) in which he urged colleagues to pay "more attention to the emotional life" and to "give emotion-focused coping the importance it deserves" (p. 140). His critique and call for a more integrative model of coping and resilience merit renewed consideration in the current debate about the value of grief work.

With these considerations in mind, our reconstruction of grief counseling affords an opportunity to achieve a kind of Hegelian synthesis of opposing views of the value of grief work, integrating the valuable elements of each. We can only begin this synthesis here by setting the stage for future work. First, it is clear that the extensive data marshaled by critics of the grief work hypothesis challenge bereavement professionals to expand their concepts of the variability of normal grief and to rethink some of the myths that have guided traditional approaches to grief counseling, such as the idea that everyone needs to intensely process and "work through" grief to cope effectively. Professionals also need to abandon a one-size-fits-all approach and adjust interventions to match the unique needs of their clients. For clients who experience a minimum of distress following their losses, counselors can serve them well by giving them permission to grieve in the way that is most natural for them, not by imposing a model of "healthy" grieving that may not be appropriate for all. Second, if iatrogenic effects for grief counseling are not empirically validated, as our current analysis suggests, and if (traditional) grief counseling is as effective as or more effective than traditional psychotherapy, critics of the grief work hypothesis will need to significantly revise their perspective to accommodate a positive role for intense emotional processing in bereavement, at least for clients who seek out such interventions.

Recent work on coping and emotions can aid in these tasks. Research in this area is beginning to explicate the construct of emotional-approach coping and how it differs, conceptually and psychometrically, from most of the emotion-related coping constructs in the current literature. For instance, Austenfeld and Stantorn (2004) argue that "emotion-focused coping"—one of the most common emotion-related constructs— has been conceptually and psychometrically confounded with distress, self-deprecation, rumination, and other ineffective coping strategies. They show how the adaptive potential of emotion-focused coping strategies is consistently documented when it is not confounded in this manner.

The study of emotion-focused coping in the grieving process can also draw on a solid foundation of earlier work on this topic, like Mahoney's (1991) summary of extensive psychotherapy research, which underscores the psychological benefits of emotional processing, and recent work by L. Greenberg and colleagues explicating the intricacies of emotional processing in therapeutic change (Greenberg, 2002; Pos, Greenberg, Goldman, & Korman, 2003). In an important article, Greenberg, Wortman, and Stone (1996) contribute the insight that the reported health benefits of emotional expression might be attributed to "enhanced self-efficacy for tolerating and regulating emotional distress" as opposed to "immersion in that distress" (p. 589). New developments in all these areas could profitably be integrated into more comprehensive models of the grieving process, such as Stroebe and Schut's (1999) dual process model of coping with bereavement, Worden's (2002) tasks of grieving, or Bonanno and Kaltman's (1999) integrative perspective on bereavement.

The critical message seems to be that people cope with loss in different ways, and therefore may have different needs for intervention and different responses to a given type of intervention. Cultural and societal issues offer an additional lens on patterns of bereavement. We need to learn more about how cross-cultural factors affect coping with loss and the efficacy of various bereavement interventions (Parkes, Laungani, & Young, 1997). Cultural background makes an important contribution to individual differences in the grieving process, as shown in recent work by Bonanno and colleagues (2005) comparing groups from the People's Republic of China and the United States. These cultural considerations become even more paramount when theory is translated into practice and we strive to match the type and level of intervention to the needs of a particular client.

It is also valuable to consider that bereavement research, theory, and practice themselves evolve within specific societal and cultural contexts. Referring to the United States, Field and Cassel (1997) note, "It seems that this nation has not yet discovered how to talk realistically but comfortably about the end of life, nor has it learned how to value the period of dying as it is now experienced by most people" (p. 265). This struggle to come to grips with death and dying, and grief and loss, may be one reason the TIDE findings and criticism of the grief work hypothesis have attracted such attention. The implication that we might be better off not talking about—

perhaps not even experiencing—our grief and loss is an appealing notion for a society that is still seeking a way around, rather than through, its loss-related experiences (Larson & Tobin, 2000).

Instead of abandoning the grief work hypothesis in favor of a bereavement model that excludes intense processing of emotions, we need to better conceptualize and measure emotional processing and the variables that determine its long-term effects. A more complete long-term research agenda would include distinguishing (conceptually and psychometrically) therapeutic processing of feelings and healthy life review from emotional discharge and negative rumination; integrative resilience from superficial adaptation and adjustment; and, in general, approach from avoidance coping. Emotional processing, positive affect, and even denial all play important roles in healthy self-regulation. We must avoid exalting one at the expense of the others if we are to make the most rapid progress toward what remains our ultimate and shared goal: finding a way to help people live with hope in a world in which loss is inescapable. ■

Dale G. Larson, Ph.D., clinician, researcher, author, is a national leader in end-of-life care and training. He is the author of the award-winning book, The Helper's Journey: Working With People Facing Grief, Loss, and Life-Threatening Illness, *and has published extensively on end-of-life conversations, stress management, self-concealment, helper secrets, anticipatory mourning, and interdisciplinary teams. He codirected an NIMH-funded national mental health skills training program for hospice workers, chaired NHPCO's First National Conference on Hospice Volunteerism, served as an Advisory Panel member for the American Psychological Association Ad Hoc Committee on End-of-Life Issues, and created the Hospice Home Page website, which received a national Award of Excellence from NHPCO. A Fulbright Scholar, Dr. Larson has also been a Summer Scholar at the Stanford Center for Advanced Study in the Behavioral Sciences and a W. K. Kellogg Foundation Expert in Residence. In 2001 he was senior editor and a contributing author for the Robert Wood Johnson–funded national newspaper series,* Finding Our Way: Living with Dying in America. *He is professor of counseling psychology at Santa Clara University, where he heads graduate studies in health psychology.*

William T. Hoyt, Ph.D., is associate professor in the Department of Counseling Psychology at the University of Wisconsin-Madison. His research interests focus on the importance of interpersonal processes for psychological well-being, with an emphasis on causes and consequences of interpersonal perceptions and on relationship-restorative processes (e.g., forgiveness). This perspective also informs his interest in research on grief and loss, and on bereavement interventions. Dr. Hoyt is also a frequent contributor to special issues on research methodology in counseling and related fields, and his work on sources of bias in observer ratings has been published in Psychological Methods. *He has a special enthusiasm for meta-analytic techniques, because of their potential to assist researchers and clinicians in making sense of existing findings in an area, and to suggest directions for future research.*

REFERENCES

Allumbaugh, D. L., & Hoyt, W. T. (1999). Effectiveness of grief counseling: A meta-analysis. *Journal of Counseling Psychology, 46*(3), 370-380.

Austenfeld, J. L., & Stantorn, A. L. (2004). Coping through emotional approach: A new look at emotion, coping, and health-related outcomes. *Journal of Personality, 72*(6), 1335-1363.

Boelen, P. A. (2006). Cognitive-behavioral therapy for complicated grief: Theoretical underpinnings and case descriptions. *Journal of Loss and Trauma, 11*, 1-30.

Bonanno, G. A. (2004). Loss, trauma, and human resilience: Have we underestimated the human capacity to thrive after extremely aversive events? *American Psychologist, 59*(1), 20-28.

Bonanno, G. A., & Kaltman, S. (1999). Toward an integrative perspective on bereavement. *Psychological Bulletin, 125*, 760-776.

Bonanno, G. A., Papa, A., Lalande, K., Zhang, N., & Noll, J. G. (2005). Grief processing and deliberate grief avoidance: A prospective comparison of bereaved spouses and parents in the United States and the People's Republic of China. *Journal of Consulting and Clinical Psychology, 73*(1), 86-98.

Bonanno, G. A., Wortman, C. B., Lehman, D. R., Tweed, R. G., Haring, M., Sonnega, J., et al. (2002). Resilience to loss and chronic grief: A prospective study from preloss to 18-months postloss. *Journal of Personality and Social Psychology, 83*(5), 1150-1164.

CFAH. (2003). *Report on bereavement and grief research.* Washington, DC: Center for Advancement of Health.

Currier, J. M., Holland, J. M., & Neimeyer, R. A. (2006). Sense-making, grief, and the experience of violent loss: Toward a mediational model. *Death Studies, 30,* 403-428.

Field, M., & Cassel, C. (Eds.). (1997). *Approaching death: Improving care at the end of life.* Washington, DC: National Academy Press.

Fortner, B. V. (1999). The effectiveness of grief counseling and therapy: A quantitative review. *Dissertation Abstracts International, 60,* (08), 4221B. (UMI No. 9944320)

Glass, C. R., Arnkoff, D. B., & Shapiro, S. J. (2001). Expectations and preferences. *Psychotherapy: Theory, Research, Practice, Training, 38,* 455-461.

Greenberg, L. S. (2002). Integrating an emotion-focused approach to treatment into psychotherapy integration. *Journal of Psychotherapy Integration, 12,* 154-189.

Greenberg, M. A., Wortman, C. B., & Stone, A. A. (1996). Emotional expression and physical health: Revising traumatic memories or fostering self-regulation? *Journal of Personality and Social Psychology, 71,* 588-602.

Grieving is an individual process. (2003, April 6). *Baltimore Sun,* Star Edition Section: Lifestyle, p. 3.

Hogan, N. S., Worden, J. W., & Schmidt, L. A. (2004). Considerations and conceptualizing complicated grief. *Omega, 48,* 263-277.

Keltner, D., & Bonanno, G. A. (1997). A study of laughter and dissociation: Distinct correlates of laughter and smiling during bereavement. *Journal of Personality and Social Psychology, 73,* 687-702.

Larson, D. G., & Hoyt, W. T. (2006, April). Deterioration effects in grief counseling: In search of the evidence. In S. Connor (Chair), *Grief counseling: Can it be harmful?* Symposium conducted at the 7th Annual Clinical Team Conference and Scientific Symposium of the National Hospice and Palliative Care Organization, San Diego, CA.

Larson, D. G., & Hoyt, W. T. (in press). What has become of grief counseling? An evaluation of the empirical foundations of the new pessimism. *Professional Psychology: Research and Practice.*

Larson, D. G., & Tobin, D. R. (2000). End-of-life conversations: Evolving practice and theory. *JAMA, 284,* 1573-1578.

Lazarus, R. S. (1979, June). Positive denial: The case of not facing reality. *Psychology Today,* 44-60.

Lazarus, R. S. (1984). The trivialization of distress. In B. L. Hammonds & C. J. Scheirer (Eds.), *Psychology and Health: The Master Lecture Series* (pp. 125-144). Washington, DC: American Psychological Association.

Mahoney, M. J. (1991). *Human change processes: The scientific foundations of psychotherapy.* New York: Basic Books.

McNally, R. J., Bryant, R. A., & Ehlers, A. (2003). Does early psychological intervention promote recovery from posttraumatic stress? *Psychological Science in the Public Interest, 4*(4), 45-79.

Meehl, P. E. (1997). Credentialed persons, credentialed knowledge. *Clinical Psychology: Science and Practice, 4*(2), 91-98.

Miller, W. R. (1985). Motivation for treatment: A review with special emphasis on alcoholism. *Psychological Bulletin, 98,* 84-107.

Neimeyer, R. A. (2000). Searching for the meaning of meaning: Grief therapy and the process of reconstruction. *Death Studies, 24,* 541-558.

Parkes, C. M., Laungani, P., & Young, B. (Eds.) (1997). *Death and bereavement across cultures.* London: Routledge.

Pos, A. E., Greenberg, L. S., Goldman, R. N., & Korman, L. M. (2003). Emotional processing during experiential treatment of depression. *Journal of Consulting and Clinical Psychology, 71,* 1007-1016.

Prigerson, H. O., & Jacobs, S. C. (2001). Traumatic grief as a distinct disorder: A rationale, consensus criteria, and a preliminary empirical test. In M. S. Stroebe, R. O. Hansson, W. Stroebe, & H. Schut (Eds.), *Handbook of bereavement research: Consequences, coping, and care* (pp. 613-645). Washington, DC: American Psychological Association.

Principe, J. M., Marci, C. D., Glick, D. M., & Ablon, J. S. (2006). The relationship among patient contemplation, early alliance, and continuation in psychotherapy. *Psychotherapy: Theory, Research, Practice, Training, 43,* 238-243.

Schut, H., Stroebe, M. S., van den Bout, J., & Terheggen, M. (2001). The efficacy of bereavement interventions: Determining who benefits. In M. S. Stroebe, R. O. Hansson, W. Stroebe, & H. Schut (Eds.), *Handbook of bereavement research: Consequences, coping, and care* (pp. 705-737). Washington, DC: American Psychological Association.

Shear, K., Frank, E., Houck, P. R., & Reynolds, C. F. (2005). Treatment of complicated grief: A randomized controlled trial. *JAMA, 293*(21), 2601-2608.

Sommers, C. H., & Satel, S. (2005). *One nation under therapy: How the helping culture is eroding self-reliance.* New York: St. Martin's Press.

Stroebe, M., & Schut, H. (1999). The dual process model of coping with bereavement: Rationale and description. *Death Studies, 23,* 197-224.

Worden, W. (2002). *Grief counseling and grief therapy: A handbook for the mental health practitioner.* (3rd Ed.). New York: Springer.

Wortman, C. B., & Silver, R. C., (1989). The myths of coping with loss. *Journal of Consulting & Clinical Psychology, 57,* 349-357.

Wortman, C. B., & Silver, R. C. (2001). The myths of coping with loss revisited. In M. S. Stroebe, R. O. Hansson, W. Stroebe, & H. Schut (Eds.), *Handbook of bereavement research: Consequences, coping, and care* (pp. 405-429). Washington, DC: American Psychological Association.

Wortman, C. B. (2006, April). The dark side of grief therapy. In S. Connor (Chair), *Grief counseling: Can it be harmful?* Symposium conducted at the 7th Annual Clinical Team Conference and Scientific Symposium of the National Hospice and Palliative Care Organization, San Diego, CA.

■ CHAPTER 10 ■

Helping Built on Personal Experience

Phyllis R. Silverman

What was special to me about coming here is that
I'm with other people whose parent died. I didn't feel so alone.
—A nine-year-old boy at the Children's Room,
a center for bereaved children and teenagers

At times of crisis and loss, there is something special about meeting and talking with others in the same situation. Helping and being helped by other people with whom one shares a common experience seems to provide an opportunity to feel hope and see new possibilities for the future. What is it about finding others like oneself that is so important, especially at times of crisis and loss in our lives? This chapter focuses on the kind of help that comes from sharing a common experience. Such opportunities can occur spontaneously as people meet in the normal course of living or they can occur in planned encounters. In this chapter, I focus on my experience with the Widow-to-Widow Program (Silverman, 1969, 2004) and what I subsequently learned about what I have come to call "mutual help" rather than "self help" (Silverman, 1976). While much of the discussion is about widowhood, the findings apply to a wide range of experiences in the life cycle (Silverman and Smith, 1984). I start with a description of the original Widow-to-Widow Program and its legacy; then describe grief from the mutual help perspective and what is involved in helping in this context. Finally, I describe some of the ways mutual help is practiced today.

The Widow-to-Widow Program

The original Widow-to-Widow Program (1966-1973) was a demonstration project sponsored by the Laboratory of Community Psychiatry at Harvard Medical School. My assignment at the time was to find a way of reducing the risk, in newly widowed persons, for developing serious emotional problems. Because we were guided by a public health perspective and because we had no way of knowing who was at risk, it seemed necessary to reach every newly widowed person in the target community. When there is danger of a disease spreading through a community, everyone is inoculated. We had no vaccine; we focused on the helpfulness of a human contact.

If a physician, nurse, or social worker reached out, we believed that newly widowed persons might get the impression that they were seen as ill. This was not the message we wanted to send. The finding that another widowed person was most helpful (Maddison and Walker, 1967) and the work in the New Careers for the Poor Program in New York City (Pearl and Reissman, 1965) pointed to a way of reaching newly widowed women. If another widowed person—perhaps a neighbor—reached out, would the new widow accept that person? What would these widows have to offer? Five women who had been widowed for several years and who lived near or in the target community were recruited to do the outreach (Silverman, 1967, 1969, 2004). We focused on women under the age of 65 years, because we assumed that senior centers offered programs for older people. (We were not correct in this assumption.) We did not include men, because we could not recruit any widowers to work with us. Men were involved in programs that developed later, such as the Widowed Persons Service sponsored by AARP. In today's world, with the focus on privacy and greater suspicion of strangers, this kind of program might not be possible. It would have to emanate from a church, funeral home, or other community agency with which mourners already had a connection. Hospice bereavement services can be seen as an outreach effort to minimize risk for the people they serve; however, hospice is involved in certain kinds of deaths and not others.

The women in our program reached out to every newly widowed woman under 65 in the target community. Using their own experience, these helpers offered neighbor-to-neighbor support in the widow's own home. The original program was active for two and a half years. It reached 300 widows in the first year and a half; of those, 61% accepted the offer of help (Silverman, 2004). Those who accepted were most likely to be women whose husbands had been ill for an extended period, women who did not work, and those with dependent children at home. Another demonstration program followed, sponsored by the Jewish Family Service. It employed Adele Cooperband (an aide in the original project) to reach out to older Jewish women in the same community (Silverman and Cooperband, 1976).

In both projects, we reached families with a wide range of backgrounds and various life experiences. A few had serious and long-standing financial, physical, or emotional problems; were accustomed to asking for help; and had established relationships with social agencies, public welfare, or psychiatric clinics. Most, however, had never had any contact with an agency or received assistance from anyone outside the family. As a result of the projects, we were able to compile a profile of every widow in the target community and demonstrate the value of "a little help from a friend." We learned a great deal about the kinds of assistance and support newly widowed women needed.

Who Accepted Help

The widows who participated in these projects had similar needs. They needed to talk with someone who would understand their feelings. They wanted information about how others had managed. Many women simply needed reassurance that they would weather the crisis successfully. Many of the women were not employed, as was much more common at that time, and had depended on their husband's wages. They now had difficulty covering living expenses. Women with children at home and those over 60 years of age received some assistance from social security. Some women asked for advice about or support in getting a job or going back to school. Others wanted specific advice about managing what money they had, and many needed help with benefits claims. Older women who couldn't drive needed transportation to get medical care; some of the younger women had to learn to drive for the first time.

Some women had difficulties with relatives who did not understand their situation. Some had children who were misbehaving and having problems at school that these mothers did not always understand were related to the children's grief (Silverman and Englander, 1975). It seemed to me that these children were even more at risk than their mothers for developing serious problems, which led to my subsequent research with children and the Massachusetts General Hospital Harvard Child Bereavement Study (Silverman, 2000; Silverman and Worden, 1992; Worden and Silverman, 1993; Worden, 1996). Some women still had adult children living at home because a marriage had failed or because of other problems. For some widows this was a blessing, while for others it created additional tensions.

As we got to know these women, we learned that four of them had histories of alcoholism and four others had histories of schizophrenia or severe depressive illness. These women were already getting help from mental health agencies, and there was little more the project could do to prevent these problems from recurring. In some instances, it seemed that it had been the now-deceased husband who had kept the family together. This was not a population that sought psychiatric help unless the problem was very severe, nor was this a time historically when counseling was generally sought for problems associated with mourning.

Widows Who Refused Help

The widows who refused help fell into two groups (Silverman, 2004): those who never became involved in any way and those who initially responded favorably on the phone but subsequently refused any contact. Thirty-five of these women, representing both groups, agreed to be interviewed after the project ended. They reported that they refused because, in descending order of frequency, (1) they were too busy with work, family, or setting their husbands' affairs in order; (2) they received plenty of support from family and friends; (3) their grown children refused on their behalf (some of these respondents said that they should have stood up to their children); or (4) they were independent and did not need support. Some of these widows were not the first to be widowed in their family or among their friends and benefited from the experience of others already in their network.

THE WIDOWED SERVICE LINE

In the early 1970s, the idea of telephone hotlines received a lot of attention. We developed the Widowed Service Line, which was staffed by two of the women who worked on the original project and involved as volunteers several of the widows served by the original program. During its first seven months of its operation, 750 people called the service line. The calls fell into three main categories: the widowed persons wanted (1) someone to listen to them; (2) to meet people; and (3) specific practical information. Most callers spoke of their loneliness and desire to meet others. Many were happy to simply find someone to listen to them (Silverman, 2004).

As with those who accepted help from the Widow-to-Widow Program, the people most likely to call the service line were those who lived alone and those who had children under the age of 16 years. The service line was an easy way to put people in touch with each other. Sometimes these people lived in the same neighborhood but did not know each other. For example, two women called who were newly widowed and pregnant, and another young caller had delivered her baby after her husband died. With the callers' permission, the volunteer arranged for the women to meet, and they formed an informal support group. Others with less dramatic stories were introduced to each other on the telephone so they could temporarily relieve their loneliness or even become friends.

Several people with very serious emotional problems called the line. Some were drinking excessively. If they acknowledged their problem, we referred them to Alcoholics Anonymous or another program. One person threatened suicide. In each of these cases, we found that the widow or widower had an active network of helpers or was involved in other programs. These callers had difficulties far beyond the capabilities of the service line and were good example of situations in which simply talking with another widowed person would not meet their needs.

The line also had silent consumers. We know that many more people read our advertisements than actually called. A widow I met socially several years later told me that she kept the phone number by her bed. She never called, but she found it comforting to know that someone was available. I assume that she was not unique.

OTHER PROGRAMS

The Widow-to-Widow Program demonstrated the value of mutual help and was a model for AARP's Widowed Persons Service. (AARP no longer maintains a national office for the service, relying on local initiative instead.) Compassionate Friends, an active national and international organization with roots in Great Britain, started at about the same time as our project (Stephans, 1973). Other independent programs have developed in cities and towns across the country and abroad in which the widowed themselves take the lead. There is no national directory of these groups. The Widow-to-Widow Program coincided with and perhaps added some stimulus to the growing self-help movement, from which many programs for the bereaved developed (Silverman, 1978; White and Madara, 2002). In our area, the program stimulated the imagination of clergy and funeral directors, who compiled a workbook on how to set up similar community programs (Silverman, 1976). The last section of this chapter describes some current programs.

Vachon (1979) replicated our program in a demonstration research program in Toronto; this led to a community-based program that existed for many years. Vachon's research documented the value of social support and of another widowed person as helper (Vachon et al., 1980). Lund (1989), stimulated in part by the original Widow-to-Widow findings, examined the consequences for elderly widows and widowers of participating in social support groups led either by peers or by professionals. His findings supported the special value of another widowed person as helper. Lieberman (1996) studied the effect of participating in a self-help/mutual aid organization and confirmed its positive impact on the widowed members. In particular, he found that the greatest benefits often accrued to the helpers. This work had an impact on the way services to the bereaved are provided in this country and abroad, although almost none of the current services involve the kind of outreach that characterized the original Widow-to-Widow Program, nor are counselors always aware of the connection.

A VIEW OF GRIEF

Over the years, research has provided new insights into the needs of widowed persons and new understanding of what it means to be bereaved. However, in 1967 this research began to challenge our understanding of bereavement as a simple time-limited process. The widows I worked with told me a different story when they said their lived experience did not always coincide with existing theory. They said they did not "recover;" rather, when they were able to look ahead (usually about two years after the death), they began to see the world in a different way than they had before.

Using a conceptual framework offered by Bowlby (1961) and Tyhurst (1958), I suggested thinking of bereavement as a time of transition (Silverman, 1966). The concept of transition provides a way of describing grief as a dynamic phenomenon that leads to an accommodation rather than recovery or "getting over it." Change is a critical element of any accommodation, and we could see how widowed persons changed over time.

To understand grief, we also have to look at the social context in which the mourner is embedded; that is, look beyond the psychological person to the world in which the person lives. In our program, we defined grief in terms of the subsequent mental illness it might cause. What was it about widowhood that would lead to mental illness? Could it be related to people losing their place in society? The role of marriage in these women's lives was central to their well-being. As we met more and more widows, we discovered that they were indeed emotionally distressed, but unless they had been psychologically ill before the death of their spouse, what they needed most was to expand their ways of coping with this stress. We could not prevent the stress, but we could help them understand what they were experiencing and find effective ways of dealing with widowhood. They also needed to find ways to redefine themselves after the loss of the role of wife. They learned that they had lost a way of life as well as a spouse, and they learned how to develop new roles, new relationships, and new ways of living in the world (Silverman, 1988). They grieved and felt pain, but they learned how to manage the pain. They found comfort in new friends and in building a different kind of relationship with the deceased, with themselves, and with the world around them (Silverman and Klass, 1996). In his work with Compassionate Friends, Klass (1988) learned from grieving parents that they did not get over their loss; rather, they found new ways of remaining connected to their deceased children through what we have come to call "continuing bonds" (Klass, Silverman, & Nickman, 1996).

Grief is not an illness that can be cured. We cannot prevent a widowed person's pain or protect that person from the disruption the death causes. We know that the rest of this person's life will not look the way it would have if the death had not occurred. The death becomes part of the person's life story and of who that person is. Bereavement changes people and forces them to look at their life differently, which in many ways leads them to behave differently and to, in part at least, develop a new sense of self. The widowed helper can be integral in this process. I learned from the Widow-to-Widow Program that the goal is to promote the ability of bereaved persons to cope with their pain and with these changes. In a sense, experience is not what happens to you but what you do with what happens to you. The help offered in this situation is not an effort to prevent grief or stress but to help people cope in ways that enhance their competence.

MUTUAL HELP

In 1964, mutual help or self-help was primarily associated with such organizations as Alcoholics Anonymous and programs established by parents for their retarded children. Recovering alcoholics helped other alcoholics and parents helped other parents. While it has been common practice throughout the ages for the bereaved to help each other, formal mutual help programs as we have come to know them were rare.

A mutual help exchange, as the term is used here, involves people who share a common problem, a problem with which one of the participants has coped successfully. The helping person has expertise based on personal experience rather than the formal education that is the professional helper's base of expertise. Borkman (1976, 1999) distinguishes between two sources of information: professional knowledge, which comes from formal learning, and experiential knowledge, which comes from personal experience. Self-help is the first step: the person becomes aware of the problem and tries to do something about it. Once the person engages someone else in sharing experiences, it becomes mutual help. A mutual help organization limits its membership to those with a specific common problem; their purpose in coming together is to offer one another help and guidance in coping with the problem or predicament. An additional benefit is that the helper, in the process of helping, may work out some aspect of his or her own difficulty, obtain new perspectives, and get a renewed sense of self-adequacy through his or her ability to help someone else.

> "You alone can do it, but you cannot do it alone" is an often-quoted saying in the literature on self-help and mutual aid…. [It] produces a special form of interdependence in which the individual accepts self-responsibility within a context of mutual aid—that is, giving help to others and receiving help from others. (Borkman, 1999, p. 196)

Informal mutual exchanges go on all the time, as people discover common experiences that until that moment they may have believed were theirs alone. Informal encounters may develop into formal organizations if people believe they have a mission to extend the exchange to others like themselves. The literature on mutual help and bereavement concentrates on the formal encounters. However, it is the informal encounters that need to be encouraged; in many ways they are the major influence on the way a community responds to grief and helps bereaved persons.

To maintain its character as a mutual help organization, a group must develop a sustainable organizational structure with officers, a governing body, and procedures for continuity (Silverman, 1980). The members determine policy and control resources, and they are both providers and recipients of service. Mutual help organizations are distinguished from voluntary philanthropic organizations such as the American Cancer Society, in which volunteers usually join to help others, not to solve a common problem. However, in a hospice volunteer program, the volunteers may bring their own experience of loss to their work. In this sense, hospice can be seen as a mutual help experience, for some.

Mutual help organizations sometimes develop when there is no match between people's needs and the help offered in their communities (Silverman, 1978). In the case of bereavement, such organizations may be a response to the community silence that grieving people often face. When friends and family distance themselves from the pain and needs of mourners, mourners seek out each other. Even in communities that offer resources for coping with grief, there may be no substitute for sharing with peers who have been there.

In a mutual help group, people can share their common experience and develop effective modes of coping with their problems in today's world. When people in this context say "I understand," they really do. The purpose of these groups is to help bereaved people negotiate a transition, to get from here to there; for example, from a hospital bed back to leading as normal a life as possible (Borkman, 1999; Silverman, 1978). For widowed persons, the goal is to go from feeling lost and overwhelmingly sad to finding new direction and meaning in life.

Learning in crises or emotionally laden situations can be enhanced in a peer context (Bandura, 1977). Hamburg and Adams (1967) pointed out that learning is made easier when the helper is one step ahead of the person in need and has experience with the problem to use as a guide. In times of stress, people tend to respond to others who have had a similar experience as role models and teachers (Silverman, 1966, 1969, 1978, 1980).

CONNECTING HELP TO TRANSITION

Lifton (1973), in a study of returning Vietnam veterans, identified factors in the helping situation that facilitated their coping with the transition to civilian life. He observed veterans helping each other and identified three essential qualities at work. He first saw that a special *affinity* developed between the veterans as they came together to share a particular (in this case, overwhelming) personal experience and try to make sense of it. He then noticed the development of a sense of *presence*, a kind of being there for each other. There was a fullness of engagement and an openness that came from knowing that the helper had shared the experience, really did understand, and could tolerate the pain. Finally, Lifton observed that members began to change roles, in a two-part process he called *self-generation*. First, the veteran who was being helped developed new insights to initiate a process of change in himself. Even as he sought help, the veteran retained major responsibility for the shape and direction of the changes he made. In the second part of the process, the veteran became willing to help others as he had been helped.

Affinity, presence, and self-generation seemed to be the necessary ingredients for facilitating a transition in widowed persons, too, as they moved between old and new self-images and values. Drawing this parallel is a good way to summarize the unique aspects of mutual help for widows and widowers. It also shows how the focus on helping relationships has changed over time.

Affinity: I'm a Widow, Too

Meeting other widowed people helps the newly widowed face their loneliness and begin to think about how to deal with change. They may be too numb to know what they need, and they often have difficulty accepting their new status. The fact that someone who has been on this road longer seems to be managing helps them be less fearful about their new situation. Receiving help from a peer tends to minimize feelings of weakness or incompetence. It was common for women in the Widow-to-Widow Program to note how reassuring it was to meet other widows, and that meeting other bereaved women made them feel less frightened. Joining a mutual help group is often the first step for people in acknowledging that they are indeed widowed.

Presence: Learning from Others Like Themselves

As time passes, the new situation may become more real and more painful. Another widowed person can provide validation for feelings and help with finding new ways of living in the world. In the Widow-to-Widow Program, a recently bereaved woman mentioned that the group helped validate the pace of her progression through grief, even while those close to her expected her to recover more quickly. People talk of developing a sense of optimism and hope as a result of this sharing. They also find role models. Participants found hope in their peers who were further along in recovery. In many cases, the information people receive is as helpful as being listened to. And learning from peers provides widowed persons not only with people who are like them, but with people they can be like in the future.

Accommodation/Self-Generation

When widowed persons begin to integrate new knowledge into a new identity, there is a change in how they connect with the group. They are more responsive to each other's needs, and the focus changes from sharing pain to learning how to build new relationships and develop a new community. Widow-to-Widow participants frequently said that they benefited from helping other widows because they felt that their shared experiences evoked a sense of empathy for the newly bereaved and gave them new confidence as they moved on in their lives.

The essence of mutual help is the exchange that takes place between people as they cope with a common problem. The relationships available in a mutual help exchange can be seen as linking opportunities (Silverman, 1981) or, in Goffman's words, a place to learn "the tricks of the trade" (1963). We identify with our peers throughout the life cycle. At each new stage or phase of life, we seek to learn from others who have gone before us. If bereaved persons cannot find anyone in their existing network who has experienced a similar death, they look outside their own network for people who can serve as a bridge between the past and the future. The resulting transitional relationships can become a permanent part of a friendship network.

CURRENT PROGRAMS AND PRACTICES

The Internet has changed the way people approach problems or periods of transition in their lives and how services are located and offered (Colon, 2004; Madara & White, 1997). The Web provides a new way for people to find each other. An Internet search finds two main kinds of resources. One is chat rooms—for example, the Young Widow chat room—where people can sign on and engage in an ongoing exchange with others. Help is also available, for example, for parents who have lost their only child or for grandparents whose grandchild has died. The second kind of resource is mutual help or self-help organizations—such as Compassionate Friends, Mothers Against Drunk Driving, and To Live Again—that have local chapters where members come together on a regular basis to support each other and to participate in various programs and activities. These local chapters survive over the years as new members join and give new life to them. Organizations that have a national office are more likely to flourish, as a central office can provide direction and support to local chapters.

Malkinson and Geron (2006) describe an initiative in Israel for parents whose children had died in automobile accidents. What began as a professionally led support group evolved into a self-help group, with members meeting on their own and using their own experience to help each other. Leah Sherman (personal communication) describes a similar situation in the Boston area. A formal, professionally led support group focuses on the needs of the newly widowed. As the group members move on in time, they are encouraged to meet on their own and fulfill their own needs for information and support. A professionally led program can thus create an environment in which participants are encouraged to continue to meet after the group ends. Caserta and his colleagues (1996) describes a health promotion program for older widowed people in Salt Lake City— preliminary data showed that about two-thirds of the participants maintained contact with each other outside the class and half noted the value of getting new information and learning new skills from their peers. These relationships extended long after the formal program ended. The role of the mental health professional in this situation is to relinquish control to the group's members and recognize their expertise.

Reach for Recovery began more than 30 years ago as an informal mutual help organization for women with breast cancer. At the time, few resources were available to help women deal with their illness and the changes in their bodies. These women reached out to each other, sharing their experience and providing support and information (Silverman and Smith, 1984). The organization was absorbed into the American Cancer Society (ACS); volunteers (breast cancer survivors) participate in a formal training program, and the ACS oversees their work, but the special help that comes from talking to someone who has been there is still very much a part of the program.

Agency-sponsored programs exist in many settings and often involve volunteers who share their own experience. For example, there are centers throughout the United States devoted to serving grieving children and their parents. They are directed by professionals, but most of the work is done by volunteers, many of whom have experienced a loss (see Dougy

Center for Grieving Children; Silverman, 2000). The quote at the beginning of this article is from a child at one of these centers; the centers provide an opportunity for grieving persons to meet others like themselves; to be in an environment where their loss is understood and where they can learn from each other.

Performing acts of caring and concern for our fellow human beings is the cornerstone in the foundation of most societies. We are social creatures, and we need each other. Kropotkin (1902) said that cooperation and mutual aid are the very essence of the human condition—they make a society viable. How can we express our needs and care for others? One way is to make available to those in need the lived experience of others like themselves

Death, dying, and grieving must be part of the community discourse. Coping with life and death invariably happens in a community of others with whom we are linked in many ways. The nature of these links determines the kind of communities we build, and how each of us understands our part in caring. ■

Phyllis R. Silverman is a Scholar in Residence at the Women's Studies Research Center at Brandeis University and an Associate in Social Welfare in the Department of Psychiatry at Massachusetts General Hospital. She has a Ph.D. from the Heller School at Brandeis and master's degrees from the Harvard School of Public Health and the Smith College School for Social Work. Her primary interests are the grieving process in children and mutual help for the bereaved. From 1964 to 1972, she served as director of the Widow-to-Widow Program and more recently served as co-principal investigator and project director of the Harvard/MGH Child Bereavement Study. Her publications include Mutual Help Groups: A Guide for Mental Health Professionals; Helping Women Cope with Grief; *and,* Never too Young to Know: Death in Children's Lives.

REFERENCES

Bandura, A. (1977). *Social learning theory.* Englewood Cliffs, NJ: Prentice-Hall.

Borkman, T. (1976). Experiential knowledge: A new concept for analysis of self-help groups. *Social Service Review, 50,* 445-456.

Borkman, T. (1999). *Understanding self-help/mutual aid: Experiential learning in the commons.* Camden, NJ: Rutgers University Press.

Bowlby, J. (1961). Processes of mourning. *International Journal of Psychoanalysis, 42,* 317-340.

Caserta, M., & Lund, D. (1996). Beyond bereavement support group meetings: Exploring outside social contacts. *Death Studies, 29,* 537-556

Colón, Y. (2004). Technology-based groups and end-of-life social work practice. In J. Berzoff & P. R. Silverman (Eds.), *Living with dying: A handbook for end-of-life-healthcare practitioners* (pp. 534-547). New York: Columbia University Press.

Dougy Center for Grieving Children. www.dougy.org.

Goffman, E. (1963). *Stigma: The management of spoiled identity.* Englewood Cliffs, NJ: Prentice-Hall.

Hamburg, D. A., & Adams, J. E. (1967). A perspective on coping behavior: Seeking and utilizing information in major transitions. *Archives of General Psychiatry, 17*(3), 277-284.

Klass, D. (1988). *Parental grief: Solace and resolution.* New York: Springer

Klass, D., Silverman, P. R., & Nickman, S. L. (Eds.). (1996). *Continuing bonds: A new understanding of grief.* Washington DC: Taylor & Francis.

Kropotkin, P. (1902; reprinted in 1972). *Mutual aid.* New York: University Press.

Lieberman, M. A., & Borman, L. D. (1979). *Self-help groups for coping with crisis: Origins, members, processes and impact.* San Francisco: Jossey-Bass.

Lifton, R. J. (1973). *Home from the war: Learning from Vietnam veterans.* New York: Simon & Schuster.

Lund, D. A. (Ed.). (1989). *Older bereaved spouses: Research with practical applications.* New York: Taylor and Francis/Hemisphere.

Maddison, D., & Walker, W. L. (1967). Factors affecting the outcome of conjugal bereavement. *British Journal of Psychiatry 113,* 1057-1067.

Madara, E. J., & White, B. J. (1997). Online mutual support: The experience of a self-help clearinghouse. *Information and Referral: Journal of the Alliance of Information and Referral Systems, 19,* 91-107.

Malkinson, R., & Geron, Y. (2006). Intervention continuity in post traffic fatality, from notifying families of the loss to establishing a self-help group. In E. K. Rynearson (Ed.), *Violent death: Resilience and intervention beyond crisis* (pp. 217-232). New York: Brunner/Routledge.

Pearl, A., & Reissman, A. (1965). *New careers for the poor: The nonprofessional in human service.* New York: Free Press.

Powell, T. J. (1987). *Self-help organizations and professional practice.* Silver Spring, MD: National Association of Social Workers.

Silverman, P. R. (1966). Services for the widowed during the period of bereavement. In *Social work practice: Selected papers, annual forum* (pp. 170-189). New York: Columbia University Press.

—. (1967). Services to the widowed: First steps in a program of preventive intervention. *Community Mental Health Journal, 3,* 37-44.

—. (1969). The Widow-to-Widow Program: An experiment in preventive intervention with other widows. *Mental Hygiene, 54,* 540-547.

—. (1976). *If you will lift the load, I will lift it too: A guide to the creation of a widow-to-widow service.* New York: Jewish Funeral Directors of America.

—. (1978). *Mutual help: A guide for mental heath workers.* NIMH/DHEW Pub. No. ADM 78-646. Washington, DC: U.S. Government Printing Office.

—. (1980). *Mutual help groups: Organization and development.* Beverly Hills, CA: Sage Publications.

—. (1981). *Helping women cope with grief.* Beverly Hills, CA: Sage Publications.

—. (1988). In search of new selves: Accommodating to widowhood. In L.A. Bond (Ed.), *Families in transition: Primary prevention programs that work.* Beverly Hills, CA: Sage Publications.

—. (2000). *Never too young to know: Death in children's lives.* New York: Oxford University Press.

—. (2004). *Widow to widow: How the bereaved help one another.* (2nd Ed.). New York: Rutledge.

Silverman, P. R., & Cooperband, A. (1976). Mutual help and the elderly widow. *Journal of Geriatric Psychiatry, 8,* 9-27.

Silverman, P. R., & Englander, S. (1975). The widow's view of her dependent children. *Omega, 6,* 3-20.

Silverman, P. R., & Klass, D. (1996). Introduction: What's the problem? In D. Klass, P. R. Silverman, & S. L. Nickman (Eds.), *Continuing bonds: A new understanding of grief* (pp. 3-27). Washington, DC: Taylor and Francis.

Silverman, P. R., & Smith, D. (1984). Helping in mutual help groups for the physically disabled. In A. Gartner, & F. Reisman, (Eds.), *Mental health and the self-help revolution* (pp. 73-93). New York: Human Science Press.

Silverman, P. R., & Worden, J.W. (1992). Children's reaction to the death of a parent. In M. Stroebe, W. Stroebe, & R. Hansson, (Eds.), *Bereavement: A sourcebook for research and intervention* (pp. 285-316). London: Cambridge University Press.

Stephans, S. (1973). *When death comes home.* New York: Morehouse-Barlow.

Tyhurst, J. (1958). The role of transition states, including disasters in mental illness. In National Research Council (Ed.), *Walter Reed Symposium on Preventive and Social Psychiatry* (pp. 1-21). Washington, DC: U.S. Government Printing Office, Supt. of Docs.

Vachon. M.L.S. (1979). *Identity change over the first two years of bereavement: Social relationships and social support in bereavement.* Unpublished doctoral dissertation, York University, Toronto, Canada.

Vachon, M. L. S., Lyall, W. A. L., Rogers, J., Freedman-Letofsky, K., & Freeman, S. J. (1980). A controlled study of self-help interventions for widows. *American Journal of Psychiatry, 137,* 1380-1384.

White, B., & Madara, E. J. (2002). *The self-help group sourcebook: Your guide to community and online support groups.* Denville, NJ: St. Clare's Health Services, American Self Help Group Clearing House. (www.selfhelpgroups.org)

Worden, J. W. (1996). *Children and grief: When a parent dies.* New York: Guilford Press.

Worden, J. W., & Silverman, P. R. (1993). Grief and depression in newly widowed parents with school age children. *Omega, 27,* 251-261.

CHAPTER 11

Meaning Breaking, Meaning Making: Rewriting Stories of Loss

Robert A. Neimeyer

Some 18 months after the death of her husband, Anna, age 62, describes herself as "drowning in a sea of grief." Far from moving toward some form of recovery, she experiences herself as "stuck" in a futile protest against the impossibility of living without John, who had been the "compass" for her life for the past two decades. Without the special caring, attunement, and structure he provided her, Anna feels "disoriented," "unreal," as if his death is "just some sort of terrible joke." John's relatively fast demise from an aggressive cancer gave her little time to adapt to the harsh reality of her impending loss, even though the couple received the competent support of the hospice nurses, social worker, and chaplain during his illness. Now, however, she feels deeply lonely and "cut off" from others, with the exception of her concerned adult daughter. She is preoccupied with burning spiritual questions regarding God's reason for taking the only man she had ever loved, leaving her with a life that is apparently "meaningless" without him. Tearfully, she describes how she has "no purpose for living" since John's death, and although she is not actively suicidal, she finds herself wishing it were she, rather than he, who had died.

■

Reflecting on the death of her college-age son, Tyler, in a motor vehicle accident, Leslie Brown[1] writes,

I ask "why" every day of my life. A scientist, my husband says that the accident was a "random" act and cannot be understood. Since I have had a more religious upbringing, I struggle to understand *why* my son was taken. I can't help asking that question in fury, and I am not alone. The other mothers who have lost children feel the same way I do. *Why?* There is absolutely no reason why. Considering the legions of despicable people who take up space on the face of this Earth while our children have gone defies any law of nature.

So I am left without any meaning in Tyler's death. Nothing is better for it; everything is worse. Here was a young man who inspired people and had recently returned from Indonesia where he had helped victims of the tsunami—a young man who was so transformed by that experience that he planned to spend two years in the Peace Corps before going on to grad school....

Today marks week 12 of his death, and I am in the process of designing his gravestone. This simply should not be. Would that I could find some meaning in this tragedy.

I, and my friends who have lost children, find solace in maintaining bonds with them. I don't see how anyone could find "closure" or "acceptance." Not in the death of one's child.

■

As Anna's psychosocial-spiritual struggle suggests, bereavement—even in the caring context that hospice provides—can profoundly challenge survivors' attempts to find some significance in the loss, ushering

---

[1] Leslie is not a client of mine in psychotherapy, but she wants to be identified. As she writes, "I would ask to be identified because I think writing about this terrible state of having lost my son is perhaps what I need to do with my life now." I appreciate her willingness to share her experience as a bereaved mother and her ongoing attempt to make sense of senseless loss.

in a protracted attempt to reconstruct a life story that retains or restores meaning and purpose. Moreover, as Leslie's experience indicates, when that death is sudden, violent, and out of phase with the family life cycle, this anguishing effort to find meaning can be even more intense and, as research documents, more complicated (Currier, Holland, Coleman, & Neimeyer, 2006). My goal in this chapter is to reflect on this struggle for meaning in the wake of profound loss, offering some insights arising in the context of my ongoing program of research and practice that carry implications for grief counseling and therapy. I offer three overarching principles of a meaning reconstruction approach to bereavement (Neimeyer, 2001), grounding each in recent research findings, illustrating each with actual case material, and offering two specific methods for grief counseling that help close the gap between abstract principles and concrete therapeutic practice.

Principle 1: Grieving entails reaffirming or reconstructing a world of meaning that has been challenged by loss.

As existential philosophers have long recognized, the human encounter with death and loss almost always raises profound issues regarding life's significance (Tomer, 1994). This does not imply that bereavement— a psychosocial transition that, after all, is ubiquitous in human life— necessarily instigates a life crisis or even a conscious search for meaning for all survivors. Indeed, recent research demonstrates that a great many bereaved persons are surprisingly resilient (Bonanno, 2004), and a minority of survivors even take the loss in stride without much conscious questioning, instead simply making the practical and emotional adaptations required to "move on" with their lives (Davis, Wortman, Lehman, & Silver, 2000). But for many of the bereaved, and especially those for whom a crippling preoccupation with their loss becomes intense and protracted (Bonanno, Wortman, & Nesse, 2004), an agonizing attempt to make sense of the loss in practical, existential, or spiritual terms becomes a dominant theme in their struggle for adaptation.

Recent theories that focus on the cognitive and emotional dimensions of troubling life transitions shed light on these divergent courses. From a constructivist standpoint, human existence is more than simply a series of disconnected experiences imposed on people by objective circumstances.

Instead, understanding life arises from our attempt to "emplot" the various episodes of our experience within a broader framework of meaning that makes them both intelligible and significant (Neimeyer, 2006c). The result of this evolving effort is a *self-narrative*, defined as "an overarching cognitive-affective-behavioral structure that organizes the 'micro-narratives' of everyday life into a 'macro-narrative' that consolidates our self-understanding, establishes our characteristic range of emotions and goals, and guides our performance on the stage of the social world" (Neimeyer, 2004, pp. 53-54).

Viewed in this light, one's sense of self emerges from an ongoing attempt to integrate various life experiences in a way that preserves the continuity of one's autobiographical memory (Boelen, van den Hout, & van den Bout, 2006) and continues to project one toward a recognizable future. Qualitative research suggests that even the death of a family member can be accommodated when survivors possess a belief system—spiritual or secular—that gives meaning to such losses. Death of a loved one can be accepted when it is seen as part of a divine plan or even an expression of worldly wrongdoing, galvanizing the survivor's long-standing efforts to crusade against injustice (Braun & Berg, 1994). In such cases, no active quest for meaning may be necessary: one need not *search* for that which was never *lost* in the first place.

For others like Anna and Leslie, however, both normative and nonnormative losses can violate the assumptive world, that network of fundamental, taken-for-granted convictions that sustain our belief in the predictability of life, the trustworthiness of others, and the beneficence of God or the universe (Janoff-Bulman, 1989). With the violation of these assumptions comes a profound disruption of the continuity and coherence of the self-narrative. The survivor is cruelly torn out of a life story that once made sense, but whose basic themes and tenets seem woefully inadequate to integrate the loss and all it implies for the bereaved person's future. The result, in the words of one bereaved mother, is a life that is "surreal, like play-acting at living." At one level, life moves forward, but without the horizon of a shared past, meaningful present, and abiding anticipation linked to the presence of the loved one. In a very real sense, the bereaved is faced with the necessity of not only making meaning of the loved one's death, but also reconstructing his or her own life's meaning as a survivor (Neimeyer, 2006c).

Research demonstrates that violent losses—the death of significant others through suicide, homicide, or catastrophic accident—are especially hard to accommodate. The survivor's inability to make sense of the death accounts for the complicated, intense grief symptoms (Currier, Holland, & Neimeyer, 2006). That is—as Leslie's plaintive questioning of *why* her son's life was extinguished in a fatal accident illustrates—such losses may have the devastating impact they do because they challenge the survivor's ability to integrate the loss into any sustaining framework of meaning. Conversely, when the bereaved are able to make sense of the loss, grief symptoms seem to be much less complicated by a sense of numbness, resentment, defensive distancing from others, or loss of essential life purpose and direction (Holland, Currier, & Neimeyer, in press). Moreover, survivors who find a positive, constructive benefit—such as reordering life priorities to give more emphasis to interpersonal relationships than private ambitions, or cultivating a sense of hard-won wisdom or empathy for responding to the suffering of self and others—seem able to mitigate the pain of loss (Calhoun & Tedeschi, 2006). In fact, meaning making (making sense of the death and finding benefit from it) appears to be so important in bereavement adaptation that it overrides the factors that intensify the level of grief: closeness of the bereaved to the deceased person, cause of death, and length of time since loss. However, there is also evidence that benefit finding may be less central and reliable a process than sense making, suggesting that finding some "silver lining" may function as a secondary buffer against bereavement-related distress when more primary efforts to impute meaning to the loss have failed (Holland et al.).

How can bereavement professionals and volunteers foster meaning reconstruction in the wake of loss? Perhaps the most obvious response is "in conversation," as meaning making is a process that unfolds between people as much as within them (Nadeau, 1997). For example, as part of a broader *Meaning Reconstruction Interview* (Neimeyer, 2002) that I use in some grief counseling situations I first explore the factual and emotional story of the loss, and then invite bereaved individuals or families to respond to questions such as the following:

- How did you make sense of the death or loss at the time?

- How do you interpret the loss now?

- What philosophical or spiritual beliefs contributed to your adjustment to this loss? How were they affected by it, in turn?

- Are there ways in which this loss disrupted the continuity of your life story? How, across time, have you dealt with this?

- How has this experience affected your sense of priorities?

- How has this experience affected your view of yourself or your world?

Such questions can be asked in an individual or group setting or used to prompt reflections in a personal journal. They help identify enduring or evolving meaning systems that can foster constructive integration of the lessons of loss. Alternatively, responses may indicate that the bereaved person is experiencing an intense disruption of meaning and is in need of more focused psychotherapeutic or pastoral work.

Another helpful procedure is encouraging bereaved persons to construct a brief biography, in the form of a "Table of Contents" of their life story, if they were to write it. In this *Chapters of Our Lives* exercise (Neimeyer, 2006a), people first spend a few reflective minutes writing down chapter titles as therapeutic homework or in session, and then share them with the therapist or members of the group in an atmosphere of (mutual) curiosity. Various facilitative questions can then be used to illuminate the autobiographical integration of loss and to envision ways that alternative stories might be constructed to grant different significance to the same life events. Such questions could include the following:

- How did you decide when one chapter ended and a new one began? What role, if any, did significant loss experiences (deaths, relationship dissolution, geographic displacement, serious illness of self or significant other, loss of job) play in marking or symbolizing such transitions?

- As you look back on how your story has developed over time, does the change seem to be more evolutionary and gradual, or revolutionary and sudden?

- If your self-narrative were a book, would it be a comedy, tragedy, history, mystery, adventure story, or romance? Or would different chapters represent "short stories" of different kinds? If so, which of them would you like to expand?

- Looking at the story, what are the major themes that tie it together? Do you notice any minor themes that pull in a different direction? If so, how might the story be different if these themes were really to have their say?

- Whom do you see as the primary author of this self-narrative? Are there any important coauthors who deserve credit (or blame!) for the way the story has unfolded?

- Who is the most relevant audience for this self-narrative? Who would enjoy the way it is written, and who would want to "edit" it?

Such reflective questions have no right or wrong answers. They invite exploration rather than evaluation, and often yield important insights into how loss intersects with life and people's sense of agency and life purpose in learning how to accommodate it.

Principle 2: Adaptation to bereavement typically involves redefining, rather than relinquishing, a continued bond with the deceased.

For most of the past century, mainstream grief theorists followed Freud's injunction that healthy mourning required a painful review and relinquishment of bonds to the deceased, understood as the "decathexis" (or withdrawal) of "libido" (or emotional investment) in the loved one (Freud, 1957). Accordingly, grief therapy was typically organized around the goals of "saying goodbye," "seeking closure," and "letting go." However, over the past decade scholars have begun to revisit these assumptions, suggesting that adaptation to bereavement could often take the form of retaining ties to the deceased, through actively recalling them in memory and conversation, seeking continuity with their purposes, and maintaining an active inner dialogue with them in a spiritual or psychological sense (Attig, 2000; Klass, Silverman, & Nickman, 1996).

The current scientific support for the adaptiveness of continuing bonds is ambiguous. On the one hand, there is little doubt that the bereaved often retain a strong emotional investment in their relationship to the deceased, and this is typically experienced as a loving connection (Hedtke & Winslade, 2003; Hogan & De Santis, 1992). On the other hand, it is not clear whether the active maintenance of such bonds mitigates the pain of physical separation: some studies suggest that a sense of the loved one's presence in the life of the bereaved is a source of comfort (Datson & Marwit, 1997), but other studies associate it with intensified grief (Field, Nichols, Holen, & Horowitz, 1999). The complexity of maintaining bonds to the deceased is reflected in the results of one well-designed study that found that overall, those widows who reported more frequently thinking of their husbands throughout the day also scored higher in negative emotion at these same times. However, for those widows who were farther along in their bereavement (a few years as opposed to a few months), this form of "continued bonds coping" was also associated with higher positive affect (Field & Friedrichs, 2004). Thus, it appears that the significance and impact of the bond may vary across time and across persons.

From a meaning reconstruction standpoint, the ambiguity in these findings implies that another (unmeasured) factor could be interacting with the strength of the bond to predict grief intensity, and recent evidence suggests that this is indeed the case. For a large group of young adults grieving a variety of family and friend relationships, stronger continued bonds coping was associated with more painful, complicated grief symptoms, *but only to the degree that the bereaved were unable to make sense of the loss* (Neimeyer, Baldwin, & Gillies, 2006). In contrast, even highly bonded survivors bore their grief more lightly when they were able to find spiritual, existential, or practical meaning in the loss. This implies that one goal of grief therapy is to consider not merely the presence or absence of an emotional tie to the deceased, but also the specific character of the postmortem relationship (Rubin, 1999) and the challenges to one's self-narrative arising from it. The following case vignette illustrates this principle and how it might be addressed therapeutically.

Terri and Steve were a couple in their 40s who sought grief therapy approximately 6 months after their 20-year-old daughter, Mindy, committed suicide. To their great credit, both acknowledged that despite the immense impact of Mindy's tragic decision, her death was "not dividing them," and each remained a great source of support for the other. However, Steve also acknowledged his anger at Mindy for "hurting so many people" and remained at a loss to understand the dark force that drew her toward her death. For her part, Terri felt "shattered" by the trauma of her daughter's overdose in a distant part of the country and was further pained by the murmured implications of church members that Mindy's destination in the afterlife was uncertain because of her hand in ending her life. As Terri stated, "I just can't understand a God who would take a child and then not let her be okay." It soon became clear that Terri faced not only a tragically imposed separation from her daughter, but a "dilemma of faith" as well.

A turning point came in our second session when Terri joined Steve in anger at Mindy and cried out, as if to her daughter, "What went wrong? Why did you make that day your last?" Terri was ready to resume a conversation with her daughter, so I suggested that she symbolically place her daughter in an empty chair and express to her what most needed to be said. Terri readily accepted the invitation, beginning with a painful lament, "How could you hurt us so? How could you cut me out?" What followed was a long and tearful tirade, in which she spoke from the broken heart of a mother who felt insufficient, angry, and inexplicably abandoned by the daughter she had loved for 20 years.

Gesturing to the empty chair, I then suggested that Terri switch places, and lend her daughter her own voice to reply to her mother's plaintive cry. As she did so, Terri's demeanor changed, and became sadder but calmer. "I felt lonely, Mom, and unworthy. I reached a place where I couldn't imagine a normal life. I had no joy, and nothing mattered." "Mindy" went on to reassure her mom that she was at peace and that she needed her mother to help others in the family understand and forgive her for what she did. In a further round of switching roles, mother and daughter concluded their moving dialogue, the implications of which we then processed with Steve.

The following week Terri was visibly transformed, carrying herself more lightly, looking well rested and smiling. Steve validated the impression that something "really life changing" had happened since the previous session. In her own terms, Terri explained that she had been able to "put Mindy away" much of the week and rediscover real closeness with both Steve and her remaining daughter. Equally remarkably, her sense of contact with Mindy, when it did occur, was itself transformed: just as a popular TV show suggested, Terri knew she was being visited by an "angel" when she unaccountably smelled sugar cookies, and spontaneously was able to ask

Mindy how she was doing "without feeling sad or anything." As they continued to "visit," Terri heard Mindy's voice in her head assuring her, "Mom, this was so not about you." Instantly, the burden of guilt she had carried vanished, and she realized that her adult daughter's life had no longer rotated around her mother as its center: "I recognized that I was not her sun anymore—I was more like her *moon*."

Concomitantly, Terri felt that she received from Mindy herself "permission not to think of her 24 hours a day." When Terri and Steve did speak about Mindy, however, it was with less anger, and more genuine wrestling with the spiritual question of "Where is she now? Is she one little bundle of energy, or did she dissipate into the universe?" Not all of these questions were addressed satisfactorily within their previous faith community, but both spouses seemed open to finding fresh answers. In the days that followed, Terri's sense of supportive "visitations" by Mindy continued: Mindy reciting a poem for her sister in Terri's dream, Terry discovering a makeup mirror decorated with Mindy's favorite painting under a hotel bed. Simultaneously, then, Terri (and to a significant extent, Steve) began to cultivate a new form of continuing bond with their daughter, while also reconstructing the meaning of her death (and life). Importantly, these changes continued to hold in the weeks that followed.

Not all grief counselors will feel comfortable orchestrating anguished conversations between their client and the image of the loved one. Indeed, the artful facilitation of such conversations requires considerable training in emotion-focused therapeutic techniques (Greenberg, Elliott, & Rice, 1993). But many counselors may find value in helping clients explore and change their connection with deceased loved ones using less demanding methods, which can nonetheless be quite powerful. One such is the *Life Imprint* technique (Vickio, 1999), which recognizes the way in which we customarily preserve our connection to many others who have touched our lives—not merely parents and grandparents—by carrying a part of them in us, appropriating their life story, in a sense, into our own. The life imprint simply involves identifying ways in which the other has left a recognizable mark on us at several levels, including our (1) mannerisms and gestures, (2) ways of speaking and communicating, (3) work and pastime activities, (4) feelings about ourselves and others, (5) basic personality, and (6) core values and beliefs. Because not all imprints are positive,

I also often invite clients to consider which imprints they want to affirm or develop, and which they would like to relinquish or change.

Another method of facilitating a connection is a *Letter Exchange* with the deceased, in which the bereaved person writes to his or her loved one, not with the intent to "say goodbye," but more commonly to "say hello again" (Hedtke & Winslade, 2003), followed by writing a response as if from the loved one. These and myriad other methods can foster the goal of cultivating a vital, but mutable relationship with the deceased, one in which new frameworks of meaning can arise from the relationship without being imposed by the therapist.

Principle 3: Narrative methods can play a role in restoring or re-storying a sense of autobiographical coherence that has been disrupted by loss.

Finally, it is worth underscoring that narrative and literary approaches can provide more than a metaphor or model for meaning making; they can generate concrete therapeutic techniques to augment individual, family, or group therapy. Perhaps the most basic of these is simply oral narrative or *storytelling*, in which the client relates an account of a loss and its impact on her or his life, while the counselor or bereavement volunteer serves an "exquisite witness" to the telling, listening more deeply and thoroughly than others are likely to (Jeffreys, 2005). For example, in her second (and last) therapy appointment following the death of her beloved mother a few months before, a recent client of mine opened by saying how greatly she had benefited from our previous session, noting, "It feels so good to be *heard*. My husband is a good listener, and he really understands, but his ministry just leaves him with so little time. And so it really helped just to be able to tell the whole story and to have another person be with me in that."

The power of witnessing is compounded when the death and accompanying grief are complicated. Thus, special group contexts for "retelling violent death" have been devised to help members speak the unspeakable and then find ways of moving beyond it, whether in words, in the case of adults (Rynearson, 1999); play therapy, in the case of children (Currier & Neimeyer, 2006); or combinations of both. Evidence for the efficacy of such procedures comes from a recent controlled trial of *complicated grief therapy* in which bereaved adults were offered a 16-session treatment consisting of three phases (Shear, Frank, Houch, & Reynolds, 2005). The first, termed "revisiting," entailed retelling the story of the loss with closed eyes as the therapist recorded the client's narration for her or him to listen to during the week at home. Distress that arose in this process was then targeted in the second phase, using methods that encouraged a constructive "reconnection" with the deceased, for example, facilitating a 10- to 20-minute imaginary conversation with the deceased, consisting of both positive and negative memories. Finally, in the phase of "restoration," clients were encouraged to redefine life goals, constructing an image of a future in which their grief was not so intense and elaborating goals for realizing this vision. Taken as a package, this form of treatment proved both more effective and efficient than standard interpersonal psychotherapy in reducing intense and debilitating grief symptoms.

Even in less systematic applications, literary and narrative methods can help people not only express, but also integrate and master complex experiences, and even reorganize their living connection with the deceased. For example, as I reflected not long ago on the death of my mother, I wrote the following poem, one of several focusing on themes of loss and human resilience (Neimeyer, 2006b):

> *Bond*
> When my mother gave up her flesh
> like a threadbare coat,
> she spread into the room
> as a vapor fills a closed space.
> Gradually,
> she permeated us,
> our sponge-like bodies
> her needed shelter.
>
> She fills us now
> as we once filled her,
> animate, moving, electric
> with quiet potential.
> The birth she seeks
> is in memory, thought,
> the dedicated act—

the ways spirit finds form.
All that we are points back
    to her,
as the branch retraced
finds trunk, or root.

What will become of her
when the rags of our bodies
fall away, and we too reach
for the haven of lives not our own?

Will a part of her, dilute
as weak tea, accompany us
in the outpouring of our souls?
Or will she find freedom from flesh,
as the cicada abandons its hard husk
to seek a final home in the air,

and release from bondage
to love?

Often the richly figurative speech afforded by poetry permits the bereaved to transcend the limits of literal language and give voice to intimate personal meanings and promote their evolution in ways that sometimes surprise the poets themselves. The frequency with which verse appears in the newsletters of bereavement support groups testifies that one need not be a professional poet to write movingly about an important loss and the bond that it affirms. Many other concrete *biographical methods* that help the bereaved articulate and honor the lives of their loved ones and their impact on their own have been described and illustrated in the meaning reconstruction literature (Neimeyer, 2002, 2001).

CONCLUSION

As bereavement theory has evolved, so too has the fund of practices to facilitate coming to terms with love and loss. My purpose in writing this brief chapter has been to sketch a few of the core principles that animate one "growing edge" of bereavement theory, namely, one that views grieving as a process of reaffirming or rebuilding a world of meaning. I hope that the clinical concepts, practical procedures, and reinforcing research I have described offer some useful inspiration for your ongoing efforts to address the meaning-breaking features of loss, and to foster the meaning-making processes of reconstruction. ■

Robert A. Neimeyer, Ph.D. is professor and director of psychotherapy in the Department of Psychology at the University of Memphis, where is also maintains an active clinical practice. Dr. Neimeyer has published 20 books, including Meaning Reconstruction and the Experience of Loss, *and serves as editor of the journal* Death Studies. *The author of nearly 300 articles and book chapters, and a frequent workshop presenter, he is currently working to advance a more adequate theory of grieving as a meaning making process. Dr. Neimeyer served as president of the Association of Death Education and Counseling and as chair of the International Work Group for Death, Dying & Bereavement. In recognition of his scholarly contributions, he has been granted the Eminent Faculty Award by the University of Memphis, and was made a Fellow of the American Psychological Association.*

REFERENCES

Attig, T. (2000). *The heart of grief.* New York: Oxford.

Boelen, P., van den Hout, M., & van den Bout, J. (2006). A cognitive-behavioral conceptualization of complicated grief. *Clinical Psychology: Science and Practice, i*(13), 109-128.

Bonanno, G. A. (2004). Loss, trauma and human resilience. *American Psychologist, 59,* 20-28.

Bonanno, G. A., Wortman, C. B., & Nesse, R. M. (2004). Prospective patterns of resilience and maladjustment during widowhood. *Psychology and Aging, 19,* 260-271.

Braun, M. L., & Berg, D. H. (1994). Meaning reconstruction in the experience of bereavement. *Death Studies, 18,* 105-129.

Calhoun, L., & Tedeschi, R. G. (Eds.). (2006). *Handbook of posttraumatic growth.* Mahwah, NJ: Lawrence Erlbaum.

Currier, J., Holland, J., Coleman, R., & Neimeyer, R. A. (2006). Bereavement following violent death: An assault on life and meaning. In R. Stevenson & G. Cox (Eds.), *Perspectives on violence and violent death.* Amityville, NY: Baywood.

Currier, J., Holland, J., & Neimeyer, R. A. (2006). Sense making, grief and the experience of violent loss: Toward a mediational model. *Death Studies, 30,* 403-428.

Currier, J., & Neimeyer, R. A. (2006). Fragmented stories: The narrative integration of violent loss. In E. K. Rynearson (Ed.), *Violent death: Resilience and intervention beyond the crisis.* New York: Routledge.

Datson, S. L., & Marwit, S. J. (1997). Personality constructs and perceived presence of deceased loved ones. *Death Studies, 21,* 131-146.

Davis, C. G., Wortman, C. B., Lehman, D. R., & Silver, R. C. (2000). Searching for meaning in loss: Are clinical assumptions correct? *Death Studies, 24,* 497-540.

Field, N. P., & Friedrichs, M. (2004). Continuing bonds in coping with the death of a husband. *Death Studies, 28,* 597-620.

Field, N. P., Nichols, C., Holen, A., & Horowitz, M. J. (1999). The relation of continuing attachment to adjustment in conjugal bereavement. *Journal of Consulting and Clinical Psychology, 67,* 212-218.

Freud, S. (1957). Mourning and melancholia. In J. Strachey (Ed.), *The Complete Psychological Works of Sigmund Freud* (pp. 152-170). London: Hogarth Press.

Greenberg, L., Elliott, R., & Rice, L. (1993). *Facilitating emotional change.* New York: Guilford.

Hedtke, L., & Winslade, J. (2003). *Remembering conversations.* Amityville, NY: Baywood.

Hogan, N., & De Santis, L. (1992). Adolescent sibling bereavement: An ongoing attachment. *Qualitative Health Research, 2,* 159-177.

Holland, J., Currier, J., & Neimeyer, R. A. (in press). Meaning reconstruction in the first two years of bereavement: The role of sense-making and benefit-finding. *Omega.*

Janoff-Bulman, R. (1989). Assumptive worlds and the stress of traumatic events. *Social Cognition, 7,* 113-116.

Jeffreys, J. S. (2005). *Helping grieving people: When tears are not enough.* New York: Routledge.

Klass, D., Silverman, P. R., & Nickman, S. (1996). *Continuing bonds: New understandings of grief.* Washington, DC: Taylor & Francis.

Nadeau, J. W. (1997). *Families making sense of death.* Newbury Park, CA: Sage.

Neimeyer, R. A. (Ed.). (2001). *Meaning reconstruction and the experience of loss*. Washington, DC: American Psychological Association.

Neimeyer, R. A. (2002). *Lessons of loss: A guide to coping* (2nd ed.). New York: Brunner Routledge.

Neimeyer, R. A. (2004). Fostering posttraumatic growth: A narrative contribution. *Psychological Inquiry, 15*, 53-59.

Neimeyer, R. A. (2006a). Narrating the dialogical self: Toward an expanded toolbox for the counselling psychologist. *Counselling Psychology Quarterly, 19*, 105-120.

Neimeyer, R. A. (2006b). *Rainbow in the Stone*. Memphis, TN: Mercury.

Neimeyer, R. A. (2006c). Widowhood, grief and the quest for meaning: A narrative perspective on resilience. In D. Carr, R. M. Nesse, & C. B. Wortman (Eds.), *Late life widowhood in the United States* (pp. 227-252). New York: Springer.

Neimeyer, R. A., Baldwin, S. A., & Gillies, J. (2006). Continuing bonds and reconstructing meaning: Mitigating complications in bereavement. *Death Studies, 30*, 715-738.

Rubin, S. (1999). The two-track model of bereavement: Overview, retrospect and prospect. *Death Studies, 23*, 681-714.

Rynearson, E. K. (1999). *Retelling violent death*. New York: Brunner Routledge.

Shear, K., Frank, E., Houch, P. R., & Reynolds, C. F. (2005). Treatment of complicated grief: A randomized controlled trial. *Journal of the American Medical Association, 293*, 2601-2608.

Tomer, A. (1994). Death anxiety in adult life: Theoretical perspectives. In R. A. Neimeyer (Ed.), *Death anxiety handbook: Research, instrumentation, and application* (pp. 3-28). Washington, DC: Taylor & Francis.

Vickio, C. (1999). Together in spirit: Keeping our relationships alive when loved ones die. *Death Studies, 23*, 161-175.

CHAPTER 12

Working with Children and Adolescents: An Overview of Theoretical and Practical Issues

David E. Balk

This chapter examines current theoretical and practical information for counselors working with bereaved children and adolescents. It addresses two questions:

1. What are the unique ways children and adolescents cope with grief, both before and after the death?

2. How can we best help these children and adolescents?

CHILDHOOD DEVELOPMENT

Bereavement affects people physically, cognitively, behaviorally, spiritually, emotionally, and interpersonally. Commentators on childhood bereavement tend to concentrate on the cognitive aspect, namely, a child's understanding of death. Cross-sectional studies demonstrate differences between younger and older children's grasp of the major components of a mature understanding of death: universality, finality, causality, and nonfunctionality. Persons with a mature understanding know that

(a) all living things eventually die, (b) death is irreversible, (c) both internal and external factors can lead to death, and (d) bodily functions cease with death (Silverman, 2000; Speece & Brent, 1996). Typically, empirical investigators consign expressions of belief in life after death to immature understanding of death and magical thinking. Counselors can use Grace Christ's (2000) five age groupings for children's understanding of death. She showed that emotional, social, and cognitive aspects of development shape children's responses to parental death. The five age groups are 3-5, 6-8, 9-11, 12-14, and 15-17. For example, here is how cognitive, emotional, and social aspects emerged in bereaved 6- to 8-year-old children.

> Children between the ages of 6 and 8 grieving a parent's death comprehended that death is irreversible, but many blamed themselves for their parent's death ("If I hadn't made Dad take me to the ballgame, he wouldn't have had a heart attack"). Separation from primary caregivers was less anxiety-provoking for 6- to 8-year-olds than for younger children. The school environment widened their social world and provided outlets.

Robert Ludwig, director of the Healing Center's programs for bereaved children at Long Island College Hospital in Brooklyn, New York, emphasizes appreciating what a bereaved child comprehends about death and accepting the limits of the child's understanding. "I don't push with finality. We have to accept that young children don't get it" (personal communication, June 27, 2006). Ludwig says children know the word "died," but they don't attribute to it all the meanings adults do. For instance, a young boy will say, "I know Daddy died, but will he come back for my birthday party?"

Because children's grasp of death varies according to cognitive developmental maturity, authors underscore the importance of using developmentally appropriate language when speaking to them about death. Ludwig said he uses analogies with young children, such as a leaf falling from a tree branch.

Linda Goldman's books (2000, 2001, 2006) are filled with examples of how to talk with children about death and loss. She uses the words "die," "dead," and "death," and argues that euphemisms create a confused understanding of death that is "a predictable influence of grief" (2000, p. 38). The following are some euphemistic explanations and Goldman's alternatives:

> "Dad went on a long trip." Goldman suggests telling how Dad died and saying that everyone feels sad but everyone will get through this hurt together.

> "Your sister is in heaven with the angels." Goldman suggests saying that the sister died and everyone will think about her a lot and remember all the wonderful things she did.

> "Grandma is watching you from heaven." Goldman suggests saying that Grandma lived a long time and died because she got very old and her body wore out.

Goldman advises giving honest responses and accurate presentations of the facts, using clear and understandable language, and demonstrating truthfulness, thereby fostering an atmosphere of confidence and trust.

Like Goldman, Silverman (2000) stresses an atmosphere in which children feel free to ask questions and adults provide truthful answers. She emphasizes "teachable moments," opportunities "to teach them that death does happen" (p. 235). The major figures using teachable moments with children are parents, but their own anxiety about death may make it hard for them to teach their children. Some teachable moments occur when a death happens far enough removed from the family that the child can learn about it "in manageable segments" (p. 236). Silverman says, "If these moments are utilized well, children learn to be respected as mourners and that they have a legitimate role as part of their community. They can touch the experience, feel its importance in their lives, and develop a vocabulary that allows them to give words to what they are experiencing" (pp. 236-237).

ADOLESCENT DEVELOPMENT

Many changes mark the transition from childhood to adolescence and from adolescence to young adulthood. Among the changes that mark adolescence are a shift in focus from parents toward peers, increased skill in interpersonal relations, growing competence in using abstract thought, interest in the meaning of existence, growth in self-concept, awareness of moral ambiguities and ironies, fluency in disclosing personal matters, skill in listening attentively to what a friend has to say, and gradual movement from unquestioning acceptance of authoritative statements to recognition of competing demands about what is true (Fowler, 1991; Josselson, 1987; 1996; Noppe & Noppe, 1996; Offer, 1969; Perry, 1970, 1999).

Three phases of adolescent development are commonly recognized: early adolescence (10-14), middle adolescence (15-17), and later adolescence (18-23). Stephen Fleming and Rheba Adolph (1986) present a conceptual framework that integrates the demands of bereavement within adolescent phases and developmental tasks. They start with the three phases of adolescent development (the age ranges vary slightly from those given above) and identify a specific task the adolescent must master in each one, as well as factors that complicate the task.

> Phase 1 (11-14). Adolescents must separate emotionally from their parents. Complications are the desire for safety and fear of abandonment.

> Phase 2 (14-17). Adolescents must gain a sense of personal mastery and control. Complications are the competing attractions of dependence and independence.

> Phase 3 (17-21). Adolescents must gain intimacy with others and commit to something besides themselves. Complications are the tension between remaining emotionally distant and becoming personally close.

Applying these ideas about phases, tasks, and conflicts to adolescent bereavement in the death of a parent illustrates the value of the model. Take Johanna, a 13-year-old girl. According to Fleming and Adolph (1986), her current developmental task is to separate emotionally from her parents. But her father died of colon cancer four months ago and thus was wrenched violently out of her life, so the emotional separation has crushing and conflicting salience. Further, the separation was not on her terms but forced on her.

Adolescents are more familiar with death and bereavement than scholars had thought. Death rates increase during adolescence as a result of vehicle accidents, homicides, and suicides. Accidents are the chief cause of adolescent deaths (Anderson & Smith, 2005). Homicide is the leading cause of deaths among middle-adolescent and young adult African-American males (Price, Thompson, & Drake, 2004; U. S. Department of Justice, 2006). Suicide has grown exponentially as a leading cause of death among adolescents, particularly among white males and—since the mid-1980s—black males (U.S. Department of Health and Human Services, 1999).

As a result of the deaths of peers and of grandparents, many adolescents are personally familiar with bereavement. Ewalt and Perkins (1979) found in a survey of more than 1,000 high school juniors and seniors that 90% acknowledged that they had been touched by the death of someone they knew. Research using convenience samples of college students found a similar pattern: 22% to 30% of college students at any one time are in the first 12 months of grieving the death of a family member or friend (Balk, 1997). The most common loss reported by college students in New York was the death of someone close to them (LaGrand, 1985, 1986).

Adolescent understanding of death is filled with ambiguity (Noppe & Noppe, 1996), mostly fueled by an increase in egocentrism (Elkind, 1967). In a way, magical thinking from childhood reenters the picture: Although adolescents understand that death is universal, they often consider themselves invulnerable. (However, these feelings of invulnerability disappear if an adolescent is in a situation in which dying is a real possibility. Adolescents stricken with a terminal illness are not cavalier, and the students at Columbine High School did not discount the possibility of their own death.)

How Children and Adolescents Cope with Grief

A number of authors (Haine, Wolchik, Sandler, Millsap, & Ayers, 2006; Sandler et al., 2003; Worden, 1996) have emphasized the importance of consistent, positive parenting for bereaved children. Positive parenting provides children with security, limits, and caring, and fosters open conversations about the death and about grief reactions. In Sandler's longitudinal research program with children who had lost a parent, consistent, positive parenting led to fewer acting-out behaviors among boys and fewer mental health problems in boys and girls (Haine et al., 2006).

Worden (1996) noted that parentally bereaved children in the longitudinal Child Bereavement Study clearly responded to the quality of the surviving parent's coping and caretaking behavior. When parents discounted their own coping, their children manifested impaired self-efficacy, became socially withdrawn, and exhibited behavioral and emotional problems that, in some cases, became full-blown delinquency. Parents with passive coping styles were clear risk factors for bereaved children's ongoing development and grief resolution. Synthesizing a major finding of the study, Worden wrote, "[A] parent who has accepted and adjusted to the loss of a spouse greatly reduces the risk of a poor grief reaction in the child" (p. 160).

In the earliest studies of sibling death during adolescence (Balk, 1981, 1983), quality of communication and emotional closeness in the family were the major influences on adolescent bereavement outcomes. Teenagers from families with a tradition of personal conversations and close attachments (called "more coherent family environments") used the family as a resource to work through problems. Teenagers in families that lacked emotional closeness and personal conversations (called "less coherent family environments") were initially insulated from many reactions to the death but over time reported enduring confusion and delayed grief reactions.

It is possible that less coherent family environments help instill the delayed grief reactions that Worden (2002) identified as one form of complicated grief. Such family environments could present a risk factor that requires counselor attention.

Dent (2005), a bereavement researcher in the United Kingdom, underscored the importance of family communication on outcomes for bereaved children and adolescents. She wrote, "Several researchers suggest that it is not so much the death that causes difficulties but the family system, which ultimately determines the long-term effects on siblings" (p. 22). Many authors agree that working with parents provides vital point of leverage in effecting positive outcomes for children following bereavement. Informative workshops for bereaved parents allow them to tell their stories and allow educators to discuss in plain language the crucial role that adult caregivers play with grieving children.

THE TASK-BASED MODEL

A well-known model (Worden, 1991, 2002) lists four tasks the bereaved person must accomplish to recover:

1. Accept that the loss is real.

2. Deal with the distress that bereavement causes.

3. Engage in a world in which the person who died is absent.

4. Emotionally relocate the deceased and move on with life. (Worden, 2002, p. 35). Worden modified Task 4 in reference to children and said grieving children need to relocate the deceased and, rather than moving on with life, "find ways to memorialize the person" (Worden, 1996, p. 15).

Worden's task-based model is the basis for several approaches to children's grief. Dent (2005) uses the model in her discussion of what children do when they grieve. Goldman (2000) modifies Worden and says bereavement requires that children handle four psychological tasks: understanding, grieving, commemorating, and going on.

In the *task of understanding*, the child makes sense of the death. Goldman notes that a child's understanding emerges out of his or her family's way of explaining death in general and clarifying the death of someone the child cared for. This task includes what Neimeyer (2001) considers the cardinal issue for coping with loss: making meaning.

The *task of grieving* refers to the acute grief reactions identified by Lindemann (1944), such as feelings of anger and guilt, disordered patterns of conduct, somatic reactions such as chills and fatigue, and cognitive distortions such as trouble concentrating and remembering things. Goldman (2000) includes anger when discussing children and the task of grieving. She writes that grieving emerges in Bowlby-like phases of "shock and disbelief, searching and yearning, disorganization and despair, and reorganization and healing"(p. 47). One can see in this task what Stroebe and Schut (1999) call the "loss orientation."

The *task of commemorating* refers to formal and informal ways children can remember the person who died. Formal commemorations include yearbook tributes, scholarship funds, and memorial services; informal commemorations include making a booklet of memories and choosing a book to donate to the school library in honor of the child who died. For a child who has lost a parent, commemorating may include maintaining an attachment to the parent. Dent (2005) insists that such attachments are essential: "Children, like adults, need to maintain bonds with the deceased, and therefore the notion of continuing bonds for children is very relevant" (p. 19).

However, some research has indicated problems with ongoing attachment to a dead parent. Some college women whose fathers had died were upset at the idea that their father could be "present" to them (Tyson-Rawson, 1996). Consider the circumstance of a child who was sexually abused by a father who died (Fleming & Belanger, 2001). Should she maintain an attachment with that abusive parent? Stroebe and colleagues (Stroebe & Schut, 2005; Stroebe, Schut, & Stroebe, 2005) suggested that in cases of insecure or ambivalent attachments, bonds should be loosened, not maintained.

The *task of going* on means becoming active again in the world of the living. Stroebe and Schut (1999) call this "the process of restoration."

The task-based model provides a schema for a teacher or counselor to assess the child's process of grieving. Robert Ludwig said he uses Worden's approach as a guide for his work with grieving children. He does not use the task terminology with children but does use the tasks for assessment and as discussion points in meetings with staff.

ANTICIPATORY MOURNING

Children and adolescents have unique ways of coping with grief before a death. Lindemann (1944) described the notion of anticipatory bereavement in which some women so anticipated that their husbands would be killed in World War II that when the men returned safely they discovered that their wives had completely detached emotionally from them. Rando

(2000) said that anticipatory mourning is bounded by six dimensions, including temporal aspects and adaptational demands. Fulton (2003) has said that the construct of anticipatory mourning lacks conceptual, theoretical, and practical meaning; Kauffman (2003), on the other hand, considers the construct of particular clinical and theoretical value, especially for understanding and treating traumatic loss.

Anticipatory mourning presents special problems for children, whose cognitive operations are still developing. They have difficulty thinking about possibilities and understanding alternatives. The concept presents other problems for adolescents, whose cognitive operations are influenced by egocentrism—they may become overwhelmed by the impact the loss will have solely on them. Anticipatory mourning raises issues about finality, and Ludwig wisely advises not pushing finality on children.

We can examine anticipatory mourning by applying Worden's task model.Watching someone deteriorate instills anticipation and can initiate accepting the reality of the loss (Worden, 2002), but this can be very troubling for children (Saldinger, 2001). Being aware that someone is dying elicits separation anxiety, and experiencing these distressing feelings is part of working through the pain of grief. Some prominent scholars place separation anxiety at the core of bereavement (Hall & Irwin, 2001; Jacobs et al., 1986). Rehearsing what life will demand following an anticipated death is one way of adjusting to an environment in which the deceased person is absent, but rehearsing strikes some as callous (Worden, 2002). Preparing oneself for an impending death can start one toward emotionally relocating the person and getting on with life. But, as Worden noted, a drawn-out period of anticipatory grief may lead someone to "withdraw emotionally too soon" (p. 139).

Clinical lore holds that humans cope better with anticipated than unexpected losses, but the empirical literature does not provide unqualified support for this assumption. Sudden deaths do not induce the enduring stresses on children of experiencing the "graphic physical, emotional, and mental deterioration of the dying parent" (Saldinger, Cain, & Porterfield, 2003, p. 168). Further, the strains of a spouse's terminal illness can adversely affect parenting (Saldinger, 2001). Unlike conventional grief after the loss of a spouse, anticipatory grief was more likely to be associated "with higher intensities of anger, loss of emotional control, and atypical grief responses" (Gilliland & Fleming, 1998, p. 541). More factors influence bereavement outcome than just advance preparation, so looking solely at anticipatory grief is simplistic (Worden, 2002).

INTERVENTIONS WITH BEREAVED CHILDREN AND ADOLESCENTS

Worden's task-based model provides a template counselors can use to plan bereavement interventions for children and adolescents. The four tasks are sufficiently specific to give meaningful direction yet flexible enough to leave room for adapting to the requirements of each child.

Bereavement interventions are no longer considered helpful just because they are well-intentioned or because of clinical lore that the bereaved need outlets that professional interventions provide. Jordan and Neimeyer (2003) raise the possibility that interventions aimed at normally bereaved persons may actually do more harm than good; however, consensus still exists that interventions can help persons with complicated grief.

Counterintuitive results about the dangers of bereavement interventions may result from poorly designed efforts. The interventions may have a questionable theoretical basis, as in efforts to move bereaved persons through Kubler-Ross's (1969) five stages of dying. The research may have been poorly designed by using highly heterogeneous samples in terms of time since the death or by gathering cross-sectional data that cannot assess changes over time. The interventions may have included persons too close to the death or too far removed from it.

It is not clear that all interventions with normally bereaved persons are contraindicated. While history suggests that over time many people do recover from bereavement, and not all bereaved persons need to talk about their loss, I believe that some people profit from intelligently designed interventions. This chapter is not the place to discuss the knowledge base a well-prepared thanatological counselor possesses, but the person should know sound counseling practices and comprehend foundational information about thanatology.

Persons who are confused over their bereavement should have the opportunity to talk about what they have experienced and what they think and feel. Given the widespread acknowledgment that children often lack cognitive capacity to comprehend fully what a death means, interventions to help them make eminent sense.

The intervention techniques discussed below are those reported by Goldman (2000), the Healing Center's interventions, and a group intervention with adolescents. These interventions are grounded in appreciation of the richness of child and adolescent development and in knowledge of the vagaries of bereavement. They build from Worden's task-based model. Another excellent source of information about helping bereaved children is the Dougy Center (www.dougy.org).

Group Work at the Healing Center

The Healing Center uses separate groups for adults and children. The adult groups focus on educating adults about grief and helping children with their grief. One can see in these adult groups Worden's ideas (1996) about various ways to include parents in counseling and educational efforts.

The children's groups have a very close ratio (1:1.5) of children to adult facilitators. The Healing Center's rationale for this ratio is that children are needy, and grieving children are needier than others. A child is never alone. The structure of the 75-minute children's group is as follows:

1. 10-20 minutes. The children and adults play games (UNO, crazy eights, hearts, charades, war) at two large tables. This part of the group is called the Holding Game and accommodates children who arrive late.

2. ~ 20 minutes. The group shifts to the Talking Circle, in which the participants sit on a carpet. A facilitator starts off by picking up the "talking stick" that lies in the middle of the circle. After speaking, the facilitator passes the stick to another person in the circle. A participant who does not want to talk may say, "I pass." The structure is reminiscent of an Alcoholics Anonymous meeting. A child says "My name is _____."

The death I have experienced is _____." Others listen to the person who is holding the stick. Topics might include "How did you find out about the death?", "When did the person die?", "How did the person die?", "What did you like about the person who died?", and "What ticked you off about the person who died?" The children decide what they are willing to share.

3. 30-40 minutes. The next part of the group is devoted to play, and all the adults take part. Activities might include dress-up, dollhouse, stories, board games, finger painting, and ping-pong. No video games, VHS tapes, or DVDs are allowed.

4. ~ 5 minutes. The group returns to the carpet for a Closing Circle.

Writing, Telling Stories, Drawing

Linda Goldman (2000, 2001, 2006) offers several techniques for engaging grieving children, such as the following.

Children are given the basic structure for completing a memory book, which helps them deal with the psychological task Goldman (2000) calls commemorating. The box provides some of the suggestions for a memory book.

My name is _____.

I am ____years old. This is a picture of me:

My special person is _____.

Here is a picture of my special person:

_____ was born on _____

and died on _____.

_____told me that _____

had died. _____ died because _____.

Source: Goldman, 2006, pp. 51-53.

Goldman offers several techniques for engaging children in the psychological task of grieving. The techniques include storytelling (for instance, beginning the story "Once upon a time there was a _____ who died") (Goldman, 2000, p. 62). Each person continues the story, one line at a time.

Other techniques are writing a letter to the person who died and drawing genograms (diagrams showing three or more generations in a family). Genograms may offer teachable moments. A 10-year-old boy, Seth, drew a genogram as a way to explore the death of his sister. The genogram "helped him to see which family members have died, which ones are still living, and which family members are those he can and cannot depend on" (p. 74). Goldman asked Seth why he had circled his grandmother as a person he could not depend on and learned that she had Alzheimer's disease, so Seth could not depend on her memory. Goldman noted, "This genogram helped to create a teachable moment with the use of a wonderful resource, *Always Grandma*, a book for children about a grandmother with Alzheimer's" (p. 74).

Group Intervention with Adolescents

Numerous interventions are appropriate for use with bereaved adolescents. While individual counseling and art therapies have value, I will focus here on working with adolescents in groups, as this is a common approach that is often adapted in educational environments.

Richard Tedeschi (1996) has written about the use of support groups for bereaved adolescents. He believes that bereavement is a life crisis with potential for growth and transformation (Tedeschi & Calhoun, 1995). In his support groups, Tedeschi links the intervention to the developmental tasks of adolescence as well as the tasks for coping with bereavement. "At the crucial ages when adolescents are learning about self-identity, how to cultivate relationships, and how to understand life events, bereavement may remove from [their]…world…the very people who play important roles in this learning" (Tedeschi, 1996, p. 295).

Because of developmental differences separating early and later adolescents, Tedeschi recommends forming groups that do not include extremes in age range or emotional maturity. However, he acknowledges that many groups "function very well with a wide range of ages, with older adolescents providing tender support for younger ones" (p. 299). He cautions against including "one or more group members who are clearly very different from the others" (p. 299), but he is referring to personality disorders rather than age differences.

In Tedeschi's framework, group size should range from five to ten members. Fewer than five members hinders the formation of group cohesion, and more than ten makes it difficult for everyone to talk during a 90-minute session. Tedeschi says there should be "ample opportunity for emotional expression before having to close up intense emotions and return to the outside world" (1996, p. 299).

The group may have an open or closed admission policy. Tedeschi favors a closed group in which the number of sessions is determined at the outset, preferably to line up with the school term. He says it is essential for group members to promise to participate in a certain number of sessions, "perhaps something like four to six, because the initial meeting may feel more painful than supportive, and it will take some time to experience some relief and learn the difficult lessons of bereavement" (p. 300). Members who decide to leave the group should promise to let the group know in advance, to permit the exchange of goodbyes and avoid "leaving group members with questions and concerns about what might have happened" (p. 300).

Tedeschi lists a variety of activities that encourage expression of thoughts and feelings in support groups for adolescents, such as writing letters, drawing, crafting collages, writing stories and poems, and creating a group mural. Rather than imposing an activity on a group, allow "the composition, needs, and reactions of the participants" to determine what they will do (p. 301).

Tedeschi discusses a number of problems in adolescent groups, including nonproductive silences and superficial discussions. Some silences are productive, allowing members to reflect on what has transpired in the group. However, silence may indicate that the group is stuck. The facilitator can deal with these moments by suggesting a topic or exercise or by frankly commenting that the group seems stuck and asking what they think would help. Other problems that might occur are attendance problems, domination or criticism by a group member, bad advice from members to each other, or a psychological disorder in a group member. These problems suggest the need for a careful intake process and skilled facilitators

CONCLUDING COMMENTS

Interventions should be grounded in appreciation for the developmental transitions that mark childhood and adolescence and sensitivity to the interplay between these developmental realities and bereavement. Counselors who use theoretical and practical information to help bereaved children and adolescents do so with a conceptual scaffolding that enables them to place bereavement in the overall context of childhood and adolescent development, and allows them to plan interventions focused on reactions to loss that occur in the midst of childhood and adolescent development. ■

David E. Balk, professor of health and nutrition sciences, directs graduate studies in thanatology at Brooklyn College of the City University of New York. He graduated from the University of Illinois at Urbana-Champaign with a Ph.D. in Counseling Psychology. Balk is an associate editor of the journal Death Studies, *and serves as that journal's book review editor. He is a member of* Omega's *editorial board. His research has focused on adolescent bereavement; at first his work looked at adolescents' responses to sibling death, and now he is examining responses to bereavement while in college. For three years he chaired the Test Committee for the Association for Death Education and Counseling (ADEC) in its work to design and administer a national exam certifying foundational knowledge of thanatology. Currently as editor-in-chief he is helping produce ADEC's* Handbook of Thanatology, *the primary resource persons will use in preparing for the national exam.*

REFERENCES

Anderson, R. N., & Smith, B. L. (2005). Deaths: Leading causes for 2002. *National Vital Statistics Reports, 53*(17). Hyattsville, MD: National Center for Health Statistics.

Balk, D. E. (1981). *Sibling death during adolescence: Self-concept and bereavement reactions.* Unpublished doctoral dissertation, University of Illinois, Champaign-Urbana, IL.

Balk, D. E. (1983). Adolescents' grief reactions and self-concept perceptions following sibling death: A case study of 33 teenagers. *Journal of Youth and Adolescence, 12,* 137-161.

Balk, D. E. (1997). Death, bereavement, and college students: A descriptive analysis. *Mortality, 2,* 207-220.

Christ, G. H. (2000). *Healing children's grief: Surviving a parent's death from cancer.* New York: Oxford University Press.

Dent, A. (2005). Theoretical perspectives: Linking research and practice. In B. Monroe & F. Kraus (Eds.), *Brief interventions with bereaved children* (pp. 13-27). Oxford, UK: Oxford University Press.

Elkind, D. (1967). Egocentrism in adolescence. *Child Development, 38,* 1025-1034.

Ewalt, P. L., & Perkins, L. (1979). The real experience of death among adolescents: An empirical study. *Social Casework, 60,* 547-551.

Fleming. S. J., & Adolph, R. (1986). Helping bereaved adolescents: Needs and responses. In C. A. Corr & J. N. McNeil (Eds.), *Adolescence and death* (pp. 97-118). New York: Springer Publishing Company.

Fleming, S. J., & Belanger, S. K. (2001). Trauma, grief, and surviving childhood sexual abuse. In R. A. Neimeyer (Ed.), *Meaning reconstruction and the experience of loss* (pp. 311-329). Washington, DC: American Psychological Association.

Fowler, J. W. (1991). Stages of faith consciousness. In F. K. Oser & G. Scarlett (Eds.), *Religious development in childhood and adolescence* (pp. 27-45). San Francisco: Jossey-Bass.

Fulton. R. (2003). Anticipatory mourning: A critique of the concept. *Mortality, 8,* 342-351.

Gilliland, G., & Fleming, S. (1998). A comparison of spousal anticipatory grief and conventional grief. *Death Studies, 22,* 541-569.

Goldman, L. (2000). *Life and loss: A guide to help grieving children.* (2nd Ed.). Philadelphia: Accelerated Development.

Goldman, L. (2001). *Breaking the silence: A guide to help children with complicated grief—Suicide, homicide, AIDS, violence, and abuse.* New York: Brunner-Routledge.

Goldman, L. (2006). *Children also grieve: Talking about death and healing.* Philadelphia: Jessica Kingsley.

Haine, R. A., Wolchik, S. A., Sandler, I. W., Millsap, R. E., & Ayers, T. S. (2006). Positive parenting as a protective resource for parentally bereaved children. *Death Studies, 30,* 1-28.

Hall, M., & Irwin, M. (2001). Physiological indices of functioning in bereavement. In M. S. Stroebe, R. O. Hansson, W. Stroebe, & H. Schut (Eds.), *Handbook of bereavement research: Consequences, coping, and care* (pp. 473-492). Washington, DC: American Psychological Association.

Jacobs, S. C., Kasl, S. V., Ostfeld, A. M., Berkman, L., Kosten, T. R, & Charpentier, P. (1986). The measurement of grief: Bereaved versus non-bereaved. *Hospice Journal, 2,* 21-36.

Jordan, J. R., & Neimeyer, R. A. (2003). Does grief counseling work? *Death Studies, 27,* 765-786.

Josselson, R. (1987). *Finding herself: Pathways to identity development in women.* San Francisco: Jossey-Bass.

Josselson, R. (1996). *Revising herself: The story of women's identity from college to midlife.* New York: Oxford University Press.

Kauffman, J. (2003) *Loss and the Assumptive World.* Philadelphia: Routledge.

Kubler-Ross, E. (1969). *On death and dying.* New York: Macmillan.

LaGrand, L. E. (1985). College student loss and response. In E. S. Zinner (Ed.), *Coping with death on campus* (pp. 15-28). San Francisco: Jossey-Bass.

LaGrand, L. E. (1986). *Coping with separation and loss as a young adult: Theoretical and practical realities.* Springfield, IL: Charles C. Thomas.

Lindemann, E. (1944). Symptomatology and management of acute grief. *American Journal of Psychiatry, 101,* 141-148.

Neimeyer, R. A. (Ed.). (2001). *Meaning reconstruction and the experience of loss.* Washington, DC: American Psychological Association.

Noppe, L. D., & Noppe, I. C. (1996). Ambiguity in adolescent understandings of death. In C. A. Corr & D. E. Balk (Eds.), *Handbook of adolescent death and bereavement* (pp. 25-41). New York: Springer Publishing Company.

Offer, D. (1969). *The psychological world of the teenager.* New York: Basic Books.

Perry, W. G. (1970). *Forms of intellectual and ethical development during the college years.* New York: Holt, Rinehart & Winston.

Perry, W. G. (1999). *Forms of intellectual and ethical development during the college years: A scheme.* San Francisco: Jossey-Bass.

Price, J. H., Thompson, A. J., & Drake, J. A. (2004). Factors associated with state variations in homicide, suicide, and unintentional firearm deaths. *Journal of Community Health: The Publication for Health Promotion and Disease Prevention, 29,* 271-283.

Rando, T. A. (2000). The six dimensions of anticipatory mourning. In T. A. Rando (Ed.), *Clinical dimensions of anticipatory mourning: Theory and practice in working with the dying, their loved ones, and their caregivers* (pp. 51-101). Champaign, IL: Research Press.

Saldinger, A. L. (2001). *Anticipating parental death in families with school-aged children.* Unpublished doctoral dissertation, University of Michigan, Ann Arbor.

Saldinger, A., Cain, A., & Porterfield, K. (2003). Managing traumatic stress in children anticipating parental death. *Psychiatry, 66,* 168-181.

Sandler, I. W., Ayers, T. S., Wolchik, S. A. Tein, J-Y. Kwok, O-M. Haine, R. A., Twohey-Jacobs, J., Suter, J., Lin, K., Padgett-Jones, S., Weyer, J. L., Cole, E., Kriege, G., & Griffin, W. A. (2003). The Family Bereavement Program: Efficacy evaluation of a theory-based prevention program for parentally bereaved children and adolescents. *Journal of Consulting and Clinical Psychology, 71,* 587-600.

Silverman, P. R. (2000). *Never too young to know: Death in children's lives.* New York: Oxford University Press.

Speece, M. W., & Brent, S. B. (1996). The development of children's understanding of death. In C. A. Corr & D. M. Corr (Eds.), *Handbook of childhood death and bereavement* (pp. 29-50). New York: Springer Publishing Company.

Stroebe, M. S., & Schut, H. (1999). The dual process model of coping with bereavement: Rationale and description, *Death Studies, 23*, 197-224.

Stroebe, M. S., & Schut, H. (2005). To continue or relinquish bonds: A review of consequences for the bereaved. *Death Studies, 29*, 477-494.

Stroebe, M. S., Schut, H., & Stroebe, W. (2005). Attachment in coping with bereavement: A theoretical integration. *Review of General Psychology, 9*, 48-66.

Tedeschi, R. G. (1996). Support groups for bereaved adolescents. In C. A. Corr & D. E. Balk (Eds.), *Handbook of adolescent death and bereavement* (pp. 293-311). New York: Springer Publishing Company.

Tedeschi, R. G., & Calhoun, L. G. (1995). *Trauma and transformation: Growth in the aftermath of suffering.* Thousand Oaks, CA: Sage.

Tyson-Rawson, K. J. (1996). Adolescent responses to the death of a parent. In C. A. Corr & D. E. Balk (Eds.), *Handbook of adolescent death and bereavement* (pp. 155-172). New York: Springer Publishing Company.

U. S. Department of Health and Human Services. (1999). *Mental health. A report of the Surgeon General.* Rockville, MD: Author.

U. S. Department of Justice, Bureau of Justice Statistics. Homicide trends in the U.S. Retrieved June 29, 2006. www.ojp.usdoj.gov/bjs/homicide/overview.htm.

Worden, J. W. (1996). Children and grief: When a parent dies. New York: Guilford.

Worden, J. W. (1991). *Grief counseling and grief therapy.* (2nd Ed.). New York: Springer Publishing Company.

Worden, J. W. (2002). *Grief counseling and grief therapy.* (3rd Ed.). New York: Springer Publishing Company.

Reflections

Keith Whitehead

I grew up living with my mother and father, but I never really had a *dad*. When I think of a father and a dad, two entirely different things come to mind. To me, my father is the person who was there to help raise me. My dad, however, is the person that I came from. I never really knew my dad. He passed away on October 9, 1989, a day before my fourth birthday. You would think that this would be a tragic event in a young boy's life and I assure you, it is.

When I was younger though, I didn't realize how much of an effect such a loss could have. When I use the term loss I mean not just the loss of the person, but more importantly, the loss of potential experiences and memories that we could have shared. Playing a game of catch or just sitting around watching television are activities that every boy wants to do with his dad. Surely you can think back and remember those days—those activities.

I, however, cannot. Now that I have grown into a young adult, I am beginning to fully appreciate the effects of these lost memories. As I grow older, I find myself thinking of my dad more and more often. You might think that losing my dad at such a young

Continued

age would be easier than if I were to lose him when I was older and, thus, had a chance to know him better, but I would disagree. I think it might even be worse—I never got to experience the simple things like playing catch or watching a ball game that other kids got to experience. It is not that I cry for him now that I am older; it is that I appreciate that the bond between a son and father is unlike any other—and it is a bond that I have never known.

Every so often his death comes to mind and troubles me, but for the most part, the experience of my father's death guides me in a straighter path. You see, my dad was a drug addict. His addiction not only hurt himself, but also hurt the people around him including the people that loved him. I was among those people but so was, worst of all, my mother. Knowing what my dad and my mother went through has kept me away from such a lifestyle. I was once with a woman that I really cared about, perhaps even loved, who had a drug problem. Because of the lessons learned from the loss of my dad, I knew I had to get out of that relationship—I just couldn't stand to see it.

There is a poem by Richard Shelton titled "Letter to My Dead Father" that I read in my college years. The poet writes that he never felt that his father loved him and that because of not receiving the love of his father, he himself cannot show love. I can understand the poem because I also never received love from my dad. He was never around and eventually my mother left him because of his addiction. Then he died. But unlike Shelton, I don't feel that I have a problem loving or showing love. In fact, I feel that in a way, I almost seek love more than I otherwise would. I know the importance of love and affection. I know that some day, when I have a child of my own, that I'll be there for him or her. Maybe I feel so strongly about this because of my dad's absence. I'm not mad at him though. I know that if he got the chance to do it all over, things would be different. At least I like to think so.

Sometimes thoughts of my dad's death creep into my mind almost subconsciously. As a songwriter, I regularly find myself writing about my dad in my lyrics. When you're writing lyrics, the thoughts come to your head unplanned. I seem to find myself, without even meaning to, writing about my dad a lot:

> My mom once asked, "Why all your songs so sad?"
> See I grew up with a father, but with no dad
> Never got to experience what most have
> So can't be all happy, but also not all so sad.

Despite all, I wasn't all alone. I did have a father figure but it's not the same. We spent time together; it was just different. The bond is different. It's not that he didn't love me or that I didn't love him, because we do love each other. I have a six-year-old half-brother and even the bond that he and our father share is different than *my* bond with our father. Even as it doesn't bother me, I do still notice, and that has to mean *something*.

I also had other people in my life that were there to watch and guide me growing up—people that cared for and loved me. People like my godfather, who was my dad's friend. He has had a very powerful and positive impact on my life. My grandmother always gave me her love. My mother basically raised me by herself, although she received financial and emotional help from others. It wasn't easy, but she did it. And she did a great job. Somehow, in the end, it all comes together. If my life were any different, I might not be the same person I am today.

Keith Whitehead is from Warwick, NY. He is currently in his junior year at Marymount College where he studies graphic design. Keith enjoys songwriting, DJ-ing, and snowboarding.

CHAPTER 13

Inner Reality and Social Reality: Bonds with Dead Children and the Resolution of Grief

Dennis Klass

Over the past several decades, we have tended to think of grief as an individual's response to significant loss, so we have conceived it as an inner process. We have laid out the stages through which people pass on their way to acceptance or resolution and have listed the tasks people must accomplish if they are to successfully work through their grief.

The definition of grief as an individual inner process, however, does not hold up to a critical examination of how people actually come to terms with significant deaths. Grief is an *inter* personal process, not an *inner* one. Walter (1994) says that traditional communities supplied rituals through which mourning was accomplished. The rituals prescribed the inner experience of the mourner. Prescribe literally means *pre-write*; thus, the community rituals supplied the narrative that was the inner experience of the mourner. With the rise of individualism, however, the old rituals lost much of their power to order mourners' inner worlds.

But the movement away from traditional rituals did not mean that the community lost its power to shape the survivor's narrative after a significant death. Walter (1996) says that in the contemporary world, grief is resolved through conversation with others who knew the deceased. The resolution of grief is not an inner process; it is an interactive process.

In this chapter, I use 20 years of ethnographic study of a local chapter of a group of parents whose children had died to show how the conversation among bereaved parents moves them toward the resolution of their grief. Illustrations in the chapter are from notes that I have taken after a meeting, transcripts of interviews, as well as poems and thoughts from newsletters or that parents gave to me. In some accounts I have changed key details to hide the person's identity. In a few places I use the person's name because they asked me to. Readers will find fuller accounts of my relationship with the self-help group, the kinds of sources I used, and the research methodology in two books in which I have reported the finding of the research (Klass, 1988,1999).

Grief can be defined as the process by which people move from equilibrium in their inner and social worlds before a death to a new equilibrium following bereavement. Equilibrium is difficult to measure but easy to sense subjectively. The parents in the study say that typically it takes three to four years before the new equilibrium seems steady enough to trust. A recurring pattern in the self-help process is that by socially sharing their continuing bond with their child, parents are able to transform the bond into the modified one they will retain into the future (Klass, Silverman, & Nickman, 1996). The more parents in this study feel integrated into the social system and can find social support in their grief, the less difficulty they have resolving their grief and the more their continuing bond with their child is integrated into their social world.

The beginning, middle, and end of the story all have to do with the answer to the question "Who is this child to you?" We will see that the question is answered by both the parent whose child has died and the communities of which the parent is a member. We will trace the transformation of the parent's bond with the deceased child. The prologue of the story is the bond with the living child. The end of the story is how the bond with the child continues in the life of the parent and the community. The middle—the part we will discuss—is how the bond is transformed. We will follow the course of the bond with the dead child in the parents' inner and outer lives as they progress through the group Bereaved Parents.

The Grief Journey

It is generally accepted that the stages of grief cannot be easily defined. Over the years, however, some language has evolved in Bereaved Parents groups through which participants locate themselves and others in their journey. They define members of the group as "newly bereaved," "into their grief," "well along in their grief," and "resolved as much as it will be." It is not a formal system, and other phrases can be used. The system was developed by the subjects of this chapter to explain their own experience, so we can use it to organize the chapter, although it may not describe grief in other settings or circumstances. In each of these phases, we will describe the bond with the child in the parent's inner world and social world.

Newly Bereaved

The Parents' Inner World

For parents, a child's death is an awful truth that seems unreal. Kauffman (1994) notes that the initial response to traumatic death is not denial but dissociation, and that the mourning process is best conceived as an interplay between integration and dissociation. The newly bereaved do not deny that their child is dead. Indeed, it is the overwhelming reality of their lives. A parent writes,

> We awaken to the sun shining in our windows—a beautiful day. But wait, was I dreaming, or is something wrong? Why do I hesitate to become fully awake? No, it isn't a bad dream, it's reality. The room is empty.
>
> He wasn't there when we went to bed. He isn't in his bed this morning. It can't be.... Our hearts are left with an empty room that will never be filled again....
>
> His presence fills the room, although we know he is gone.... Today is a bad day. The door is closed. Someone is pretending it never happened. Will it be open again tomorrow? It's hard to say, as we are just trying to make it through today. So we turn our heads when we go by. The urge to beat on the door and cry out "Please come back!" is almost too much to bear.

As the reality sinks in, parents often have intimations of the future bond they will have with the child. In a poem, a mother describes a recurring dream in which it seems that the child is still there. But when she reaches out to touch him, he disappears. The mother's interpretation of the dream is that the child is sending a message that he has not yet gone and is still with her. We can see that the child and the parent are not separated, because the poem shifts from the parent's dream to the child's dream, and the mother feels herself in the child's dream just as the child is in hers. The child's presence is projected into the future.

> For in your dreams each night,
> God lets my love shine through.
> God sends you all the pictures,
> for in your mind to view,
> of all the precious times we had,
> and all the love we knew.

■

During early grief, parents often establish a connection with the dead child through a linking object (Volkan, 1981); this connection will transmute over time and may be long lasting. Three years after her 21-year-old daughter died, a mother wrote,

> Raggedy Ann and Andy still sit there, perched on top of a
> bookshelf in what used to be E's room....Years ago I tried to
> throw them away, and my then-teenaged daughter indignantly
> rescued them from the trash. "Not Ann and Andy!" she cried,
> settling them in her room.... E is gone now...her beautiful,
> promising young life snuffed out by a drunk driver.... Our lives
> have been changed, and so has E's room. We use it primarily
> as a computer/word processor room now, but many of the
> reminders are still there, including Raggedy Ann and Andy.

The Parents' Social World

The disequilibrium and dissociation parents feel in their inner life also exists in their social world. Newly bereaved parents care that other people share the loss. Parents in the groups reported whether people came to the funeral, whether a memorial was planned at the school, and whether other people were deeply affected by their child's death. But for a significant number of parents, the pain they feel is not reflected in their community, and it seems that neither the child nor the child's death has social reality. Many people refrain from mentioning the child's name in their presence; inquiries about how they are doing imply that their grief is not so terrible, that the child can be replaced by a new baby, or that God loves the child in heaven better than the parent could have loved the child here. When a child dies, it seems to parents that their lives have stopped while other people's lives go on. The sense of isolation can be bitter.

> Thick layers of gauze,
> Its contents, my heart.
> A clinical perspective for friends,
> Enough so the blood does not drip.
> Only at the solitary presence of his tiny grave,
> Do I sit and unwind all the layers
> and view the deep gash.
> It will never heal...I will only wrap it differently with time.

One of the reasons for the existence of Bereaved Parents is that the mainline culture or the parents' community affiliations may not adequately address their experience, which is that the child is dead but the parent is still bonded to the child. A constant theme in self-help groups' newsletter articles is an appeal to friends and family to understand and accept the parents' feelings and behavior.

> Please don't tell us to turn off our memories, to snap out of it, that he/she is dead and life has to go on. Our love for them doesn't end with death....Yes, we fully realize that he/she is dead, gone forever, and that's what hurts.
>
> Please have patience with us. Try to understand why we are acting or feeling the way we are today. In a small word or gesture, let us know it's all right with you for us to love, to cry, to remember. We aren't doing it to make you uncomfortable or to gain sympathy. We are just trying to cope.

INTO THEIR GRIEF

The Inner World

The complexity of the parents' bond with the dead child is expressed in the complexity of their grief. A parent's daily psychic and social worlds may involve the child in various ways. There are differences, for example, in how a child's death affects the parent's work life. For some parents, work is an island in a stormy sea—tasks and relationships on the job seem "normal." Other parents find work difficult and their performance diminished. The difference seems to be the extent to which their selfhood at work has involved the child. If work is relatively easy, the transition from work to home may be marked by a surge of emotion. A midlevel executive said she functioned well at the office, though she was occasionally teary. However, during the drive home, she became overwhelmed by the thought that her son was gone forever. A salesman said he had to control his grief, because he was expected to be his old self with clients. He was fired from one job when his grief impaired his production, and he had a hard time finding another. His wife kept her job but was moved to a position where little was expected of her. The marriage was strained because his wife interpreted his controlling his grief as evidence that he hadn't really loved the child.

Before the new bond can be established, many parents must spend time separating conflicting images of the child. For example, when a troubled teenager dies of a drug overdose or gang violence, the parent has the images and feelings from those years, but also the images and feelings of a happy preteen child. This is especially difficult for parents whose functioning remains highly dependent on the availability of the child (Horowitz, Wilner, Marmor, & Krupnick, 1980; Rynearson, 1987). In a few cases in our study, the child was directly integrated into the self-system rather early in the grief process. For example, a newly recovering alcoholic's 15-year-old daughter K. was shot as a bystander in a holdup, and he was having trouble maintaining his sobriety. Even as a child, K. had been the one person in the family who "could tell me off when I was being stupid. She would just say, 'Dad, cut the crap.'" About six months after her death, he was standing at the grave when he heard a voice say, "Dad, why are you acting this way? This is what you were like when you were drinking." K. became his constant inner companion, helping him control his rage and maintain his hard-won sobriety. After several years as an active member of Bereaved Parents, he could separate himself from direct dependence on K. She became part of his "good self," which expressed itself by helping other bereaved parents.

As parents begin to let go of the images of the living child, some find that the first point of connection between them and their dead child is the pain of their grief and the pain the child knew. In an interview, a woman told of her two-year-old daughter who died after several months in the hospital. The child had had blood drawn many times and feared the procedure, for it always hurt her. A few months after the death, the mother donated blood at a clinic.

> As I went in, I found myself saying over and over, maybe even out loud, "Look at Mommy, she can have them take blood, and she will be a big girl so it will not hurt. See, J., Mommy is going to be a big girl." When they stuck me, it really hurt. I've given blood a lot and it never hurt like that. When I told my mother about it, she said, "This may seem strange, but I think that was J. who was hurt." I think she's right. I cried all the way back to work, knowing what she had suffered.

> ■

The child's pain can be felt in many ways. A woman whose daughter had an incurable degenerative disease said, "I never let myself experience her pain," because the medical staff had urged the mother to be the voice of hope and determination. When her daughter cried and wanted to give up, it was the mother who insisted she get up and try again. "Well," the mother said in an interview, "I know the pain now." Several parents whose children had committed suicide repeated the phrase "Suicide is a way to pass the pain."

As parents begin to establish the enduring bond, they often have a sense of a double connection: They are bonded to the child as he or she was when alive and bonded to the child who is immortal. They still feel the amputation, but they also feel the new bond. The disassociation they felt early in their grief is transformed in a way that allows them to let go of the earthly child and keep the heavenly. One mother attended the funeral of F. (a friend of her dead son J.). The friend's mother said she had had a vision of J. in heaven welcoming F. J.'s mother said, "I know he's in heaven, but I still miss him. I just want to hold him."

As parents come to terms with memories of their child, they often must deal with ambivalence. Bonds with the child that are of the less-than-good self or that are extensions of attachments to negative figures in the parent's history produce more difficult griefs, for example, if it feels to the parent like the child is repeating the substance abuse from which the parent has recovered after much effort, or if the parent sees the child acting in ways that are like the parent's own father against whom the parent had rebelled. Sometimes it is simply a matter of purging the negative memories and holding the child in an idealized light. Some parents need to face their guilt over what they now see as less-than-adequate parenting. It is not unusual for ambivalence and guilt to lead to severe marital conflict. For example, the son of a strict Pentecostal couple died from a drug overdose. His mother attributed his use of drugs to the father's strict discipline and distant emotional relationship with the boy. She blamed herself only for acquiescing to her husband's child-rearing ideas. The difficulty was resolved after the mother, as part of her anger at her husband, acted out a part of her own "bad" self in a brief affair. In coming to terms with the resultant guilt, she was able to admit and deal with her negative memories of her son.

The Social World

As parents separate the living child from their selves and come to terms with ambivalent bonds with the child, they are aided by integrating the child into their social world. Most Bereaved Parents activities are rooted in shared bonds with each other's children. Membership in the community means membership as a bereaved parent, a person whose life is not as it was before and who must be related to differently than before. The dead child is also a member of the community, and is valued, remembered, celebrated, and loved.

Sharing their bond with the child begins with sharing the pain of their child's death. Sharing pain is summed up by a phrase that recurs in members' accounts of what they need from others: "Just be there." "Being there" means being with the parent in such a way that the reality of the death and the pain are not the parent's alone. The phrase is used somewhat differently when members describe how the group is helpful to them. They say the people who can really understand are other bereaved parents, for they have "been there."

Sharing the pain also means sharing ways to relieve some aspects of the pain, especially in the social world. Often meetings are devoted to practical issues; for example, how to include the child in the holidays. These issues can be approached in various ways; each approach is really a stance, a way of being-in-the-world. One mother made a holiday wreath for the front door with many colored ribbons, including a black one. "It's there," she said. "If they want to see it and mention it, they can. It is not me that didn't bring it up."

Finding the answers to practical problems helps parents develop new stances in their family and community. It is common for parents to report that they have to teach family and friends how to relate to them. Often what they teach is what they have learned at Bereaved Parents. A member wrote a poem addressed to those who would help her:

Please listen to me,
Hear what I'm saying.
Not just the words that come from my mouth…
Listen with more than your ears....
If you rush me with good advice
and tell me not to worry, I'll clam up.
I'll think you don't understand....
So please,
Accept my problem and take a share....
Be here with me
And cry with me
And then I'll know you've truly listened
And heard, and understood.
Then—I'll be comforted.

■

Bereaved Parents has developed activities and rituals through which members can connect with each other's pain and, thus, with each other's children. In a Saturday cemetery tour, members visit the graves of each other's children. They go by van so everyone can be together. At each grave, the parent of that child has prepared something to introduce the child, such as pictures, favorite things, songs, and so on. Virtually every member of the group has experienced the lonely sorrow of standing at their child's grave. In the cemetery tour, "My child is dead and buried" can transmute into "Our children are dead and buried."

When the pain and the child's death are integrated into the social network, the experiences through which parents maintain contact with their children can be socially validated. Seeing, hearing, and sensing the presence of dead children is not often part of modern social reality, but many bereaved parents have such experiences daily. Early on, the group did not have a language to talk about this phenomenon, and attempts to share were often very tentative. However, as the group matured, these experiences were routinely reported and integrated into the fund of knowledge about grief. The group maintains the Bereaved Parents principle of not holding to any doctrinal position; it validates these experiences by saying that they are real but are different for different people, and what is learned in the experience is for the parent, not for everyone. Nearly every year in most chapters, one meeting is devoted to these experiences, and several members have become well-read on the topic. At national and regional meetings, sessions on "strange events and experiences" are well attended.

WELL ALONG IN THEIR GRIEF

The Inner World

Bereaved Parents members begin to find a new equilibrium in their lives in terms of their bond with their child. The movement toward the new equilibrium is often cast in terms of letting go and holding on. The idea of letting go of the pain in exchange for a clearer, comforting bond with the child is one of the central insights in Bereaved Parents. Rather than identifying with the child's pain, the parent identifies with the energy and love that were in the living child. In a speech at a holiday candlelight service five years after her son's death, a mother reflected on her progress:

I was afraid to let go. Afraid that I would forget the details of him, the peculiar color of his eyes, the shape of his nose, the sound of his voice.... In a strange way, my pain was comforting, a way of loving him, familiar.... Finally, I had to admit that his life meant more than pain; it also meant joy and happiness and fun—and living. The little voice in my heart was telling me that it was time for me to let go of him.... When we release pain, we make room for happiness in our lives. My memories of S. became lighter and more spontaneous. Instead of hurtful, my memories brought comfort, even a chuckle.... I had sudden insights into what was happening to me, the pieces began to fit again, and I realized S. was still teaching me things.

■

One of the clichés of bereavement work is that grief is the price we pay for love. In a newsletter article, a father wrote, "If the price I pay for loving D. is the pain and sorrow I now have, I still think I got a bargain to have had him for 13 years."

■

The developing bond with the dead child is often quite explicitly linked to the parents' thoughts about their own healing. In the newsletter, a father reported that when he began running, his 17-year-old daughter had encouraged him to keep it up by registering both of them to run a five-kilometer race. She was killed in an accident 2 weeks before the race. He ran wearing her number. After that, she became part of his running.

Every time I ran, I took a few minutes to think about D. and how I was dealing with her death. I was alone with no distractions but the pounding of my feet, and I could focus on her and my feelings. I tried to coach myself a bit, inch myself toward the light. That done, I often moved on to report silently to her about what I'd been doing lately, about what I thought of the weather, how my conditioning was going, what her younger brothers were up to. Frequently, I sensed she was nearby, cruising at my elbow, listening.

The Social World

Socially sharing the bond stabilizes it in the parent's life. One mother whose living children have moved away reflected in the newsletter on how she stays connected to all her absent children, including the one who is dead. She finds she does it in similar ways. However, while she can hold her living children on her own, she needs Bereaved Parents to help hold the bond with the dead child. In the group, she says,

> Mention of your child's name won't cause an awkward gap.
> You know, the kind that makes you feel somehow you shouldn't
> have said anything. How can anyone else know that your child
> is still real? That they were real and are real? I want to scream
> sometimes that my boy is real! See, he's here in my heart ....
> The little one is not so clear in my mind anymore, but he's real.
> How many children do I have? Three. My daughter is married
> and living in New York. And the boys? Well, one will always be
> four and a half. I heard him laughing the other day in the giggles
> of some preschoolers.

■

The bond with the child is an integral part of the parent's membership in Bereaved Parents. As the coordinator of the annual picnic wrote in the newsletter,

> Our children lost are the heart and soul of our picnic. It is for
> and because of them that we come, and it is for them that we
> have our cherished balloon release—a time set aside in our day
> to remember and include our special children. Helium-filled
> balloons are passed out, along with markers, giving us all one
> more chance to tell our children the things we most long to
> say—mostly, "I love you." We stand as one, but each involved
> in his own thoughts, prayer, and emotions as we release
> hundreds of balloons to the sky and they disappear to a
> destiny we are certain they will reach.

■

The children are the heart and soul of the group because it is the shared bond with their dead children that binds the members to each other. The children are in the midst of the group, not simply in the hearts and minds of the individual parents. Because the bond with the child is shared in the group, the parents can be in touch privately with their children but can also tap into the strength of the group. One balloon sent into the sky would seem lonely and fragile. Hundreds of balloons, each addressed to a different child, are sure to get through.

Ritual is also part of the meetings. At the beginning of the meeting, the parents introduce themselves, giving their name and then their child's name and something about the child's death. Parents often add a sentence or two about how good or bad the month has been. They may note that a significant date, such as a birthday or death anniversary, is coming up. At the end of the introductions, the cumulative effect of all those names and all that pain is a deep quiet, often punctuated by the soft sobs of a newly bereaved person. Most chapters have one meeting each year in which members pass around pictures of their children and tell stories about them. At national and regional meetings, there are long lines of picture boards. Parents from around the country often begin talking as they stand looking at the pictures of the children. Cards and phone calls come on the children's birthdays and on their death anniversaries.

For those who become core members and then leaders in the group, this work connects them with their child in a way that actualizes both their child's and their own better self. In a meeting to develop leadership skills, a woman said that in Bereaved Parents she is "continuing who M. was." She described M. as a person who was always helping others. She has many memories of M. on the phone talking to friends who needed someone to listen. Now, especially as she talks on the phone with a newly bereaved person, this mother feels close to her daughter. The facilitator of a newly formed meeting talked about her son as a helper. He had been in a peer-counseling group and had spoken on behalf of DARE, a drug prevention program. Helping others was part of who her child was; therefore, helping others makes the child real in her life. She said she felt challenged getting the new meeting going—organizing, doing the publicity, and running the meeting. But she sometimes felt her son looking over her shoulder saying, "Go for it, Mom. You can do it." A third meeting facilitator talked about her son as the one who brought the vitality into the family. Now, when she feels blue, she thinks of him saying, "Come on, let's get going." She said,

> You know, sometimes I just sit downstairs at the computer. I call it my "nothing time," because I just play the same game over and over. I hear him, almost pulling at my chair, saying, "Come on, Mom, get going! Get out of here and do something!" I want to just sit there and do nothing, but I feel as though he's pushing me to get involved in this group, to do something, to get out of my lethargy.

■

As they learn to share their child in Bereaved Parents, members find ways to include the child in their other communities. One woman reported that six years after her daughter's death, she decided she wanted the child included in the family Christmas gift exchange.

> Last year I shocked my sister, who usually organizes the name exchange. I called her and said, "I want J.'s name in the exchange, too." Well, there was silence on the phone. So I explained that whoever gets J.'s name can make a donation to a charity in her name. Her name was included and, for the first time since she died, I felt she was part of things.

RESOLVED AS MUCH AS IT WILL BE

The Inner World

Members of Bereaved Parents are adamant in their conclusion that "you don't get over your grief." They often add, "but it doesn't stay the same." The message to newly bereaved parents is "It will always hurt, but it will not hurt the way it does now." What, then, can resolution mean?

At an "alumni gathering," the group went around the room doing the ritual of introduction. There was a lot of humor. The fourth person, who had been a group facilitator a few years earlier, paused for a moment after she introduced her child and said, "Gosh, it feels so good to say that and not cry. Look: We're doing this and we're laughing." Several people said they were moving on with their lives, noting that they were "not even on the mailing list any more." Occasionally they still cry. Their sadness is part of them; they can recognize it and not be afraid of it. In a newsletter, a mother wrote about "older grief."

Older grief is gentler.
It's about sudden tears swept in by a strand of music.
It's about haunting echoes of first pain, at anniversaries.
It's about feeling his presence for an instant one day
while I'm dusting his room.
It's about early pictures that invite me to fold him in
my arms again.
It's about memories blown in on wisps of wood smoke
and sea scents.
Older grief is about aching in gentler ways, rarer longing,
less engulfing fire.
Older grief is about searing pain wrought into tenderness.

The bonds between parents and children are complex, so transforming the bond can be a long and exhausting task. Eventually, the parents in the study were able to establish the bond with their dead child as part of their ongoing life. One of the paradoxical feelings often mentioned in meetings is that the end of intense grief is itself a kind of loss. Moving on with life has an ambivalence for bereaved parents, but the ambivalence is somewhat mitigated by the enduring continuing bond with the child. Betty Johnson wrote a poem for the newsletter:

Time roars on, but I rear back,
Resisting, afraid to move on and leave you behind.
I was safe with you, unafraid in my own realm.
If I heal, will you be gone forever?
Your leaving opened new worlds.
I have time now and my days and energies no longer
revolve around your needs.
I want you to come with me into the future.
Your youth protected my youth, but now new beginnings
eclipse the past.

My eyes strain as they search my heart for distant memories.
But your face fades as I reach out to you.
All that remains are warm feelings, smiles, tears and
Glimpses of your love, left in the wake of your parting.
Will you forgive me if I go on?
If you can't make this earthly journey through time with me,
Will you then come along in my heart and wish me well?

■

Parents in the group often tie the resolution of their grief to their bond with their child. The parents' newfound interest in life is often described in terms of the child's presence. As the child comes along in their heart to wish them well, many report that the peace they have found in their resolution is what their child would have wished for them.

It was an unmistakable thrill
That moment I first noticed
I think more about his life now
Than about his death!
It's just what he would have wanted!

The Social World

Part of the resolution of grief in Bereaved Parents is making the pain count for something, or, to put it another way, making the parent's life, especially the experience of the child's death, count for something. In making their own life meaningful, they make their child real. One of the ways parents can make their lives count is to help others. The organizational life of Bereaved Parents depends on some people staying and leading the group as a way to expressing the change in their lives that their child and their grief have made. A man who led the committee planning the candlelight ceremony wrote, "I wanted most to do it for J. All that I do now I do to honor his memory and his life." He continued,

We do need to find a positive outlet for all the anger and pain.
Find a charity, or a cause that has personal meaning; get involved
with Bereaved Parents; plant a garden; get into shape; do something that illustrates the positive effect that your child had on
you—even if you are the only one to see it.

■

Early in their membership in Bereaved Parents, parents can bond with their child in their affiliation with the group. Over time that bond changes—as the bond with the child becomes more solid, the bond with the group becomes less focused. In a meeting of a committee rethinking the organizational structure, discussion centered around the idea that the group works best when there is a steady turnover of meeting facilitators. Two former facilitators said they knew when the time had come for them to move on from that job. A woman whose daughter had been dead two and a half years and who had just taken on the task of facilitating a meeting said, "I don't understand. The time I give to Bereaved Parents is my A time." She thought of the energy and care she gives the group as care and energy she would be giving to the child. She worried, "So, what does it mean to move on? Do I lose my child? Does that mean I won't have that any more?" A veteran who no longer attends meetings replied,

No, you don't lose that. It has been 13 years for me. I was like you when I was facilitating the meeting. That was my connection with B. It was real direct; when I was doing Bereaved Parents work, it was for B. I can't say exactly when it changed or how, but now he is there all the time. He's just there; he's part of me. It isn't my connection with Bereaved Parents that connects him to me. But Bereaved Parents gave me something important when I needed it and I want to give something back. Sometimes it's good for me to be very involved and other times it seems like I should pull back more. Right now I feel like getting more involved again. But that's because it feels right to be part of something good. B. is part of that, but B. is part of many things in my life.

The dynamic creates some moments of irony. A man was honored for extraordinary service to the organization and received a long standing ovation. He said, "I just had a funny thought: If T. were here, he'd be proud. But if he were here, this wouldn't be happening."

■

However, irony is not often expressed, because the interactions in the life of the group have an authentic feel. The tasks are important and difficult. Members take long calls from the newly bereaved; spend two days a month with a small group, folding and labeling newsletters for mailing; or make calls all over the city to solicit donations for the picnic/balloon release. Meeting facilitators prepare for several days for a meeting, then spend hours debriefing each other as they try to keep abreast of members' progress and the complex interactions in the meetings. A woman who chaired the holiday candlelight service said it had been as much work as the wedding she planned for her living daughter.

The organization has proved itself to these parents. Affiliation with other bereaved parents allowed them to find resolution in their grief. In giving back to others, their experience is part of their better selves. Dead children are often melded into the parents' better selves in a way that makes the children seem like teachers of life's important lessons. The father of a child born with multiple congenital heart defects who lived "2,681 days" ties his present activity in Bereaved Parents to those lessons:

> He not only taught me the importance of what really matters
> in life but, through his death, also how we can make even more
> use of his life. Because of J., we make ourselves available to other
> bereaved parents who are at some point on death's desolation
> road.... So whenever people ask if I'm done grieving for my
> precious son, I answer with much conviction: "Most assuredly so.
> But I will never be done showing my appreciation for having
> been blessed with such a gift."

■

Early in their grief, parents searched for a community in which they could keep their bond with the child. They were angry when their child was not included in their interactions with friends and family. Sharing the bond with their child with others was an important part of transforming that bond. For those who stay with Bereaved Parents as leaders, the bond with the child is part of their work in the group. As their grief resolves, parents find that the bond is a natural part of many of their social affiliations. At one meeting a father whose son had been dead more than 10 years said that, early in his grief, people seemed afraid to talk to him about his son. But as he is more resolved, the boy becomes part of many spontaneous conversations. At work he keeps a piece of metal from his son's welding class on his desk as a paperweight.

> For a couple years there, you could just see people trying not to look at it, let alone mention it. Now someone will see it and ask, and when I tell them what it is and why I keep it there and what it means to me, they just accept it and seem comfortable with how I feel about my son.

Then the conversation moves on to business. Thus, the child is integrated into the parent's social world in similar ways that a living child would be.

Phenomena that indicate active interaction with the dead child— for example, a sense of presence, hallucinations (though the parents might argue that "hallucination" is an inappropriate word here), belief in the child's continuing active influence on thoughts or events, or a conscious incorporation of the characteristics or virtues of the child into the self— are no longer occasions for the parents to be concerned about their own sanity. The phenomena are accepted as a positive aspect of everyday life. On the 20th anniversary of her son's death, Margaret Gerner, founder of St. Louis Bereaved Parents, reflected in the newsletter on his place in her life and sent him a message of love and care:

> Arthur is still a big part of my life, even today. As a family...
> we don't hesitate to mention him, even to strangers, if he fits
> into the conversation....We tease about him. Pictures get crooked
> on the wall and we say "Arthur's been at it again."...We ask his
> help. Something big is in the wind for one of us and we tell
> Arthur to "get working on it."...
>
> Arthur's death has had a tremendous impact on my life.
> His death has been an impetus for positive change and growth
> for me.... I had Arthur for only a few short years, but he has
> given a special love to my life. He can't receive my love, but
> I can send it to him by giving it to others.

Arthur, years ago, in my heart, I let you go—to run and play in
Heaven and not to have to worry about how I'm doing. Now, on
the 20th anniversary of your death, again my heart is stopping
by Heaven's playground just to say hi and tell you
how much I love and miss you.

CONCLUSION

Grief is the process by which persons move from equilibrium in their inner
and social worlds before a death to a new equilibrium. For bereaved parents
in a self-help group, moving to the new equilibrium is largely a process of
transforming the bond they had with the living child to the continuing
bond they will maintain with the dead child in their ongoing life. The
transformation of this bond is not just an inner process. That is, grief is not
an individual psychological phenomenon. Rather, grief is resolved though
interactions in a community. In this chapter, we have traced the interaction
between the bereaved parents' inner reality and the social reality of the self-
help community. We have seen that as the reality of the child's death and
the reality of the parents' continuing bond with the child are made part of
socially shared reality, the parents can transform the bond with the dead
child in their inner worlds.

The lesson from the self-help group for those of us whose children
have not died is simple. We can help by becoming part of the bereaved
parents' community. We can be there. That means opening ourselves to the
reality of the child's death so that we experience the pain not as the parent
feels the pain, but as we might feel the pain of a friend's hard time. In our
own way, we can share the reality of the parents' bond with their dead child.
We can ask how the child lives on for them and make room for that reality
in our lives.

The message of this chapter to bereaved parents is the same message
every caring person should be giving them: Your child has died. The world
will never be the same. Your child's death has made the world a poorer
place for all of us. As your child lives on for you, we hope we can learn to
let the child live on for all of us. If we say stupid or insensitive things
because we are afraid of your pain, please forgive us. Help us make your
child's death and your continuing bond with your child a part of our

relationship with you as your friend, your neighbor, your coworker, your family member, or even as your psychotherapist. If you will help us do that, we can deepen ourselves as people while we walk with you toward the resolution of your grief.

> *Any man's death diminishes me,*
> *because I am involved in mankind; and, therefore,*
> *never send to know for whom the bell tolls; it tolls for thee.*
> (John Donne, Meditation XVII)

■

Dennis Klass earned his doctorate in the psychology of religion at the University of Chicago. He received the Kemper Award for Outstanding Teaching at Webster University and the Missouri State Governors Award for Excellence in Teaching. He has been active in the study of death, dying, and bereavement since 1968 when he was an assistant in the famous Death and Dying Seminar led by Elisabeth Kubler Ross at the University of Chicago Hospitals. A licensed psychologist in Missouri, Klass had a clinical practice with difficult and complex bereavements. He is on the editorial boards of Death Studies *and* Omega, Journal of Death and Dying, *a member of the International Work Group in Death, Dying, and Bereavement, and on the board of the Association for Death Education and Counseling.*

Klass is the author of Parental Grief: Resolution and Solace *(Springer, 1988) and* The Spiritual Lives of Bereaved Parents *(Brunner/Mazel, 1999). He is the coeditor, with Phyllis Silverman and Steven Nickman, of* Continuing Bonds: New Understandings of Grief *(Taylor Francis, 1996) and the coauthor of* Dead but not Lost: Grief Narratives in Religious Traditions *(AltaMira, 2005). Klass has written over 50 articles or book chapters on death and grief and on the psychology of religion.*

Klass retired to Truro, on Cape Cod, after a long career as a university professor. In his retirement Klass gardens, golfs, kayaks, watches the trees grow, and occasionally gathers oysters.

REFERENCES

Horowitz, M., Wilner, N., Marmor, C., & Krupnick, J. (1980). Pathological grief and the activation of latent self-images. *American Journal of Psychiatry, 137*(10), 1157-1162.

Kauffman, J. (1994). Dissociative functions in the normal mourning process. *Omega, Journal of Death and Dying, 28*(1), 31-38.

Klass, D., Silverman, P. R., & Nickman, S. (Eds.). (1996). *Continuing bonds: New understandings of grief.* Washington, DC: Taylor & Francis.

Klass, D. (1988). *Parental grief: Resolution and solace.* New York: Springer.

Klass, D. (1999). *The spiritual lives of bereaved parents.* Philadelphia: Brunner/Mazel.

Rynearson, E. K. (1987). Psychotherapy of pathologic grief: Revisions and limitations. *Psychiatric Clinics of North America, 10*(3), 487-499.

Volkan, V. (1981). *Linking objects and linking phenomena: A study of the forms, symptoms, metapsychology, and therapy of complicated mourning.* New York: International Universities Press.

Walter, T. (1994). *The revival of death.* London: Routledge.

Walter, T. (1996). A new model of grief: Bereavement and biography. *Mortality, 1*(1), 7-25.

CHAPTER 14

Death of a Parent of an Adult Child

Miriam S. Moss and Sidney Z. Moss

In this chapter, we explore the impact of the death of an elderly parent on the surviving adult child. The death of a parent can be an important loss at any age. When the parent of a young or adolescent child dies, society tends to see that parent as too young to die, and the death is viewed as stressful and untimely for the child (Silverman & Worden, 1993). When an old parent dies (we are defining "old" as over age 65), the social view of the death generally is quite different. Adults tend to accept the fact that their parents will die. The deaths of old persons are perceived as normal and expected. The adult child is generally not dependent on the parent to meet his or her daily needs or to be a central source of support in adapting to the world. Most often, the child is no longer living with the parent; for many, their daily lives are separated by hundreds of miles. Adult children tend to have developed strong ties and commitments to a spouse or partner and to their own children.

In this chapter, we describe major demographic changes over the past century, then examine the significance of a parent's death and some reasons why the topic has not been extensively studied. Because we view the death of an old parent as a process, not an event, we review some of the themes that have emerged regarding anticipation of the death of a parent. We discuss the impact of the parent's death on the adult child's sense of self, differences in the bereavement processes of sons and of daughters, reactions to parent death in several contexts, and the impact of the death on the family system. Finally, we try to reconcile seemingly contradictory themes that have emerged from our research and that of others.

BACKGROUND

The past century has seen a dramatic increase in longevity. In the United States in 2003, three out of every four deaths (74%) were of persons 65 years or older (Hoyert, Heron, Murphy, & Kung, 2003). The death of a parent is the most common form of bereavement for adults in western societies. Uhlenberg's (1996) analyses of life tables over the past century showed that parent deaths are occurring at a later point in the life course. In 1900, only 22% of persons age 40 had two living parents; by the end of the century, 58% of persons age 40 had two living parents. Seen another way, in 1900, more than one in four 40-year-olds had no living parent; in 2000, fewer than one in twenty 40-year-olds were orphans. For 50-year-olds, the proportion of orphans dropped from over 60% in 1900 to less than 20% in 2000. Finally, in 1900, only 8% of 60-year-olds had a living parent, compared with 44% of 60-year-olds in 2000. Thus, more and more adult children are experiencing their parents' deaths toward the end of middle age.

The death of a parent is significant for many reasons. The tie with a parent is a unique, nonreplaceable, long-lasting bond; there are no former parents or ex-parents. The parent is a mythic figure and a symbol of the family. Parents and children have a shared history and often a shared worldview. Elements of the tie have continued through decades, involving mutual protection, nurturing, guidance, affection, and interdependence. The child's identity is rooted in the bond.

Academic researchers and clinicians who work with bereaved persons have traditionally focused on the impact of deaths that are not normative. Thus, they have tended to ignore the impact of the death of an elderly parent on an adult child. The lack of attention to this topic has various causes. Several researchers have reported that a parent's death evokes a less intense emotional response than the death of a child or a spouse (Leahy, 1993; Sanders, 1980). Generally, parents are *expected* to die when they are old. Young people tend to avoid the recognition that they will become old. In many ways, old people represent an existential threat for the young, reminding them of the fallibility of the body, the transitory basis of self-esteem, and the inescapability of death (Martens, Goldenberg, & Greenberg, 2005). Experiencing the end of an elderly parent's life is not seen as a major life task in middle age, when marriage, raising children, and establishing a career are central issues. Further, there is little evidence that bereaved adult children seek counseling after their parent has died. We suggest that the concepts of ageism and disenfranchised grief can help us understand the neglect of this topic.

Ageism affects the ways people think, feel, and behave in response to a person's chronological age. Older people often are less valued than younger people. They may be viewed as frail, rigid, sexless, isolated, possibly confused, and homogeneous. Scholars agree that any notion of a "typical" old person is likely to be wrong; for example, more than half of all people older than 80 live relatively independently in the community. Old persons are often seen as out of the context of time, a perception that devalues the person's past as well as his or her future. Although there are no hate groups against old people, ageism is socially acceptable and pervasive, and many explicit and implicit stereotypes exist regarding old age (Levy & Banaji, 2002). When old people internalize this ageism, they devalue themselves just as they are devalued by others. There is much evidence that older people tend to be marginalized; they are stripped of responsibility and power, and ultimately of their sense of worth (Nelson, 2005).

Ageism is so common in our culture that it is overlooked, yet it cannot be ignored when we examine the impact of an old parent's death. Disenfranchised grief is the grief people experience when they incur "a loss that is not or cannot be openly acknowledged, publicly mourned, or socially supported" (Doka, 1989, p. 4). If old persons are less valued, then grief for their death is also less valued, its significance is diminished, and the adult child's expression of bereavement is expected to be neither intense nor lengthy.

Although many books have been written about the impact of parental death, they are generally anchored in the authors' personal experience of a parent's death, and few focus exclusively on the death of an old parent. In the following sections, we discuss the findings of several research papers and a three-year longitudinal study that was the basis of the first scholarly book on this topic (Umberson, 2003).

OUR RESEARCH

We have been involved in qualitative and quantitative research and writing about parental death for over two decades, most prominently as part of a research team funded through the National Institute on Aging. We have focused on adult children whose second parent died within the previous six to nine months; thus, both parents of all study participants had died. Initially, we interviewed more than 100 daughters of recently deceased women; subsequently, we interviewed more than 200 adult sons and daughters with regard to their deceased mother or father. The first study participants were volunteers from the community; in the second study, participants were recruited through a random sampling of death certificates in Philadelphia County.

ANTICIPATION OF A PARENT'S DEATH

There are many signals, in addition to advanced age, that a parent is approaching the end of life: retirement; the parent's inability to do what he or she used to do; the physical changes of grey hair, wrinkles, and slower pace; and the onset or complications of a chronic disease. Even the sudden death of an active, alert 75-year-old parent does not come as a total surprise. Many people have early childhood fantasies of being an orphan, and throughout the years, people experience the deaths of the parents of friends and acquaintances. There is an underlying sense of anticipatory orphanhood. Four-fifths of the daughters we spoke with said they began to grieve before their mother died; more than half said they had grieved "a lot."

Anticipation of a parent's death is not necessarily tied to the duration of an illness, the trajectory of decline, or the medical diagnosis of a terminal disease. In fact, after repeated crises and remissions of chronic illness, when an old parent is dying the family members may expect yet another recovery, because the parent is seen as invincible. A person whose parent has died after a long illness may perceive the death as sudden or unexpected (Bass & Bowman, 1990).

If a parent becomes frail or is seriously ill, the adult child generally tries to hold on to the parent. Threats of separation tend to intensify the bond. Not infrequently, there is increased interaction between the adult child and the parent when the future is uncertain. As part of the process of holding on, the child may set goals such as family plans for future events that could encourage the parent to live longer. At the same time, the adult child has a tendency to let go of the parent as he or she imagines what it will be like after the parent has died. When the adult children we interviewed recalled the time before their parent's death, several themes emerged: partial grief, adaptation anxiety, and uncertainty. These themes reflect both emotional and cognitive responses to the parent (Moss & Moss, 1996).

Many adult daughters recognized their mother's decline, and contrasted her present functioning with that in the past. They spoke of feeling a deep sense of loss, of partial grief for their living parent (Berezin, 1977). Many recalled that they were more upset about the parent's increasing frailty than about the prospect of the parent's death. A third of the daughters said they had been so overcome by grief for their mother before she died that they couldn't say or do some of the things they would have liked. This uncontrolled grief was not correlated with the mother's physical or mental functioning; rather, it was associated with adaptation anxiety (Moss & Moss, 1996). Adaptation anxiety emerged in two ways. First, two-thirds of the daughters said they worried about how the mother would handle her decline and dying. Second, over half of the daughters said they were concerned about how they would adjust and manage after the mother's death.

For most older people, at the end of life there is no well-defined trajectory as in cancer deaths. Most deaths of old people are not due to cancer, rather, old people most often suffer from chronic diseases—such as heart, circulatory, and respiratory conditions—in which the terminal course is uncertain. The lack of a trajectory is further complicated by the fairly common illusion of the parent's invulnerability, which has been bolstered by decades of resilience.

Adaptation anxiety reflects the tension between the fear of the impending loss and the urge to maintain the bond. The theme of holding on and letting go is pervasive. Partial grief, while acknowledging the decline, allows the adult child to emphasize the continuity of the parent's strength and competence. At the same time, uncertainty about the process and timing of dying and death allows the adult child to think simultaneously about the living parent and the dying parent.

REACTIONS AFTER THE PARENT'S DEATH

In general, adult children have no clear role models for how they should react to a parent's death. Although they may have memories of their parents' ties with their grandparents, most recall little about how their parents responded to the deaths of their own parents. In the context of ageism and disenfranchised grief, it is not surprising that the bereaved adult child's expressions of grief and loss are muted.

Impact on the Self

Although it has been suggested that, on losing the last parent, the child ceases to be a child and becomes an adult, children have generally spoken of the continuity of their ties with their parents—they see themselves as both adults and adult children. In our research involving adult children whose last parent had died, many children spoke of feeling a sense of orphanhood. They perceived that they had lost the parent's physical presence and also lost a "buffer" against their own death. They felt an increased sense of personal mortality (Douglas, 1990).

We suggest that the tie with the parent tends to persist throughout the child's life. Thoughts of mother or father reaffirm one's sense of being a child of that parent. The parent's death does not mark the end of the parent's legacy. The parent's values, the expectations the parent had for the child, the behaviors the parent modeled in the various stages of life, and the place of the parent in the collective family identity continue.

The quality of the earlier relationship with the parent may play a role in how the child responds to the death. If the relationship was one of rejection, abuse, parental alcoholism, or mental health problems, the child may feel a sense of relief (Umberson, 2003). At the same time, the child may mourn the loss of the imperfect parent and may regret not having been able to resolve problematic aspects of the relationship before the parent died. Umberson (2003) reported a significant increase in depression among bereaved children compared with children who had not experienced the death of a parent.

Gender

Much of the early literature on bereavement in general was based on the experience of women, usually widows, which resulted in a feminized model of grief. Bereaved persons were thought to emphasize intense investments in social relationships, to be expressive, and to find comfort in social support and sharing of emotions. A male style of grief tends to be more instrumental, to prize self-control over emotional expression, and to emphasize action or agency, individualism, and the maintenance of personal privacy. It is not surprising that recent literature has found that gender of both the parent and the child plays a role in the child's reaction to the parent's death (Moss, Resch, & Moss, 1997).

Women have been found to react to the stress of bereavement with a greater tendency to depression, while men exhibit more use of alcohol (Umberson, 2003). In our research, we found that daughters were more likely than sons to express emotional upset and somatic responses, and to report a continuing tie with a deceased parent. Sons reported more acceptance of the parent's death than daughters—a more cognitive response.

In an in-depth examination of the reactions of sons to a father's death, we found themes that are not adequately described in the feminized model of grief. We found four interrelated themes as the bereaved men sought to maintain their manliness: control, action, cognition, and privacy (Moss, Rubinstein & Moss, 1997). Other researchers have suggested masculine styles that are generally congruent with our findings (Martin & Doka, 2000). They note men's instrumental style compared with the expressive style more often seen in women.

Men tend to control their expression of grief in several ways. Rather than holding on to the parent with feelings of sadness, they express their grief primarily through memories of the deceased that recur over time. A man may talk about the end of his father's life in mechanistic or sports images: "He ran out of gas" or "He came to the end of the game." Men may model themselves on their fathers' nonemotional responses to loss, creating an intergenerational legacy. They tend to see any emotional component of grieving as short-lived and a prelude to action.

Men's instrumental style emphasizes doing things rather than yielding to a feeling of passivity and dependency. They talk about taking care of funeral arrangements and financial matters, and use themselves as models to help female relatives master their own emotions. Rather than expressing his feelings, a son is likely to find meaning in a review of his father's life and of his relationship with his father. Finally, men tend to avoid public expressions of feeling and often speak of finding private times and places where they can grieve.

Different Contexts of the Death

In our research on daughters and mothers, we explored how certain things—such as the mother's living arrangement or quality of life—can affect the daughter's experience of bereavement (Moss, Moss, Rubinstein, & Resch, 1993). We focused on four groups of elderly deceased mothers: those who received considerable caregiving from a daughter who lived with them, those who lived in a nursing home, those who were relatively healthy and lived fairly independently, and those who lived at least several hundred miles from the daughter.

Considering the daily interaction with their parent and the potential burdens of caregiving, it is not surprising that daughters who had been heavy caregivers tended to report more health problems after the death, more emotional upset, and stronger continuing ties with their mother. At the same time, caregiving children have also been reported to feel more relief and less stress (Umberson, 2003). They, like the children of parents who lived in a nursing home, had a greater sense of acceptance of the death. Some research suggests that this acceptance results from the powerful influence of society's tendency to disenfranchise the child's grief.

For an elderly person, moving to a nursing home is often seen as a step toward death. When parents had been nursing home residents, children tended to express less emotional upset after the death, to control their expression of grief, and to report weaker ties to the deceased parent. And yet, other research has found that almost half of surviving children whose parents died in a nursing home said they had a harder time adjusting to the death than they had anticipated (Pruchno, Moss, Burant, & Schinfeld, 1995). The latter study also reported that the more upset the child was about the nursing home experience, the more emotionally upset he or she was after the parent's death.

The daughters of women who had lived in the community and been relatively independent tended to express the most intense grief and the least acceptance of death. There was a strong sense of untimeliness and shock. Not only did they lose the mother of the past and the present, they lost the fulfillment of their expectations for the future. Although daughters may wish to have their mothers die without deterioration and suffering, many of the daughters in our study implied that they wished they had had more warning of the imminence of death.

Finally, we found that when the mothers lived far away, the daughters' reactions to the loss were not significantly different from the reactions of daughters in the three other groups: daughters who lived with and cared for their mothers, daughters whose mothers lived in a nursing home, and daughters whose mothers had lived independently. This suggests that ties and the meaning of relationships, at least between daughters and mothers, tend to remain strong in spite of distance.

The death of a parent who had suffered from considerable dementia has been found to be less stressful and emotionally upsetting (Aneshensel, Pearlin, Mullan, Zarit, & Whitlatch, 1995), although the adult child grieves both for the former strong and vital parent and for the parent who suffered from dementia.

Family

The death of a parent is a loss that is most fully understood in the context of family (Nadeau, 1998). All the adult children we interviewed spoke of the significance of siblings and other kin—living and dead—as they described the impact of their parents' death. Generally, we interviewed only one surviving adult child in each family, but in one family we had lengthy individual interviews with four of the surviving children (Moss & Moss, 2001). The themes that emerged from this large Irish-American family were striking. The children described their deceased 90-year-old mother as the center of the family, the bond or glue that held them together. Each adult child saw his or her tie with the mother as inseparable from his or her role in the family. For example, each sibling spontaneously reported that, in a unique and important way, he or she was the mother's favorite child. All four siblings accepted the diversity of strengths and weaknesses among them. For each bereaved sibling, the tie with the mother remained strong, as did ties with other deceased family members. The sense of family crosses the boundary between living and dead.

Our finding that family ties tend to remain strong was similar to other research that reported that after a parent's death, most relationships among the survivors remained unchanged, and those that shifted tended to become closer rather than more distant (Scharlach & Fredriksen, 1993). However, Umberson (2003) found that while sibling ties tended to remain unchanged and adult children's relationships with their own children were strengthened, a parent's death had a significant detrimental effect on many marriages.

Many important aspects of a parent's death are beyond the scope of this chapter. We list them because they need to be explored further: how the quality of the long-term relationship between child and parent affects the child's reaction to the death; the unique dynamics of cross-gender dyads (son-mother, daughter-father) compared with the more frequently studied same-gender dyads; how family members renegotiate the psychosocial space left by the deceased parent; and the nature of intergenerational legacies in families as their members adapt to the loss of parents.

Two Important Aspects of the Death of a Parent

Two other factors play a major role in the adult child's experience of a parent's death: (1) race/ethnicity, and (2) distinctions between the death of the first parent and the death of the second parent.

The role of ethnicity and religion in the bereavement process of the adult child has been little explored. Umberson (2003) found that the response to a parent's death does not differ much across racial groups. A careful analysis of our mother-daughter data (Smith, 1998) examined the loss within the socio-historical context of the African-American experience. Several themes emerged among bereaved African-American daughters, who stressed not only the emotional impact of the loss for themselves and their families but also ways the loss was felt in the black community. The importance of extended kinship groups is associated with the broad impact of the mother's death. Many daughters saw their social status as rooted in their mother's relationships in the African-American community. A number of these daughters spontaneously reported that they had provided care for their mothers and thus did not feel guilty after the death. Daughters tended to idealize their mothers and see them as symbols of strength and connectedness in the black family and community.

In our study, spirituality was a major resource for black daughters in coping with death. It was expressed in the sense of a personal God, a belief in the afterlife, and the expectation of a future reunion with the mother. These beliefs supported the daughters as they sought meaning in their mothers' deaths. More research and understanding are needed of the ways members of various cultures and subcultures in the United States react to and find meaning in the death of an elderly parent.

As Marshall (2004) has suggested, for most adult children, parent death is a two-stage transition—from being a child of living parents through the death of the first parent to the death of the second parent. For some adult children, the death of the first parent may be the initial experience of the loss of a close family member. A child's grief for the first parent is often deeply affected by the grief of the surviving parent. There is a sociocultural sense that different survivors have different degrees of legitimacy in expressing their grief; for example, a widowed spouse may be perceived as having more right to grieve than an adult child. Thus, the child may attempt to control his or her expression of grief. With the loss of the first parent, the child often places high priority on providing support and care for the surviving parent. When adult children are interviewed about the death of their second parent, they are likely to spontaneously compare the impact of that death with their experience (often more than a decade previously) of the death of their first parent. Somewhat surprisingly, after the death of the first parent, many adult children report that they have no increased awareness of the fact that the surviving parent will also die. They continue to hold on to the role of adult child.

FINAL THOUGHTS

Two separate polarities recur in the literature that examines the impact of the death of an elderly parent. First, there is a tendency to focus on the extent to which the adult child has recovered from the loss versus a focus on a life course process of maintaining a tie with the parent. Second, there is an emphasis on a major transformation of the adult child's sense of self versus an emphasis on the continuity of personal identity.

Recovery tends to imply a sense of decathexis and distancing from the grief associated with the death of a parent, as well as a reduction in the salience of the parent in one's life. We have found that for most bereaved children the emotional pain of the loss declines over time, although the connection with the parent continues. An internal dialog with the deceased parent tends to persist, along with associations and memories connected to people, places, and things that are linked to the parent. Shared values are often recalled, as well as old conflicts and disagreements. The sense of family identity, that was rooted in early childhood and evolved over decades, continues. In each of these processes, there is a viable tie with the deceased parent and a simultaneous pattern of holding on to the parent and letting go. This can be seen in the child's experience of holding on to a possession that had been owned or valued by the parent, while at the same time being confronted with the fact that the parent is no longer alive. Whether the parent represented approval or disapproval, was a model with whom the child identified or rebelled against, the image of the parent remains. The parent lives on symbolically in the adult child's world.

The second polarity that recurs in the literature on parent death focuses on upheaval and transformation of the child's self and continuity of self. Our research participants tended to emphasize a strong sense of continuity in their personal identity, their relationships with others, and their worldview. They were able to stand on their own after the parent's death, much as they had when the parent was alive. As many researchers in gerontology have noted, continuity of self is a major factor in aging (Atchley, 1989; Kaufman, 1986). The meanings adult children find in the loss of a parent are generally congruent with their past and present views of themselves, their family, and the world. The resiliency of the bereaved adult child can be profound. Surely, some adult children may feel a developmental push toward new ways of being in the world, but the response to the loss typically reflects the essence of the survivor's self-image. ■

Miriam S. Moss, M.A., is a faculty research scientist at Arcadia University, Glenside, Pennsylvania. For 35 years, until 2004, she was senior research sociologist at the Abramson Center, formerly the Philadelphia Geriatric Center. Her major research focus has been on the interface between gerontology and thanatology. She is a member of the International Work Group on Death, Dying and Bereavement, a fellow of the Gerontological Society of America, and a corecipient of the Richard Kalish Award.

Sidney Z. Moss, DCSW, is a clinical social worker and a faculty research scientist at Arcadia University, Glenside, Pennsylvania. Since 1989, he has been involved in research projects on the death of an elderly parent and on bereavement in long-term care settings. He is a member of the International Work Group on Death, Dying and Bereavement, and a corecipient of the Richard Kalish Award of the Gerontological Society of America.

REFERENCES

Aneshensel, C. S., Pearlin, L. I., Mullan, J. T., Zarit, S. H., & Whitlach, C. J. (1995). *Profiles in caregiving: The unexpected career.* New York: Academic Press.

Atchley, R. C. (1989). A continuity theory of normal aging. *Gerontologist, 29,* 183-190.

Bass, D. M., & Bowman, K. (1990). The transition from caregiving to bereavement: The relationship between care-related strain and adjustment to death. *Gerontologist, 30,* 35-42.

Berezin, M. (1977). Partial grief for the aged and their families. In E. M. Pattison (Ed.), *The experience of dying* (pp. 279-286). Englewood Cliffs, NJ: Prentice Hall.

Doka, K. J. (1989). Disenfranchised grief. In K. J. Doka (Ed.), *Disenfranchised grief: Recognizing hidden sorrow* (pp. 3-11). Lexington, MA: Lexington Books.

Douglas, J. D. (1990). Patterns of change following parent death in midlife adults. *Omega, 22,* 123-137.

Hoyert, D. L., Heron, M. P., Murphy, H. R., & Kung, H. C. (2003). Deaths: Final data for 2003. National Center for Health Statistics, National Vital Statistics Reports, 54, #13 [Online]. Retrieved June 21, 2006 from www.cdc.gov/nchs/data/nvsr54/nvsr54_13.pdf.

Kaufman, S. R. (1986). *The ageless self: Sources of meaning in late life.* Madison, WI: University of Wisconsin Press.

Leahy, J. H. (1993). A comparison of depression in women bereaved of a spouse, child or a parent. *Omega, 26,* 207-217.

Levy, B. R., & Banaji, M. R. (2002). Implicit ageism. In T. D. Nelson (Ed.), *Ageism: Stereotyping and prejudice against older persons* (pp. 49-75). Cambridge, MA: MIT Press.

Marshall, H. (2004). Midlife loss of parents: The transition from adult child to orphan. *Ageing International, 29,* 351-367.

Martens, A., Goldenberg, J. L., & Greenberg, J. (2005). A terror-management perspective on ageism. *Journal of Social Issues, 61,* 223-240.

Martin, T. L., & Doka, K. J. (2000). *Men don't cry...women do: Transcending gender stereotypes of grief.* Philadelphia: Brunner/Mazel.

Moss, M. S., & Moss, S. Z. (1996). Anticipating the death of an elderly parent. In J. D. Morgan (Ed.), *Ethical issues in the care of the dying and bereaved aged* (pp. 113-129). Amityville, NY: Baywood.

Moss, M. S., Moss, S. Z., Rubinstein, R. L., & Resch, N. (1993). Impact of elderly mother's death on middle aged daughters. *International Journal of Aging and Human Development, 37,* 1-22.

Moss, M. S., Resch, N., and Moss, S. Z. (1997). The role of gender in middle-age children's responses to parent death. *Omega, 35,* 43-65.

Moss, S. Z., & Moss, M. S. (2001). Four siblings' perspectives on parent death: A family focus. In J. Hockey, J. Katz, & N. Small (Eds.), *Grief, mourning and death ritual* (pp. 61-72.). Philadelphia: Open University Press.

Moss, S. Z., Rubinstein, R. L., & Moss, M. S. (1997). Middle-aged son's reaction to father's death. *Omega, 34,* 259-277.

Nadeau, J. W. (1998). *Families making sense of death.* Thousand Oaks, CA: Sage.

Nelson, T. D. (2005). Ageism: Prejudice against our feared future self. *Journal of Social Issues, 61,* 207-.221.

Pruchno, R. A., Moss, M. S., Burant, C. J., & Schinfeld, S. (1995). Death of an institutionalized parent: Predictors of bereavement. *Omega, 31,* 99-119.

Sanders, C. M. (1980). A comparison of adult bereavement in the death of a spouse, child, and parent. *Omega, 10,* 303-322.

Scharlach, A. E., & Fredriksen, K. I. (1993). Reactions to the death of a parent during midlife. *Omega, 27,* 307-317.

Silverman, P. R., & Worden, J. W. (1993). Children's reactions to the death of a parent. In M. S. Stroebe, W. Stroebe, & R. O. Hansson (Eds.), *Handbook of bereavement: Theory, research, and intervention* (pp. 300-316). New York: Cambridge University Press.

Smith, S. H. (1998). *African American daughters and elderly mothers: Examining experience of grief, loss, and bereavement.* New York: Garland Publishing.

Uhlenberg, P. (1996). Mortality decline in the twentieth century and supply of kin over the life course. *Gerontologist, 36,* 681-685.

Umberson, D. (2003). *Death of a parent: Transition to a new adult identity.* New York: Cambridge University Press.

CHAPTER 15

Grief Counseling with Families: Meaning Making in the Family During the Dying Process

Kathleen R. Gilbert

"There is no more emotionally connected system than the family,
if for no other reason than because no one can ever truly leave it"
(Rosen, 1990, p. 17).

B ut what is a family? And what role does family play in making
meaning through the dying process?

Families are made up of two or more individuals who share a common
history and unique connections that extend beyond a simple sense of
responsibility and commitment to each other. These individuals may be
connected through traditional kinship ties; that is, they may be joined by
blood, marriage, or adoption. On the other hand, their bonds may be pure-
ly relational, as for all intents and purposes they take on the characteristics
of legally established families. For example, cohabiting couples might be
remarkably similar to married couples, whether they are opposite- or
same-sex couples. And long-term friends might think of themselves more

as siblings than friends and might be regarded as uncles or aunts by each other's children. Regardless of the structure, family characteristics that appear to be critical to meaning making during the dying process are intimacy, commitment, continuing engagement, and a history of interactive meaning making

Language, meaning, and interaction are critical to our definition of family (Gubrium & Holstein, 1990). One person's idea of family may not be consistent with another's—even if they grew up or now live in the same household. Each person identifies his or her family based on their own perceptions. As Gubrium and Holstein suggested, family is not so much a thing as it is a way of interpreting interpersonal ties.

"Family" is defined in this chapter fairly expansively, with an emphasis on its function as a meaning-making environment: a place where members are able to test their understanding of their own or their family member's dying, the dying process itself, and what all of this means for their own experience of life and death.

As Rosen (1990) implied, families are also part of our history and future. So in addition to immediate ties, the bonds of family may extend through generations, and those we identify as family members—living, dead, and yet to be born—have the potential to inform our meaning-making process. Their role in meaning making is further complicated by the fact that family bonds may be voluntary or involuntary, wanted or unwanted, central to our thoughts or held to the side. Our family influences us throughout our lives, whether we like it or not.

THE FAMILY AS A SYSTEM

For any family system to operate, certain functions must take place and roles played (Rosen, 1990). Each family has its own way of doing this, with its unique structure, relationships, roles, responsibilities, and interaction patterns (Rando, 1984; Walsh, 2006). Individuals may perform many roles in their family. If a person serves one or more roles that are central to the family's ongoing operation, the more disruptive is the loss or impairment of that person.

Through their ongoing interactions, families maintain a certain balance and achieve some sort of predictability in their day-to-day lives.

However, maintaining balance can be challenging on an everyday basis, because families must deal with ongoing, normative change from such simple things as aging of family members and the evolving relationships within the family (Doka, 1993). When a family member is dying, the family may be thrown into disarray—it certainly enters into a state of heightened stress. The relative stability that has been established in the family is disrupted, and the family must somehow regain some sense of stability and shift the various responsibilities among family members to continue functioning (Walsh, 2006).

The family's ability to adapt to a terminal illness or a death is affected by a variety of factors (Murray, Toth, & Clinkinbeard, 2005): the timing of the illness or the death in the life cycle; the nature of the illness or death itself; and the degree to which the loss is acknowledged or, possibly more significant, the degree to which it is disenfranchised (Doka, 2002), stigmatized, or both. In addition, if the family is experiencing concurrent stressors, if the ill or dying person is central to the family's operations, or if there is conflict between the person who is dying and others in the family, the family will be more vulnerable. Families with a variety of resources within and outside the family and families that are open, flexible, and cohesive are better able to handle the various stressors related to the illness and death (Murray et al., 2005).

THE DYING PROCESS—MOVING TOWARD A DEATH

In a sense, we all begin our dying process when we are born. As Parkes, Laungani, and Young (1997) noted, albeit somewhat humorously, "Life [is] an incurable disease which always ends fatally" (p. 7). However, most people see the dying process as beginning when a life-threatening illness or condition exists. The point at which the individual, medical professionals, and family members become aware of the life-threatening nature of the condition will not be the same for everyone concerned. The afflicted individual may recognize symptoms and seek medical care. Or the individual may ignore symptoms, and it may be up to family members to encourage the individual to seek medical advice. In some cases, the individual's condition may become very advanced before anyone becomes concerned, because family members may attribute changing behaviors and conditions to something other than illness. Realization of a terminal illness may not occur until the condition is recognized and labeled by a physician.

In my own family, I recall visiting my dying father with my then-nine-year-old daughter. I saw my father's physical condition as evidence that he was very near death and expected that my next visit would be for his funeral. That was, in fact, the case. My daughter, on the other hand, said with great sincerity, "Grandpa looked really good today. I think he's getting better." Although I saw a man ravaged by pain, with every organ in his body failing, my daughter saw her beloved grandfather who had smiled and squeezed her hand—evidence that he was gaining strength he had not had at the last visit.

Although this chapter focuses on the family's response, it is important to keep in mind that the dying individual is at the center of the experience. Doka (1993) identified a series of recognizable phases through which the dying individual moves. They are the *prediagnostic, acute, chronic,* and *terminal phases* of dying. Each of these phases is associated with a number of behaviors. However, as Doka reminds us, these behaviors may show up in a different phase of the dying process or may never become an issue for the dying individual. The following brief information on these phases is taken from Doka, and he provides more detailed information on each phase in his book.

The *prediagnostic phase* begins before the illness is diagnosed and involves someone recognizing symptoms or behaviors that could indicate a serious illness or life-threatening condition. The person with the illness or a family member or friend may be the first to recognize the symptoms. A spouse or partner might notice changes in a mole on the individual's back and encourage the individual to "get it checked out." Alternatively, a child might come home from a school lecture on the dangers of smoking and present her own lecture to her father, a long-time, heavy smoker. Ultimately, the focus is on recognizing warning signs and responding to them.

The *acute phase* centers on the crisis of diagnosis, and many questions must be dealt with at this time, including medical, psychological, and interpersonal decisions. In many cultures, medical decisions must be made by the ill individual unless he or she is a minor or incapacitated. In other cultures, particularly those found in Asia (Matsumura, et al., 2002), medical decisions are made by the physician in concert with family members. If the diagnosis is a terminal condition, the individual is typically not told because of the fear that this will cause him or her to lose hope. Who may be involved in the nonmedical decisions depends on who has been told the true nature of the illness. The individual may initiate discussion with other family members, or he or she may prefer to handle such decisions alone. It is not uncommon in this phase for the ill individual to maintain an illusion of ignorance about the true nature of his or her condition.

The *chronic phase* involves the individual's struggle to live with the illness and treatment while also attempting to live as normal a life as possible within the confines of the illness. The progression of the illness may not be linear or constant; often, it will be punctuated by a series of medical crises. This is often the period of time during which family members come together or move apart. It may become difficult for the family to maintain a unified attitude as family members deal with the unique meanings they attribute to the potential, anticipated, or expected loss of the ill family member.

The *terminal phase* is often the shortest. It is in this phase that death is considered inevitable. Death, rather than life, becomes the focus for the individual and the family.

In his discussion of these phases, Doka (1993) noted that individuals may not experience all of these phases. Some may recover from their illness, even, in rare cases, after entering the terminal phase. In each phase, the individual and family members may respond in ways that may not seem sensible. For example, some family members may hold themselves at an emotional distance, unable to deal with a rollercoaster of emotions, and find themselves struggling to trust the individual to live.

In a family-centered model that roughly parallels Doka's, Rosen (1990) described a series of phases in families similar to those of dying individuals. These are the *preparatory phase, living with the fatal illness,* and *final acceptance.* The phases described here are not time limited, nor are they directly associated with the course of the illness. Rather, the model focuses on the emotional response of the family to the illness and its implications for the family's ability to function and remain as a system.

Preparatory Phase

Fear and denial of the seriousness of the illness are common, especially early in this phase. Yet even after diagnosis, families or individual family members may be unwilling to accept it and may choose alternative, less threatening explanations for the individual's symptoms. The illness may be highly disruptive to normal family operation, and the family may become highly disorganized, particularly if members have few resources on which to draw. Feeling threatened, the family may turn inward and protective of itself and of its members. Anxiety, according to Rosen (1990), may be higher at this time than at any other point in the dying process. This is a crisis situation for the family, and the shock to the system can be overwhelming. Alternatively, the family may function in a resilient fashion to adapt to meet the support needs of family members (Walsh, 2006).

Living with the Fatal Illness

This phase begins with the family's efforts to adapt to the fact that a family member has a terminal illness. This phase can be quite long, and the family members may settle into their new roles, adjusting to the altered needs for the family system to function well. The family may become less disorganized during this phase, but the reorganization may not be healthy if, for example, family members isolate themselves and refuse offers of help. This may be particularly true if the illness has an element of stigma associated with it.

Family members carrying out caregiving roles may adapt and become comfortable in that role. This is an important adjustment, because a great deal of the care for the terminally ill is provided by family members (Mezey, Miller, & Linton-Nelson, 1999). Other roles may shift throughout this phase, including those of the terminally ill person. Roles will be abandoned and, in many cases, picked up by others in the family. This is to be expected, because roles in the family shift as the demands of the illness shift. Sometimes this need to shift roles will be a problem. If other essential functions in the family—for example, the care of healthy children—receive less attention, the family's ability to deal with ongoing responsibilities may suffer. Other related and unrelated stressors are active in the family at this time. Commonly described stressors are concern about finances, resource availability, and caregiving.

Final Acceptance

Usually the shortest phase, final acceptance involves the recognition of the fact that the individual's death is inevitable. Some family members may say goodbye, although not all family members are equally willing to accept that death cannot be forestalled. In fact, some family members may not accept this reality until after the person has died. Others may overanticipate the death and may emotionally separate before the individual has died. In this phenomenon, labeled *social death* (Sudnow, 1967), the dying person is seen to be "already dead," which may result in him or her becoming more and more isolated as others move on with their lives and are less socially engaged with the individual. Several years ago, a student of mine who had experienced the conflict that could be tied to this phenomenon described her relationship with her maternal grandmother, who had suffered from Alzheimer's disease, and with her mother. Over the years before her grandmother died, my student's mother had increasingly questioned her for "bothering to visit an old lady who doesn't even know who you are. The woman we knew is dead. That's not my mother in that bed. That's not your grandmother." In talking with me shortly after her grandmother's death, my student said, "Dr. Gilbert, my grandma knew who I was. I saw her a week before she died. She recognized me. She knew who I was. She called me by my name. She wasn't dead to me."

The family that may have become well organized during the phase of living with the illness often becomes disorganized and in shock in the final acceptance phase. Roles and relationship patterns they established during the previous phase no longer work or work poorly. Family members may come together out of personal fears or out of a need for support from people close to them. On the other hand, they may withdraw from each other in a self-protective move.

The family may become anxious about what others will think of them, which can pressure the family to move to extremes of closeness or distance. Communication is an essential tool for helping the family to maintain a sense of connection during this time (Walsh, 2006). The degree to which family members are able to develop a shared perspective is a factor that can help family members to feel connected, even if they are really "at different places" in their efforts to cope with the final phases of dying and death of a family member. This is especially true if the family's tendency is to protect each other from "unpleasantness" or pain. Rosen (1990) recommended that professionals working with families encourage them to come together as a "team" at this time, and to recognize that, if they choose, they can separate in a healthy way at a later time.

Throughout the dying process, the dying individual and family members will undoubtedly deal with what is referred to as *anticipatory mourning* (Rando, 2000). This controversial conceptualization of grief has evolved over time, and a detailed discussion of this concept will not be possible here. Although the term seems to indicate that what is being mourned is one's own impending death or for the family, the ultimate death of their loved one, it is more more complex than that. Anticipatory mourning involves the grief that is associated not only with the loss of a loved one, but also the ongoing losses of functions, relationships, opportunities, and other aspects that are specific to that family's particular situation.

With my own father's dying, I found the progression of potential, anticipated, and expected death helped me to cope throughout the dying process. Initially, when it appeared that he might recover, I grew more aware that he had the potential of dying sooner than I was ready for. As his condition worsened, I began to anticipate what life without him, my only living parent, might be like. As he became overwhelmed by his illness, I progressed to seeing his death as expected. I believe my father, as the dying person, added another aspect of the dying process: wished-for death.

The dying process within the family, then, consists of the interplay of individual family members acting in the social and relational context of the family, with each member affecting and being affected by the others. Therefore, a great deal is happening simultaneously as each family member attempts to come to grips with the situation. Intense emotions are experienced, and, for each family member, the reality of a future without the dying person will be faced, accepted, and integrated into each survivor's world view.

MEANING MAKING: AS INDIVIDUALS AND AS FAMILIES

One does not simply experience life; instead, people construct models that help them to understand their past and present experiences and to predict what might happen in the future (Kelly, 1955). As Kelly and other constructivists suggested, we function as "personal scientists," testing hypothetical models of the ways in which life operates against the norming models of others (Raskin, 2002). Our models also are socially constructed (Hollander & Gordon, 2006; Neimeyer & Neimeyer, 1994); as social animals, we use our social network, including our family, as a tool for confirming our internally constructed model of reality. Through interaction with others, our subjective views may be confirmed and given an objective reality that seems to be independent of the social setting (Berger & Luckman, 1966). Alternatively, our views may not be confirmed, and we may find ourselves questioning our own beliefs and continuing our search for the "truth" of the situation (Gilbert, 1996). This is true for both the dying person and the members of that person's family.

What we understand as death and dying are social constructions (Gilbert, 1996; Gilles & Neimeyer, 2006; Nadeau, 1998), which means that they are defined using words, concepts, and ways of thinking available in the culture (Kastenbaum, 1998). Because this meaning is socially constructed, dying and death can mean different things to different people, and the meanings can change over time for each person.

The family's involvement in meaning making is an ongoing, everyday part of family life (Gubrium & Holstein, 1990). It is a naturally occurring aspect of human relationships, one that precedes the dying and death of a family member and one that will continue after that event. In their daily interactions, family members receive information from others in the family about what has happened, is happening, and will happen in their lives (Reiss, 1981). Sometimes this information is direct and clear; sometimes it comes only from interpreting others' behavior (White & Klein, 2002), and that interpretation may be inaccurate.

The process of making meaning begins in infancy (Hollander & Gordon, 2006; Miller & Mangelsdorf, 2005) and continues throughout life. Meaning making is interactive. One need only listen to children as they develop a narrative about what death and dying mean to get an idea of this interactivity: "Grandma, what does it mean to be dead? Am I going to be dead? I saw a bird on the road and its guts were hanging out. Do people get dead like that, too?" or "Daddy, Lucas's brother lost all of his hair and is really skinny and he puked on Lucas and it was gross and Lucas said he's dying. What is dying, Daddy? Lucas started to cry when he said dying, like it was bad. Daddy, I ate a bug and puked last week. Am I dying, too? Will I lose my hair and get skinny, too?" One can picture the adults in this child's life answering questions and confirming or correcting the child's perceptions while the child asks questions over and over in an effort to get a handle on the difficult concepts of death and dying. By asking questions and absorbing the responses, children form an idea of what these concepts mean to the adults in their lives and come to incorporate them into their interpretation of death and dying (Miller & Mangelsdorf, 2005).

In adulthood, a more subtle version of this process of social confirmation can be observed. The serious illness of a family member might trigger a couple's discussion of their expectations about end-of-life decisions they should make about each other. The partners may test their ideas about life and death, quality of life, and expectations about how they should be treated as they approach death. Couples who discover that they hold conflicting views about end-of-life issues may begin in disagreement—and eventually may modify their own opinions.

Thus, as they encounter new information in their environment, family members compare their impressions and attempt to confirm their beliefs, opinions, hunches, and theories with each other. As noted earlier, subjective views held by family members that are confirmed by others in the family are given objective reality; that is, family members come to see their views as a truthful reflection of reality because significant others also see them that way (Berger & Luckman, 1966; Fowlkes, 1991). If this does not happen, family members may question their own or others' perceptions and look elsewhere for information (Gilbert, 1996). Family members also may "agree to disagree" and elect not to discuss points of contention.

The single most important resource for families dealing with any stressor is the ability of the family to communicate, although this may become increasingly difficult for the dying person. Shared meanings—that is, mutually validated views—facilitate communication, provide structure and meaning to family interactions, and serve as the basis for familial coping behavior (McCubbin & Patterson, 1983; Nadeau, 1998; Reiss, 1981). For many of the processes family members need to carry out, as well as for shared meaning, open and supportive communication is essential (Walsh, 2006). The belief that the family holds a shared view can help the family cope with a loved one's dying: when a family member is approaching death, shared views can reduce uncertainty about what is going on and can clarify rules for behavior in the family—individuals in the family may feel less alone and confused about how to react. Thus, the meaning of the dying of the family member and the responses of family members to the dying process are shaped by the system of beliefs within the family.

Shared meaning making is a tremendously valuable resource for families dealing with loss (Nadeau, 1998). The urge to find or establish shared beliefs in the family is quite strong, even when family members encounter information that contradicts their sense that other family members hold the same view as they do. Shared time and activities help to facilitate this sharing, with the added bonus that the activities alone may have a mood-lifting effect, especially if the activities involve physical activity. They also provide an opportunity effect; that is, the simple act of being together provides opportunities to family members to build a shared view.

Unfortunately, family members have only each other's behavior and imperfectly communicated information on which to base their beliefs about shared views. Moreover, family members' shared history and expectations may skew their interpretation of the information communicated. It is, therefore, not surprising that conflict occurs. Family members may find old issues they thought they had resolved reemerging with a vengeance and may return to old battles. During the height of the AIDS epidemic, I spoke with a man who had lost his partner of several years. They had seen themselves as married and had lived together for several years until a few months before his partner's death. He and his partner had long before cut off all contact with his partner's family because of its strong disapproval of their gay relationship. Any contact with the partner's family resulted in their blaming him for "turning their son gay." When his partner was hospitalized, the partner's parents banned him from the hospital, and he was unable to be with his loved one at the time of his death. The man's one saving grace throughout was his own family, which had been supportive and caring and had shared the view of these two men as a couple.

The same potential for conflict or collaboration on attributed meaning may occur with a variety of decisions that are made in the family: choices made about end-of-life care, advance care planning, wakes, funerals, and periods of mourning. These decisions, coming during a period of significant transition for the family, are associated with high stress (White & Klein, 2002). In her study of end-of-life decisions, Gauthier (2005) found that family concerns were an important factor in the decision making of terminally ill patients. Increased dependence, the need to relocate to be near family, accommodating the needs of family caregivers, the economic burden on family, and communication were all social concerns of the terminally ill that were associated with family function—and that made decisions more difficult.

THE FAMILY AFTER DEATH

Although this chapter primarily focuses on the dying process in the family, death is the outcome. After a family member has died, the family must respond in a way that is supportive for the ongoing function of the family. Walsh and McGoldrick (2004) proposed that to successfully adapt to the loss of the family member, the family must *recognize the loss as real* and *reorganize and reinvest in the family system.*

Recognize the Loss as Real

Family members must acknowledge the reality of the loss while each family member shares his or her grief. To do this, family members must share emotions and thoughts with each other. They must allow different family members to express their grief in different ways, without judgment. When the loss is disenfranchised, others may not find it appropriate to acknowledge the reality of the loss. In the case of the man whose partner died of AIDS, his own parents acknowledged his loss and recognized it as real. The response of the parents of his partner did not.

Reorganize and Reinvest in the Family System

As stated earlier, the family system is destabilized by the loss; yet for the family to continue to function, order and control must be reclaimed. Family members must reconstruct what family means to them and the roles and responsibilities of the person who died must be reassigned or given up. However, abandoning these roles and responsibilities, no matter how functional this ultimately might be, will heighten stress in the family. Family life may seem chaotic at this time, and there may be battles over how the family will be reorganized. Differences in grieving may contribute to a feeling of being out of sync among family members (Gilbert, 1996). To get in sync, families might reframe their differences as strengths rather than weaknesses. The family must reinvest itself in normal developmental evolution, particularly if this was put "on hold" as the family dealt with the terminal illness. Tasks that were carried out as a matter of course in families must again be carried out. Those previously assigned to the deceased must now be reassigned. For example, a family in which Dad used to sit at the head of the table at holiday dinners, and lead the family in prayer before the meal might specifically identify one family member to take over that task, perhaps the oldest son, after Dad's death. Another family might shift the role to someone seen as the most religious. Still another family might rotate the task among members. This reclaiming of a normal life may be seen by some as abandonment of the deceased loved one. Efforts to avoid mention of the deceased may inhibit communication, contributing to a sense of secretiveness in the family. Family members should let each other hold onto memories without fear that this will keep them stuck in the past (Klass, Silverman, & Nickman, 1996).

Open communication is essential to completing the tasks of grieving (Gilbert, 1996; Nadeau, 1998; Walsh & McGoldrick, 2004). This process may be slow, as each family member has strong needs and limited resources after a loss. Family members, who are already more emotional because of their loss, may not recognize each other's different grief styles as legitimate. Rituals like funerals, religious rites, and even family holidays can be used to facilitate the process of recognition, reorganization, and reinvestment in the family (Imber-Black & Roberts, 1992).

Rituals often become more valuable to the family during this time of loss, but they can help throughout the dying process. Rituals are composed of metaphors, symbols, and actions that are "packaged" in a highly condensed, time- and space-bounded, dramatic form to establish and maintain family identity (Imber-Black, 2004). Family rituals serve five functions: *relating*, issues of expressing and maintaining relationships;

changing, transitions for self and others; *healing,* recovery from relationship betrayal, trauma, or loss; *believing,* voicing beliefs and making meaning; and *celebrating,* affirming deep joy and honoring life with festivity (Imber-Black & Roberts, 1992).

In their overview of cultural variations in approaches to end-of-life decisions and associated rituals, Searight and Gafford (2005) described a wide range of approaches to decision making in the family, including whether or not the dying person should be involved in the decision-making process or even if the dying person should be informed that a decision needs to be made. In a world that allows greater mixing of culturally diverse individuals and the blending of cultures in families, issues of meaning may become intense at these times (Klessig, 1992).

Implications for Practice

Clearly, the family experience of the dying process is a complex one. Each family member will be dealing with his or her own issues, concerns, and needs, while also attempting to come to terms with the ongoing changes in the family. At the same time, they may be trying to act in a supportive way toward other family members. Communication between family members is essential as family members work to make sense of what is going on in their family. Sharing information, making time to be together, and working as a team all contribute to a sense of shared focus in the family. Awareness of the variation in meaning for individual family members, along with acceptance of differences in coping style, will reduce the extent to which each family member feels disenfranchised or stigmatized in the family. From this, positive family interactions and individual meaning making can be promoted.

Practitioners working with families going through the dying process can best help by doing the following:

- Emphasize the importance of communication within the family. For some family members, it may be necessary to "institutionalize" this communication in some sort of ritual expression. If the family can arrive at a common sense of mission, it will be easier for the family to function well throughout the dying process and to reconstitute itself after the loss.

- Work with families to help them understand that individual family members who had idiosyncratic reactions to events in the past will continue to do so now, that events will have different meanings for each of them, and that these idiosyncrasies may actually serve as strengths through the dying process.

- Emphasize respect for differences, whether for each member's different methods of processing information or for some members' periodic need for privacy as they work through the process.

- Point out that it is essential for family members to reframe each other's behavior, looking for strengths in differences or ways of separating out differences that are difficult to accept from other characteristics that are valued.

- Some family members may prematurely disengage from the dying individual, resulting in the isolation of the individual. Encourage the family to work as a team to reduce the likelihood of that happening. Help family members to understand why some members are becoming less involved and encourage them to assist disengaged members to better cope with the situation.

As they move through the dying process, families may feel overwhelmed and overburdened. If they are provided with support like that available through hospice, they will be better able to cope with the stresses associated with the dying process. ■

Kathleen R. Gilbert, Ph.D. is an associate professor of applied health science at Indiana University–Bloomington, where her work has been focused on interpersonal dynamics associated with loss and grief, especially in the family. She developed and regularly teaches one of the first fully on-line, credit-bearing courses on grief in a family context. She was elected to the International Work Group on Death, Dying and Bereavement and is a Fellow in Thanatology in the Association for Death Education and Counseling. She has published books, book chapters, and articles and has presented papers on a variety of topics associated with death, dying, grief, and loss.

REFERENCES

Berger, P., & Luckman, T. (1966). *The social construction of reality.* New York: Doubleday.

Doka, K. J. (1993). *Living with life-threatening illness: A guide for patients, their families and caregivers.* New York: Lexington Books.

Doka, K. J. (2002). *Disenfranchised grief: New directions, challenges, and strategies for practice.* Champaign, IL: Research Press.

Fowlkes, M. K. (1991). The morality of loss: The social construction of mourning and melancholia. *Contemporary Psychoanalysis, 27,* 529-551.

Gauthier, D. M. (2005). Decision making near the end of life. *Journal of Hospice & Palliative Nursing, 2,* 82-90.

Gilbert, K. R. (1996). "We've had the same loss, why don't we have the same grief?" Loss and differential grief in families. *Death Studies, 20,* 269-283.

Gilles, J., & Neimeyer, R. A. (2006). Loss, grief, and the search for significance: Toward a model of meaning reconstruction in bereavement. *Journal of Constructive Psychology, 19,* 31-65.

Gubrium, J. F., & Holstein, J. A. (1990). *What is family?* Mountain View, CA: Mayfield.

Hollander, J. A., & Gordon, H. R. (2006). The processes of social construction in talk. *Symbolic Interaction, 29,* 183-212.

Imber-Black, E. (2004). Rituals and the healing process. In F. Walsh & M. McGoldrick (Eds.), *Living beyond loss: Death in the family.* (2nd Ed.) (pp. 340-357). New York: W. W. Norton.

Imber-Black, E., & Roberts, J. (1992). *Rituals for our times: Celebrating, healing, and changing our lives and our relationships.* New York: Harper Collins.

Kastenbaum, R. J. (1998). *Death, society, and human experience.* (6th Ed.). Boston: Allyn and Bacon.

Kelly, G. A. (1955). *A theory personality: The psychology of personal constructs.* New York: W. W. Norton.

Klass, D., Silverman, P. R., Nickman, S. L. (Eds.). (1996). *Continuing bonds: New understandings of grief.* Washington, DC: Taylor & Francis.

Klessig, J. (1992). The effect of values and culture on life-support decisions. *The Western Journal of Medicine, 157,* 316-321.

Matsumura, S., Bito, S., Liu, H., Kahn, K., Fukuhara, S., Kagawa-Singer, M. L. K., Wenger, N. (2002) Acculturation of attitudes toward end-of-life care: A cross-cultural survey of Japanese Americans and Japanese. *Journal of General Internal Medicine, 17,* 531-539.

McCubbin, H. I., & Patterson, J. M. (1983). The family stress process: The double ABCX model of adjustment and adaptation. *Marriage and Family Review, 6*(1/2), 2-38.

Mezey, M., Miller, L. L., & Linton-Nelson, L. (1999). Caring for caregivers of frail elders at the end of life. *Generations, 23,* 44-51.

Miller, P. J., & Mangelsdorf, S. C. (2005). Developing selves are meaning-making selves: Recouping the social in self-development. *New Directions for Child and Adolescent Development, 109,* 51-59.

Murray, C. I., Toth, K., & Clinkinbeard, S. S. (2005). Death, dying, and grief in families. In P. C. McKeney & S. J. Price (Eds.), *Families and change: Coping with stressful events and transitions* (pp. 75-102). Thousand Oaks, CA: Sage.

Nadeau, J. W. (1998). *Families making sense of death.* Thousand Oaks, CA: Sage.

Neimeyer, G. J., & Neimeyer, R. A. (1994). Constructivist methods of marital and family therapy: A practical precis. *Journal of Mental Health Counseling, 16,* 95-104.

Parkes, C. M., Laungani, P., & Young, B. (1997). Introduction. In C. M. Parkes, P. Laungani, & B. Young (Eds.), *Death and bereavement across cultures* (pp. 3-9). London: Routledge.

Rando, T. A. (1984). *Grief, dying, and death: Clinical interventions for caregivers.* Champaign, IL: Research Press.

Rando, T. A. (2000). Anticipatory mourning: What it is and why we need to study it. In T. A. Rando (Ed.), *Clinical dimensions of anticipatory mourning* (pp. 1-13). Champaign, IL: Research Press.

Raskin, J. D. (2002). Constructivism in psychology: Personal construct psychology, radical constructivism, and social constructionism. In J. D. Raskin & S. K. Bridges (Eds.), *Studies in meaning: Exploring constructivist psychology* (pp. 1-25). New York: Pace University Press.

Reiss, D. (1981). *The family's construction of reality*. Cambridge, MA: Harvard University Press.

Rosen, E. J. (1990). *Families facing death: A guide for healthcare professionals and volunteers*. San Francisco: Jossey-Bass.

Searight, H. R., & Gafford, J. (2005). Cultural diversity at the end of life: Issues and guidelines for family physicians. *American Family Physician, 71*, 515-522.

Sudnow, D. (1967). *Passing on: The social organization of dying*. Englewood Cliffs, NJ: Prentice Hall.

Walsh, F. (2006). *Strengthening family resilience*. (2nd Ed.). New York: Guilford Press.

Walsh, F., & McGoldrick, M. (2004). Loss and the family: A systematic perspective. In F. Walsh & M. McGoldrick (Eds.), *Living beyond loss: Death in the family*. (2nd Ed.). (pp. 3-26). New York: W. W. Norton.

White, J. M., & Klein, D. M. (2002). *Family theories*. (2nd Ed.). Thousand Oaks, CA: Sage.

■ CHAPTER 16 ■

Countering Empathic Failure: Supporting Disenfranchised Grievers

Dana G. Cable and Terry L. Martin

INTRODUCTION

In recent years, grievers have become more willing to seek out support to help them cope with their loss. But a griever may encounter some obstacles in acquiring the support he or she seeks and needs. This is particularly true if there is a failure to recognize that support is necessary. A person may experience what is to him a significant death, but society may not view the loss the same way. Additionally, the griever may not feel empathy for himself, believing that his reactions to the loss are not "normal." In these cases, a loss of self-esteem may result.

A Note About Empathy

Many lay people (and some counselors) confuse empathy with sympathy. Whereas sympathy implies sharing deeply in the other's experiences, empathy stresses the need for boundaries. As Rogers (1959) observes, empathy is "to perceive the internal frame of reference of another with accuracy and with the emotional components and meanings which pertain thereto as if one were the person, but without ever losing the 'as if' condition. Thus, it means to sense the hurt or the pleasure of another as he senses it and to perceive the causes thereof as he perceives them, but without ever losing the recognition that it is as if I were hurt or pleased and so forth" (pp. 210-211). A failure to empathize can lead people to base their assessment of the importance of the loss to the griever on their own inability to generate a response set identical to that of the griever.

DISENFRANCHISED GRIEF

Doka (2002) suggests that in cases where there is a lack of public empathy, we are dealing with *disenfranchised grief*—losses that are not or cannot be acknowledged openly, mourned publicly, or socially supported. Examples of such situations are plentiful. If one has a significant death in the family, such as a spouse or a child, time is usually allowed off work for the funeral and mourning, and one receives support from others. However, if one's best friend or former spouse dies, there may be no provisions for mourning or support.

Doka (2002) lists five reasons that grief may be disenfranchised. In some instances, the *relationship may not be recognized*. We are usually quick to acknowledge relationships such as parent, child, spouse, and others based on kinship ties. But relationships such as friend, coworker, in-law, former spouse, and same-sex partner are often not acknowledged by society. These grievers may receive very little support.

A second situation arises when the *loss is not recognized*, as in prenatal death, death of the very elderly, abortion, or pet loss. In these cases, others may minimize the loss. For example, a woman who has had an abortion may be confronted with the attitude that she chose the death and thus caused any grief she might feel. On the other hand, because many people do not consider a fetus to be a human life, they might feel no need to support the griever.

The third instance occurs when *the griever is not recognized*. Society perceives some persons—such as young children and those with developmental disabilities—as not able to grieve because of their lack of understanding of death.

The circumstances of the death may cause grief to be disenfranchised. Families often work very hard to avoid having a death labeled as suicide. A stigma is attached to suicide; thus, society may not support the grievers, perhaps considering them to bear some responsibility for the death.

The fifth example of disenfranchised grief relates to *the ways in which some individuals grieve*. This disenfranchisement can be seen in the patterns identified by Martin and Doka (2000). We discuss this more fully below.

Rando (1993) adds a sixth situation in which disenfranchised grief may occur. She suggests that there are deaths in which *the social group members are defensive or try to protect themselves against anxiety*. Examples would include deaths that involve mutilation or deaths that are stigmatizing, such as a death from autoerotic asphyxiation. This category is similar to Doka's fourth type.

Kastenbaum (2004) speaks of *hidden grief*. He is referring to grief that may go unrecognized or unacknowledged by others because the mourner keeps the loss or the feelings about the loss to himself or herself. This might occur among hospice staff or nurses in a critical care unit or nursing home. They experience grief over the death of their patients but are concerned that if they show it, they may be seen as no longer effective in their work and unable to separate themselves from their patients.

In each of these instances of disenfranchised grief, stigma is attached to the loss, or the griever feels that the grief must remain unnoticed.

A final view of disenfranchised grief derives from the work of Martin and Doka (2000). They identify two primary styles of grief: *intuitive grief*, in which experiencing and demonstrating affect is the major modality for grieving, and *instrumental grief*, in which cognitions and behavioral reactions define the griever's responses. In both styles, gender role theory plays an important (though not definitive) role. Since most counseling approaches recognize and support affective (feeling) responses as the key to healthy grieving, many instrumental grievers may find themselves disenfranchised. This is especially true of female instrumental grievers, who do not conform to the stereotype of women being more "feeling-oriented" than men. Often, these instrumental women are viewed with suspicion and labeled as cold or unfeeling. On the other hand, some men are very intuitive grievers; they may find themselves being supported by those who like the idea of the androgynous male and disregarded by those whose ideal male is strong, silent, and unemotional.

In all these cases, the underlying common element is that the needs of the mourner are not met. In some of these situations, the mourner may not even be permitted to have a role in the dying process or the rituals of death. While others are receiving support, disenfranchised grievers are excluded and must deal with their grief alone and without social support.

The fact that disenfranchised grief is unacknowledged may intensify the reactions of the mourner. All the normal feelings of guilt, anger, and so on may occur, but with no outlet. In the case of instrumental grief, the absence of intense feelings about their loss may lead these grievers to conclude that they are defective in some way. The disenfranchised mourner may not be able to participate in the rituals of death or show emotions freely. Instrumental grievers may be criticized by others for their lack of emotion and may find themselves isolated in their grief. In these cases, there may be no closure on the relationship. The grief may become complicated and require grief therapy.

"Complicated grief" is the term typically used to describe grief situations that raise special problems. In the past, such grief was described as pathological, abnormal, or unhealthy. Use of the word *complicated* removes the negative implications while recognizing that the grief situation is special and complex.

COUNSELING DISENFRANCHISED GRIEVERS

Assessment is the first step in counseling disenfranchised grievers. In some cases, the assessment focuses on the situations surrounding the loss; in others, it focuses on the griever's behavior. In both cases, the counselor should inquire about the circumstances of the loss and the reactions of others, and listen very carefully to the language the griever uses. Unfortunately, many counselors begin by saying, "Tell me how you are feeling about your loss." This immediately implies that the griever should talk only about affective reactions. While all grievers have some degree of affect regarding their loss, instrumental grievers in particular may sense that the counselor is not interested in any responses other than feelings.

A better approach is to inquire, "How did you react?" or "How did you respond?" This allows the griever to choose the domain of experience in which to discuss the loss and conveys a sense of validation.

In counseling someone who has experienced disenfranchised grief, the first step is to legitimize the person's reactions. In many cases, society has given them a sense that their grief is not legitimate. Grievers should be educated about the various forms of disenfranchised grief so they can see that their reactions are valid, that the relationship was an important one, and that they have the strengths to adapt to the loss.

Unrecognized Relationships

In cases in which society does not recognize the relationship, the counselor must help the griever understand that, despite the lack of support from others, the relationship was important to him or her and the death represents a significant loss. The counselor must be careful not to confuse his or her own valuation of the relationship with that of the griever. In fact, if the counselor cannot accept or understand the significance of the relationship, it may be necessary to suggest that someone else should work with this griever. As therapists, we cannot always set aside our own values, but we can recognize and acknowledge the right of every person to value relationships as he or she sees fit.

For example, in the case of the death of a former spouse, others may assume that because the relationship had ended, there will be little or no grief and hence no real need for support. However, even relationships that end bitterly were at one time important and, presumably, good. We cannot expect a person to deny the past and forget what was good in the relationship.

One of the authors worked with a woman at the time of her ex-husband's death nine years after they divorced. The relationship had not been a good one; on several occasions, the wife had gone to a shelter for battered women. When she finally divorced her husband, everyone supported her. When he died, everyone told her that now she would never have to deal with or even think about him again. However, in therapy, she related that during the years of abuse, she had always believed the relationship would get better. Even after the divorce, she kept alive a fantasy that, one day in the future, they would get back together and the relationship would be what she had always hoped for. His death effectively ended that dream. The counselor's sensitivity was essential to provide the woman with an understanding of her feelings and to give her the support she was not receiving elsewhere.

Unrecognized Loss

Pet loss can illustrate the need for special skills in supporting grievers whose loss is not generally recognized. When a pet dies, most people understand that the owner feels bad. But the typical response is "When will you get a new one?" The counselor must be sensitive to the significance of the loss. For many people, their pet is their confidant, their child, their companion. The authors run a support group for pet loss through the local Humane Society. The grief experienced by participants is every bit as great as that experienced by persons in other types of grief support groups.

Other losses that often go unacknowledged are romantic breakups among young people (LaGrand, 1989) and divorce (Martin, 1989). Paying attention to these non–death-related losses has been criticized as diluting the importance of death in disenfranchised grief (Cable and Martin, 1999), but people who experience such losses often encounter the same lack of understanding and support. In the case of divorce, society may view the failure of the marriage as preventable. This perception is seen in the weakening of kin relationships, the failure of the faith community to provide support, and the absence of ritual marking the transition from couple to single persons.

One of the most difficult situations in which loss is not recognized is abortion. The issue of abortion itself is controversial. Most people consider abortion a choice and may be reluctant to acknowledge that it is really a loss. However, even when abortion is chosen, there are usually mixed emotions. The counselor must have the skill to acknowledge that a loss has taken place and the sensitivity to not make this acknowledgement seem accusatory. Often, the girl or woman simply needs someone to help her with her conflicting feelings about the choice she has made.

Unrecognized Griever

In the third type of disenfranchised grief, the griever—for example, a child—is not recognized. Children are often denied the opportunity to participate fully in the rituals that surround death. When they express their grief, they may be told to "be brave." The counselor must be sensitive to the fact that children can and do grieve. Just like adults, they need an opportunity to express their grief and receive appropriate support.

Today, many hospices sponsor programs like Camp Jamie at Hospice of Frederick County, Maryland. The camp was developed to allow bereaved children ages six through fourteen years to gather together with skilled and sensitive adults to share their grief and receive support from the adults. The weekend program, though short, has had a dramatic effect on many grieving children. The staff is sensitive to the fact that parents and others in the child's life are so enmeshed in their own grief that they often cannot provide the help the child needs. The camp experience allows the children to receive support without feeling that they are burdening their families.

Defensiveness of the Social Group

In the cases Rando (1993) cites (in which the social group tries to protect itself against the anxiety the death evokes), the counselor must be particularly sensitive. For example, a death by autoerotic asphyxiation may produce anxiety or denial in the griever. Forcing a bereaved person to acknowledge the cause of death may serve no real purpose and should not be pushed until the person is ready to deal with the issue. The counselor must try to understand what the facts of the death mean to the griever.

Unwillingness to Express Grief

The hidden grief cited by Kastenbaum (2004) often involves professionals who fear that if they allow themselves to experience their grief, they may be perceived as unable to be objective and continue in their work. Program directors, facility administrators, and support persons need to understand the significance of loss for these professionals. They must be skilled at allowing them to open up and express their grief yet sensitive to the fears they have about the possible consequences of sharing their grief with others.

Unrecognized or Unsupported Grief Behaviors

Affirmation of the griever's experience is paramount. Some strategies can support the griever's own way of reacting to the loss. For an instrumental griever, the emphasis should be on cognitive and behavioral strategies. Moos and Shafter (1986) identify the following as effective strategies:

- Logical analysis and mental preparation
- Cognitive restructuring
- Cognitive avoidance
- Information seeking

Martin and Doka (2000) emphasize the importance of problem-solving activity. Problem-focused activity can

- Provide an outlet for the physical ventilation of grief.
- Address problems created by the loss.
- Provide a feeling of control in an otherwise chaotic situation.

Recently, one of the authors worked with a middle-aged man who was caring for his dying wife. He sought professional support when he was criticized by his stepdaughter for not showing his "deep feelings" about the impending loss. This husband was providing all the nursing care to his wife and managing a household, while continuing to work full time. His relief was palpable as he learned that he was grieving in a very active and cognitive way.

For grievers who are affectively oriented, affective regulation and creating a safe environment for affective discharge can be beneficial. One man, after the death of his infant son, was treated with disdain by his supervisor when he was discovered openly weeping in his office. By learning how to regulate his grief and finding a safe haven for its expresion, he regained a sense of self-control and was able to behave in an "appropriately male" fashion at work.

Conclusion

Society often fails to provide grievers with the support they need following a death. All too often, we define loss on the basis of our personal evaluation of its significance, rather than attempting to understand the loss from the griever's perspective. Counselors and others who work with grievers must be sensitive to the personal construct of a loss as seen by the griever. Developing a true sense of empathy is essential to working with all bereaved persons, but especially with those whose grief has been disenfranchised. Only then can we meet grievers where they are and help them work through the grief process so they can move on in their lives. ■

Dana G. Cable is a professor of psychology and thanatology at Hood College in Frederick, Maryland, where he is director of the M.A. in Thanatology program. He is a licensed psychologist and a fellow in thanatology, death, dying, and bereavement. Since 1973 he has maintained a private clinical practice specializing in grief and death-related issues. In 1993, he received the Clinical Practice Award from the Association for Death Education and Counseling. Dr. Cable is on the Editorial Board of the American Journal of Hospice and Palliative Care. *He is a frequent presenter of programs on grief for professionals throughout the United States.*

Terry L. Martin is an associate professor of psychology and thanatology at Hood College. He is a licensed clinical professional counselor. Dr. Martin maintains a private counseling practice and also serves as consultant to hospices, nursing homes, hospitals, and various government agencies. His published work includes chapters in Kenneth J. Doka's Disenfranchised Grief *(1987, 2002) and chapters in earlier books in the Living with Grief series. He coauthored (with Kenneth Doka)* Men Don't Cry…Women Do: Transcending Gender Stereotypes of Grief *(2000).*

REFERENCES

Cable, D. G., & Martin, T. L. (1999, April). *Grief diluted versus grief distilled.* Presentation, Annual Conference of the Association for Death Education and Counseling, Pittsburgh, PA.

Doka, K. (Ed.). (2002). *Disenfranchised grief: New directions, challenges, and strategies for practice.* Champaign, IL: Research Press.

Kastenbaum, R. J. (2004). *Death, society, and human experience.* (8th Ed.). Needham Heights, MA: Allyn and Bacon.

LaGrand, L. E. (1989). Youth and the disenfranchised breakup. In K. Doka (Ed.), *Disenfranchised grief: Recognizing hidden sorrow* (pp. 173-185). Lexington, MA: Lexington Books.

Martin, T. L., & Doka, K. J. (2000). *Men don't cry…women do. Transcending gender stereotypes of grief.* Philadelphia: Taylor and Francis.

Martin, T. L. (1989). Disenfranchised: Divorce and grief. In K. Doka (Ed.), *Disenfranchised grief: Recognizing hidden sorrow* (pp. 161-172). Lexington, MA: Lexington Books.

Moos, R. H., & Shafer, J. (1986). *Coping with life crisis: An integrated approach.* New York: Plenum Press.

Rando, T. A. (1993). *Treatment of complicated mourning.* Champaign, IL: Research Press.

Rogers, C. R. (1959). A theory of therapy, personality and interpersonal relationships, as developed in the client-centered framework. In S. Koch (Ed.), *Psychology: A study of science* (Vol. 3, pp. 184-256). New York: McGraw Hill.

The Importance of Self-Care

Part III concluded with a discussion of disenfranchised grief. That chapter was a strong affirmation that many individuals who may not share a biological or legal tie with a person who is dying or deceased may be touched by grief.

Those grieving individuals include, of course, hospice and other health care professionals. Such professionals may form bonds, intensified by crises, with both dying patients and their families. Hence the loss becomes deeply personal.

Joyce Davidson's very sensitive chapter illustrates that point. Her chapter not only offers wisdom on ways to work with persons who are dying and their families, it shows the subtle bonds that develop among patients, families, and staff.

Self-care has always been addressed within the Living with Grief® series, both in the books and on the teleconferences. It is often said that hospice and other health care professionals are far better at taking care of others than they are at taking care of themselves.

Mary Vachon's chapter addresses this issue. Vachon has been a pioneer in the field of death studies. While she has made substantial contributions in many areas of palliative care, a significant focus of her work has been on the professional stress experienced by those who work with dying individuals. Vachon is sensitive to the range of losses professionals experience as they work with dying persons, and she offers effective methods for coping with loss on both individual and organizational levels. The latter is an exceptionally important point. Self-care is not just a responsibility of the individual; organizations have a responsibility as well to create environments where the care of staff is seen as a vital component of the care that staff can provide.

It is for that reason that the Hospice Foundation of America always concludes each book with a list of resources. It is a challenge but also a calling and privilege to assist persons who are dying and grieving. Yet, it is work that need not be done alone. ▪

CHAPTER 17

Lessons Before Dying

Joyce D. Davidson

Shay* was a 36-year-old, scruffy, street-smart survivor with advanced ovarian cancer. She lived from pillar to post and was noncompliant with her treatment, causing frustration in those attempting to treat her. Emergency room visits supplanted scheduled office visits. She refused to acknowledge the severity of her disease. This time she had been admitted to the hospital for pain control and tachycardia; her anxiety was through the roof, and her street smarts were failing her. I was doing an internship in palliative-care counseling and was asked to see if I could calm her down. I entered her room with trepidation; I had never met her, but I knew she was considered a basket case. If more experienced people had trouble dealing with her, I doubted that I had much to offer. She was sleeping (whew!) so I sat beside her bed and slipped my hand under hers. Without moving or opening her eyes, she said, "Is there someone like you here 24 hours a day?" She became one of my first powerful teachers. There have been so many since.

Like most of you, I have been with many patients and families during the final steps of their journey. And like you, I have witnessed a broad spectrum of personalities and needs. Some patients are so much more gratifying to work with; they make the frustrations of the difficult cases easier to bear. We have all experienced those glorious moments of revelation, reconciliation, and redemption. But it is often the difficult patients who teach us the most, and I believe our stories are among the greatest gifts we have to offer each other.

* *All names except my father's have been changed.*

Mr. Seymour was an irascible old man who had achieved enviable business success and prosperity, but his family relationships were in shambles. The hospice intake coordinator wrote TYRANT! at the top of the intake cover sheet, and that pretty much said it. His family was terrified of him. His three grown children had moved as far away as they could without falling into the ocean. Everyone on the hospice team approached him with trepidation.

But Mr. Seymour enjoyed the diversion of company. He wanted control, of course, and so I let him have it, or at least the illusion of it. He loved to talk about his mother and siblings, all idealized and long dead. In his mind it was his living family that had failed him. He was candid about how disappointed he was in his children; none of them had his business acumen. His son Cal was a particular disappointment. Even though he was a successful physician, he had never learned the proper way to balance books, much less run a business, despite his father's best efforts.

Despite that, Cal took time off from a busy practice and flew across the country to be with his father in those final weeks. He wanted very much to find a kernel of something in his father that he could love and admire and pass along to his own sons.

In one of my visits, Mr. Seymour recited his favorite quote: "I shall pass this way but once; therefore, any good that I can do or any kindness that I can show to any human being, let me do it now. Let me not defer nor neglect it, for I shall not pass this way again."

"That's beautiful," I said. "What a wonderful legacy to leave your children and grandchildren."

"Oh, I've never said it to them. What's the point?"

"Well, you've taught Cal about business and balancing books. Don't you think this is worth telling him so he can pass it on to his sons?" Mr. Seymour made no reply.

But, according to Cal, a few nights later at the dinner table his father recited the quotation out of the blue.

"That's wonderful, Dad," Cal said. "Would you say it again so I can write it down for my boys?"

"Aw, what's the point?" Mr. Seymour muttered.

But he repeated it as Cal wrote it down.

Cal really searched for ways to share meaningful time with his dad. He had read *Tuesdays with Morrie*, "but my dad's not a Morrie kind of guy," he said. I suggested that shaving his father might be an intimate but safe activity, as his father could no longer shave himself. Cal liked the idea. Later he told me that he had loved the role reversal and tenderness and usefulness of it. When he was finished, his father rubbed his hand over his face and said, "Cal, when you've finished shaving yourself, do you feel to see if you've missed a spot?"

"Why yes, Dad, I do," said Cal, pleased at this continuation of father-son sharing.

"Well then, why didn't you do that for me?" his dad asked gruffly.

Cal related that to me with wry resignation. It was so typical of his dad. But in the months after his father's death, Cal spoke with fondness and gratitude of having had those opportunities to shave his father, and of being entrusted with the quotation that his father had loved, even if Mr. Seymour had not seemed to be guided by it.

And so I learned the value of "the least possible contribution," Avery Weisman's (1979) theory that stresses the value of finding gratification in those small acts or gestures, often unexpected, that make a small contribution to a patient's or family member's experience.

My colleague Susan tells the story of her first day of work as a palliative-care counselor in a large teaching hospital. She was sent to visit a terminally ill patient and asked him the question we should always ask: "Is there anything I can do for you?" "Well," he said, "I would love a cup of hot coffee, because the coffee's always cold by the time the food tray arrives." So Susan picked up the Styrofoam cup on his tray and set out to find a microwave, which took awhile because she didn't know her way around the hospital. As she nuked the coffee, the cup exploded inside the microwave. Flustered, she cleaned up the mess and then set out to find the cafeteria, which again took awhile. But she finally returned to the man's room with a cup of hot coffee. As he wrapped his hands around the cup and held his face over the steam, he let out a contented sigh.

The next morning Susan arrived at the hospital to learn that the man had died overnight, and she realized the significance of the small offering of hot coffee. She had experienced, on her very first day of work, the gratification of the least possible contribution. It can be as simple as offering lip balm, or nuking a cold cup of coffee—or suggesting that a son shave his father.

Doug Manning (1999) has written a beautiful statement regarding sorrow: "Large sorrows hit us out in the open and we are well aware of their effect on our lives. Small sorrows creep in unaware and silently collect in the bottom of our soul" (p. 30). Being aware of the small sorrows, both for patients and families and for ourselves is an important tool in working with dying patients.

But I have also come to realize that the flip side of that coin has to do with large joys and small joys. Anyone who works for any length of time in hospice and palliative care knows the profound joy of the big moments of transcendence, but often we overlook or undervalue the small moments that might not have occurred without us. They are more powerful than we know, and treasuring them fosters resilience and enhances our clinical practice and our lives.

At times we go into disheveled and chaotic homes and lives, you and I, and we are challenged to find equanimity and meaning in such a setting. In hospice we like to say that we meet patients and families where they are, but that is ever so much easier to do when we like where they are.

The Delaneys were a raucous family whose three generations shared a crowded, squalid apartment in New York City. The grandfather was the hospice patient, and he, along with the rest of the family, talked loudly and simultaneously with the others. Their overlapping, confrontational conversation unnerved me. It took me a while to figure out how to even follow it, let alone contribute to it. I considered it a contemplative moment if only one person was speaking at a time.

So what was I to do? What was my role? Was it even worth being there? After each visit I left the apartment feeling as if I had been ringside at Madison Square Garden. How was that doing anyone any good? But I kept going, and I kept my expectations low. I accepted their offerings of junk food and tried not to think about how unsanitary the kitchen was.

Over time I realized that my role was to bear witness to the Delaney family's struggle, to hold their anxiety and dysfunction in my heart, and to withhold judgment. It was so easy to judge them, and so much more difficult not to. My visits continued for more than a year. Did I effect great change? No, but I showed up. I grew to care about them deeply. I tried to be a calm and compassionate presence. I was steadfast. I look back on those visits now with tremendous gratification. What I offered was a safe space for them to spread out the puzzle pieces, even if they never quite got the puzzle put together. And while I believe my visits were helpful for the Delaneys, they taught me so much more than I taught them.

In Walter Wangerin's eloquent story, "The Making of a Minister" (1984), he tells of Arthur Forte, who lived the last year of his life "in a rotting stuffed chair" in the front room of his squalid house. Arthur, "dead the third year of my ministry, poor before he died, unkempt, obscene, sardonic, arrogant, old, lonely, black, and bitter—but one whose soul has never ceased to teach me. . . . From Arthur, from the things this man demanded of me . . . I grow. My perceptions into age and pain are daily sharpened. My humility is kept soft, unhardened. And by old, dead Arthur I remember the profounder meaning of my title, minister. It is certainly time, now, to memorialize teachers, those undegreed, unasked, ungentle, unforgettable" (pp. 64-65).

You may be familiar with the story of the little boy lying in bed in the dark who calls out to his parents, "I'm scared. Come in here and be with me." His father calls back, "There's no need to be afraid, son, God is in there with you." After a pause the boy replies, "But I need someone with skin on!"

We can be that for others, every one of us.

Shay, the young woman with ovarian cancer, taught me the power of touch, and hundreds of other patients have affirmed it. A dying person may be "skin hungry" from being touched only when they are poked or prodded by their doctors and nurses. But how do you assess whether the patient is receptive, and how do you know when it's appropriate? After shaking hands or briefly holding their hand, I might say, "Your hands are dry; would you like me to put some lotion on them?" If they agree, I put lotion on their hands, giving them a light hand massage, which allows me to assess how they respond to touch. Over the years, almost without exception, patients have asked if I would come back and do it again. It can be a powerful way to connect with a patient who has difficulty communicating, and it can be an effective way to put a patient at ease. There have been times when the nonverbal connection seemed to make the patient more comfortable talking to me, and other times when the touching was our only way of really connecting. I do it consciously and with intentionality, because I understand its power.

I had to learn early on to leave my own thoughts and distractions at the door. Before I open the door to a hospital room or a home, I take a moment to close my eyes, exhale deeply, and visualize the release of whatever thoughts might distract me from being fully present with the person on the other side of the door. It helps me feel more connected from the outset. With each new patient, I have no idea what I will find once I open that door, but what I do know is that I can't "fix" it—I can only be attentive and assess where they are and what I can do to best support them.

"You don't have to be larger than life to help people in the darkest moments of their lives," says author and crisis counselor Diane Ackerman (1997). But, she adds, it does require that we "listen athletically, with one's whole attention, and it is physically exhausting. It feels like a contact sport" (p. 9).

In his day, Rev. Dawson was a force to be reckoned with—a strong, compassionate leader and a masterful orator. His competence in matters both professional and personal was impressive and reassuring; he was the one everyone turned to.

Now, in his 94th year he was frail and dependent on the care of his 90-year-old, 90-pound wife, herself a marvel of competence that permitted him to live at home longer than anyone had imagined possible—until he suffered a series of small strokes that launched a 911-hospital-nursing home journey. Transient confusion complicated his ability to recover, as well as the ability of the hospital and nursing-home staffs to assess and care for him. An extreme case of sundowning was tortuous and apparently intractable; no one seemed to be able to relieve it, and it caused both the patient and the family significant suffering. They refused to leave him at night, since that was when the worst things happened, and they fought a Herculean struggle to keep him in his bed. His wife and daughter were exhausted, sleep-deprived, and at the end of their rope. He begged them to take him home, and they promised they would as soon as the doctors released him. "They can't keep me here without a warrant!" he exclaimed.

No one had mentioned hospice, but because his daughter was a hospice professional she pursued it; she had to persuade not only her mother but also the nursing home staff that it was appropriate. The staff seemed befuddled, but the director of nursing looked over the case— *really* looked over the case—and determined that, while the patient had no single terminal condition, a sufficient number of co-morbidities rendered him hospice-appropriate. She called in hospice, and everyone breathed a sigh of relief. The daughter reassured her mother that hospice would take care of everything.

In a timely manner, the hospice nurse, social worker, and chaplain all showed up. They were frazzled; they had had three intakes in this nursing home that day, which they discussed in front of Rev. Dawson's family. The daughter knew that was unprofessional and ill advised, but she said nothing. She didn't want to rock this boat. It was her mother's first experience with hospice, and the hospice people were warm and friendly and talked about the patient's comfort and gave hugs.

The hospice workers touted a topical compound that would be "better than" the standard hospice medications of liquid morphine and Ativan. The daughter was dubious, but they persuaded her to wait and see. On Thursday afternoon, Rev. Dawson was drowsy when the hospice doctor visited. That night and the next, the patient's agitation, confusion, and pain were worse than ever. The process of applying the topical compound distressed him further.

On Friday, the doctor again visited, but the patient was once again napping after a sleepless night. The doctor decreased the patient's night-time medications. Later in the day, as the patient became more agitated, the daughter asked the hospice to switch medication, but the staff told her that the hospice doctor wouldn't prescribe a different drug when the topical compound was already on board.

The daughter asked to take her father home, and the hospice staff said it would take several days to arrange. The hospice nurse hugged her, called her "sweet lady," and suggested that perhaps *she* should try the topical antianxiety medication.

A continuing series of hospice missteps and unfulfilled reassurances resulted in a hellish weekend. On Monday morning, the nursing home director of nursing (the one who had earlier determined the patient was hospice appropriate) witnessed the patient's obvious distress and advised the family to change to another hospice. In the meantime, she prevailed on one of the nursing home physicians to order stat doses of morphine and Ativan. Within minutes, Rev. Dawson was calm and restful. As his body relaxed and the distress melted from his countenance, his family registered profound relief as well. Within hours the patient was under the care of a new hospice. Two days later his family took him home on hospice, where he died peacefully a week later. They had kept their promise to bring him home.

Things don't always go right, not even in hospice. I learned more from that one case where things went off the rails than I had ever learned before. I learned that we can say all the right things, have the vernacular down pat, and still get it wrong.

And I learned it from "the other side of the bedrail." I was that daughter. The painful realization that no one was really, really hearing what we said was agonizing, for my father's comfort and dignity were in the balance. I anguished that I could not do for my own father what I had done for so many others.

But now I realize that my role changed everything. I was not a hospice professional then. I was a daughter. I needed people to step in for me. We needed someone to "listen athletically" to us, and it was the nursing home director of nursing who did that, not the hospice team.

In a lecture I attended years ago, the author Joan Borysenko (1996) said that we in the health care community encounter people with life-threatening illness and their families when they are no longer who they have been and are not yet reborn into who they will become. We meet them, she said, in "the space between no longer and not yet." In this frightening territory both the patient and family are suggestible and search for clues in everything we do and say and how we do and say it, which creates the potential for us to do either great good or great harm. And so it is of utmost importance to be both sensitive and mindful in our interactions with them.

I knew that before, but I understood it in a new way when I was the one in the alien, frightening place. I looked back at the times in the past when I had dismissively referred to an anxious family member as needing Ativan—not to their face but certainly to other team members—and I know now that I missed the mark.

The French philosopher Simone Weil (2001) has said that "The capacity to give one's attention to a sufferer is a very rare and difficult thing. It is almost a miracle; it is a miracle. Nearly all those who think they have this capacity do not possess it. Warmth of heart, impulsiveness, pity are not enough."

The great and humbling privilege of companioning a dying person and his/her loved ones demands tenderness and bravery, but there is profound meaning and significance in each journey. And we are the richer for it. ■

Joyce D. Davidson, M.S., C.T., is a hospice and palliative-care counselor, as well as a crisis and trauma counselor, in New York City. She is also a member of the faculty of the New Jersey Medical School, a frequent speaker on the topics of end-of-life care and grief/bereavement, and has a private practice in grief counseling. She has coedited several HFA Living with Grief series books with Kenneth J. Doka, including Living with Grief, At Work, At School, At Worship; Caregiving and Loss; *and* Living with Grief: Who We Are, How We Grieve.

REFERENCES

Ackerman, D. (1997). *A slender thread.* New York: Random House.

Borysenko, J. (1996). Fourth annual governing board lecture, Morristown Memorial Health Foundation, Morristown, NJ.

Manning, D. (1999). *Share my lonesome valley: the slow grief of long-term care.* Oklahoma City: Insight Books.

Wangerin, W. (1984). The making of a minister. In *Ragman and other cries of faith,* 73-79. San Francisco: Harper Collins.

Weil, S. (2001). "Reflections on the right use of school studies." In *Waiting on God.* San Francisco: Harper Perennial Classics.

Weisman, A. (1979). *Coping with cancer,* 57-66 . New York: McGraw Hill.

CHAPTER 18

Caring for the Professional Caregivers: Before and After the Death

Mary L. S. Vachon

The stress related to dealing with people in crisis and loss—
sometimes it affects me more than other times—
they touch your heart. It's not a stressor that makes
me want to leave the work, but it needs to be acknowledged.
—A palliative care nurse

As professional caregivers working with persons who are dying and with their family members, we can become involved and experience significant grief both during the dying process as well as after the death, yet the grief we experience is often unrecognized by ourselves as well as the systems in which we work. Not all caregivers experience or acknowledge experiencing grief, and certainly no caregivers should continue to experience considerable grief following the death of each person in their care. Dealing with grief can be difficult, but it can also cause us to grow as people, as well as professionals.

Barnard, Towers, Boston, and Lambrinidou (2000) state, "Palliative care is whole-person care, not only in the sense that the whole person of the patient (body, mind, spirit) is the object of care, but also in that the whole person of the caregiver is involved. Palliative care is *par excellence*, care that is given through the medium of a human relationship" (p. 5). Furman (2006) notes that in a holistic model of care, three levels of presence govern our relationships and tasks with patients:

- *Physical presence*, or "being there" for the patient, which includes your routine nursing interventions and tasks

- *Psychological presence*, or "being with" the patient, conveyed through communicating, assessing, caring, and accepting the patient

- *Therapeutic presence*, in which you connect with your patient on a human level, using all resources of your body, mind, and spirit.

Katz (2006) speaks of countertransference as "…an 'abbreviation' for the totality of our responses to our work—emotional, cognitive and behavioral—whether prompted by our patients, by the dynamics incumbent to our helping relationships, or by our own inevitable life experiences"(p. 6). She notes that scientific research has shown that the whole is greater than the sum of its parts, which demands that we face the fact that we as "experts," cannot responsibly divorce ourselves from this whole, nor from the alchemical reaction that occurs when two individuals engage together at what is, perhaps, the most vulnerable time in a human's existence.

The compassionate care of the dying requires the ability to give of oneself without being destroyed in the process. Learning how to do this takes time and requires that caregivers come to know themselves intimately, learning what may trigger a sense of loss and grief and how to best care for themselves in order to grieve appropriately and move on with caring for others. Goleman (2006), who wrote the book *Emotional Intelligence*, recently published *Social Intelligence*, in which he quotes a study by Strazdins (2002) showing that nurses whose work made them more distressed lost track of their mission, had poorer physical health, and most strongly wanted to leave their jobs. However, if a nurse had nourishing relationships with patients and frequently left feeling that she had improved their moods, she herself benefited emotionally. He suggests that a compassionate medical setting will recognize that nurses and others who operate at the front line of pain and despair need help to "metabolize" that inevitable suffering, rendering them more emotionally resilient.

This chapter will review the literature on loss and grief in caregivers—showing that loss and grief are related not only to the deaths of patients—discuss caregivers' responses to the deaths of patients and other losses, and review selected interventions designed to help caregivers cope with their experiences of grief and loss.

OVERVIEW

In a large, international study of occupational stress in close to 600 caregivers caring for the critically ill, dying, and bereaved (Vachon, 1987), feelings of depression, grief, and guilt constituted the single greatest manifestation of stress across all professional groups. The feelings were closely intertwined and were usually experienced in response to a loss that involved bereavement. This loss could be the death of a patient, but might also reflect a loss of self-esteem or a loss of social support from significant others, including team members. The loss may be of original ideals or of "good people" to work with. Caregivers may also feel they have failed at their work or have failed to live up to their original standards (Maslach, 1982). The individual meaning that is consciously or unconsciously ascribed to the particular loss determines whether an individual will experience grief—the emotions associated with loss causing bereavement.

Papadatou (2000) and Papadatou, Martinson, and Chung (2001) note that the losses may extend beyond the deaths of patients, including the following:

- Loss of a close relationship with a particular patient
- Loss due to the professional's identification with the pain of family members
- Loss of one's unmet goals and expectations
- Losses related to the caregiver's personal system of beliefs and assumptions about self, life, and death
- Past unresolved losses or anticipated future losses
- The death of self

LOSS AND GRIEF ASSOCIATED WITH PATIENT DEATH

Constant exposure to death and loss may leave staff with grief overload and considerable distress. However, participating in the death of some patients may also result in intense positive experiences that promote professional development (Saunders & Valente, 1994). More exposure to patients' deaths has been linked to higher reports of stress and burnout in physicians and nurses (Escot, Artero, Gandubert, Boulenger, & Ritchie, 2001; Kash et al., 2000; Marino, 1998; Payne, 2001). Constantly confronting the death of others causes caregivers to repeatedly re-evaluate their own mortality and reexamine the meaning of life and death (Mount, 1986). Wakefield (2000) notes that grief is like a powder keg. Caregivers may not be aware that they have been challenged by grief, but the effects of grief can be explosive and can cause problems at any time. Yet caregivers are expected to carry on "as usual" once a patient has died.

Saunders and Valente (1998) found that nurses felt that they handled their grief effectively if they helped the patient die a *good death*, which included:

- Relieving the patient's distress and symptoms to the extent allowed by current knowledge and technology

- Realizing that patients had the chance to complete tasks related to their important relationships

- Believing they had delivered the best possible care to the patient

- Feeling that the patient's death did not violate the natural order

- Feeling that the death was contextually appropriate (e.g., natural deaths in oncology)

Although resolving the grief took longer than many nurses anticipated, they were proud of managing symptoms and facilitating family communication, and this comforted them in their own grief.

In an international study of grief in pediatric nurses (Papadatou et al., 2001) in Greece (N = 39 oncology and ICU nurses) and Hong Kong (N = 24 nurses working on the general pediatric ward, pediatric intensive care unit, or neonatal intensive care unit), 93% of the nurses reported they were grieving during or after the death of a patient. Only three nurses reported avoiding involvement with patients to protect themselves from being affected by their death. These nurses remained emotionally detached and distant and did not grieve when children died. The nurses who allowed themselves to experience grief described it as being a continuous, ongoing fluctuation between focusing on the loss and pain, and avoiding or repressing it. Responses that put them in touch with their loss and pain involved sadness; depression; despair; recurring thoughts about the deceased and the dying conditions; the experience of guilt feelings; and a need to cry, to pray, to temporarily withdraw from daily activities, and to share their experiences with colleagues or loved ones or attend the child's funeral to bring closure to the relationship. Responses that helped them to repress or avoid their feelings involved systematically controlling their feelings, becoming involved with clinical duties and activities, and distancing themselves from the actual dying or death scene.

Patterns of Grief

The major patterns of professional grief in an early study (Vachon, 1987) included anticipatory grief, denial of grief, distorted grief, and chronic grief. *Anticipatory grief* occurred when the caregiver had a close relationship with the patient and began to grieve the patient's loss before the patient actually died. *Denial of grief* can be difficult to assess, as different cultures expect different manifestations of grief. An emergency nurse said, "It's a weird thing with death—it just doesn't bother me. I didn't cry with deaths in my own family—they just didn't bother me. Recently when the hospital chaplain died and I had to care for him in emergency, I didn't cry either. I cried, however, when my dog died" (Vachon, 1987, p. 158).

Sometimes, instead of being manifest, grief becomes distorted or *masked grief.* It may consist of manic behavior or "life-affirming" behavior that masks grief—such as caregivers going out drinking together after a death. Caregivers may also become physically ill in response to unrecognized grief.

Grief may become *chronic* with multiple losses, either close together or over an extended period of time. Chronic grief may result in preoccupation with death, a sense of generalized depression, and misgivings about the caregiver's own competence. Writing during the AIDS epidemic, Cho and Cassidy (1995) stated that multiple losses might result in chronic grief because there is no time to finish grieving for one person before another death occurs. In addition, many caregivers were experiencing personal grief as well as professional grief.

Disenfranchised grief occurs when a loss is not or cannot be openly acknowledged, publicly mourned, or socially supported (Doka, 1989, p. 4). Health care professionals may experience disenfranchised grief because they are exposed to multiple losses but may not have the socially sanctioned right or role of grieving persons (Lev, 1989). Their grief may not be recognized or acknowledged by their colleagues or their administration, which might expect them to immediately become involved in caring for another patient after a patient close to them has died.

Factors that may interfere with a caregiver's ability to grieve professional losses may be both social/environmental and personal/psychological (Marino, 1998). Rando (1984) suggests a number of factors that may contribute to a failure to grieve, including social negation of the loss, isolation from social support (visiting nurse agencies in which opportunities for support or debriefing may be limited), assumption of the role of the "strong one," the need to be in control, a feeling of being overwhelmed by multiple loss, and the reawakening of old losses.

Grief and Institutional Transformation

Caregivers who have been in hospice and palliative care since the early days of the movement often feel that they are no longer able to give the type of care they used to give. For many, this feeling constitutes the death of a dream, and they grieve the loss. Russ (2005) is an anthropologist who did field work in hospice in the 1990s. She proposes that in hospice settings, the exchange and distribution of valued resources—money, care, touch, stories, and love—may be viewed as bearing in their design this *foundational burden of reconciliation* between life and death. Like many service organizations, "hospices operate at the interstices of two different economies: one characterized by an ethic of pure gift, sacrifice, and charity; the other by standards of efficiency and discipline, cost containment, and profit making. [Russ describes] the ways that paid caregivers navigate between these two economies—one valorizing loss and expenditure; the other, economy and gains—in their interactions with patients and in their embodied experience and negotiation of care" (p. 129). Russ describes how a discourse about restraint and the need to set limits to compassion took hold among paid caregivers in the 1990s. She explores, as well, how paid hospice caregivers sometimes transgressed those limits in an effort to maintain and perceive the value of their care.

> (T)here are these people dying. Regularly. And so, to me, the question becomes: What is important? What is real? And that's the question that I think about from moment to moment. Except when I'm too full of grief, when I can't think of even that....
> So, there is a desire for direct experience in caring. And it's true that it's frustrated in hospice work—the reality of it, that is. It is because most of the people I meet at Comfort of Home and also in the field don't place a value on the experience. It seems to me that most of them have a job.... That isn't to say that good works aren't done, because they are, all the time. In fact, sometimes I think they are done in spite of, maybe even to correct (laughs) the general climate (p. 144).

Unless the caregivers were burned out, most described their own experience of caring, as well as the patient's experience of dying, in terms of a "gift," insisting that they gained far more than they gave.

"Economic metaphors for burnout, such as feeling 'spent' or 'consumed,' indicate the potential for excess and the need for caregivers to exercise restraint. However, even as caregivers felt it necessary to 'shut down,' they also felt a concern that hospice and palliative care programs were becoming an 'institutional' space defined more by the physical work of caring than by the emotional or spiritual labor" (Russ, 2005, p. 146).

An admission nurse in a palliative care program said,

> The regulations to admit to the Palliative Care Team are so different. The patient and the physician are not willing to admit to hospice—to put them into hospice. There are lots of regulations. I get called because we do the support that others don't do. I have to make up "skilled needs." Emotional issues don't get resolved quickly—social issues and emotional issues take lots of time. You can teach a monkey to do an IV—the emotional stuff, that's what is really hard.

Another nurse from the same palliative care program said,

> We used to have a support group; they stopped it. I went a few
> times and felt it was helpful. It felt safe to share how we were
> feeling. As our caseloads went up, we had less time to attend.
> We now have no mental health days. I have worked in hospice
> for six years. The organization does less and less for the people
> who work here with each passing second. I guess that is the way
> it is in health care in general. Most of the people I know have
> their own ways of coping with these issues outside the hospice.
> Management seems to have less and less empathy for those of
> us doing direct service. (Vachon, unpublished research, 2006).

Grief Associated with Personal Loss

A history of unresolved or current grief can make a caregiver more
vulnerable to feelings of complicated grief. Dr. Peter Selwyn (1998), a
hospice physician, writes of unexpectedly getting in touch with his own
previously unresolved grief at a workshop led by Dr. Elisabeth Kübler-Ross:

> My father died suddenly at the age of 35, when I was 18 months
> old.... My father most likely died by suicide and not, as I
> had grown up believing, in a bizarre accident in which he
> inexplicably lost his balance and fell out of a window....
>
> It was not until more than 30 years later—when I was confronted
> with the deaths of all these young men and women (from AIDS)
> whom I could no more save than I could save my father—that
> I began to come to terms with this primal loss (pp. 106-107).

Recent personal bereavement and unresolved grief from deaths
prior to coming into a children's hospice were associated with high stress
(Woolley, Stein, Forrest, & Baum, 1989). In a study of palliative care nurses and administrators, a significant correlation was found between job
satisfaction and absence of loss in the past year (Krikorian & Moser, 1985).

Mills and Aubeeluck (2006) did a small (N = 5) study of nurses caring
for ill family members. The nurses had difficulty dealing with boundary
issues, as they would recognize that the family member was going to die

long before the family member might have been given the prognosis. Being expected to provide family members with information and treatment options was challenging. Maintaining boundaries within the work situation was also a challenge: "Your personal life is dragged into your work in such a bizarre situation. That wouldn't normally happen" (p. 162).

Nurses described positive aspects of their role as caregiver, particularly when their family member died. The nurse caregivers articulated issues that are often identified by informal caregivers—such as potential losses, anticipatory grief, adapting to life without their loved one, communication issues—yet issues such as professional and personal boundaries appear to be specific to nurses (and probably other health professionals).

A Developmental Framework in Working with Death and Dying

Dr. Bernice Harper (1994), a social worker, developed a model, Comfort-Ability Growth and Development Scale in Coping with Professional Anxieties in Death and Dying. Her model proposes that learning to be comfortable in working with dying patients and their families must be preceded by a growth and developmental process or sequence, including cycles of productive change, observable behavior, and feeling. She describes stages experienced by social workers engaged in a supervisory process. Many caregivers in hospice are not given such supervision but learn through mentoring or by "fending for themselves." For many caregivers without high-quality supervision the process Harper describes may take much longer, and many caregivers may not progress beyond the model's early stages.

STAGE I INTELLECTUALIZATION 1-3 MONTHS

The caregiver provides practical help. Generally the caregiver relates on an intellectual basis, rejecting any emotional involvement.

STAGE II EMOTIONAL SURVIVAL 3-6 MONTHS

The caregiver experiences trauma, often accompanied by guilt and anxiety.

STAGE III DEPRESSION 6-9 MONTHS

The "Grow or Go" stage

- Mastery of self is a real challenge in this stage; it requires a growing acceptance of death and an orientation to the reality of death and dying.

■ The caregiver may experience extreme anxiety, grief, and depression; question his or her usefulness and real ability to contribute and to be helpful; and express anger, hurt, and inability to come to terms with the situation. The pain, mourning, and grieving are a part of not accepting the loss and then a moving forward to accept death and dying.

STAGE IV EMOTIONAL ARRIVAL 9-12 MONTHS

■ This stage is marked by a sense of freedom from the debilitating effects that inhered in the previous stages of the experiential growth process. The caregiver is now largely free from identifying with the patient's symptoms, free from the preoccupation with his or her own death and dying, from guilt feelings about his or her own good health, and from incapacitating periods of depression.

■ The caregiver is not insensitive; rather, the caregiver's sensitivities have sharpened. Although not free from pain, the caregiver is typically free from its incapacitating effects. At this stage the caregiver has "appropriate" emotions and has the sensitivity to grieve and the resilience to recover. "In other words, one has reached the stage at which one has the control to practice the art of one's science" (p. 71).

STAGE V DEEP COMPASSION 12-24 MONTHS

■ This stage involves self-realization, self-awareness, and self-actualization. The developmental process involves the caregiver "doing for himself." This growth process contains all the elements of Stages I through IV plus personal values, self-reliance, and the realistic acceptance of life and death.

■ "Stage V is the culminating point of all the growth and development that has previously transpired. The learning process was anxious, traumatic, painful, and depressing, but the product of the process in terms of professional growth and development is rewarding" (p. 83).

■ The deep compassion felt by the caregiver toward the dying person is translated into constructive and appropriate activities based on a human and professional assessment of the needs of the dying person and the family.

Stage VI The Doer 8-10 years beyond Stage V

- The caregiver demonstrates inner knowledge and wisdom, inner power, and inner strength. "…There is reinforcement, enhanced wisdom and knowledge to the understanding of death and dying. There is less and less misunderstanding of death. The professional and caregiver see, understand, and accept death as a part of life's transitions" (p.122). "In order to use what you know, you must know what you use" (p. 99).

- Burnout is not a point at issue. Professional growth and development of seasoned health care professionals prevent burnout because these professionals take each stage and each phase of growth and development in stride and grow in the process.

- To some extent, Doers have learned how to gather from the universe what they need to do their work. Their patients recognize something in them and feed back this information, which can then be used to help others.

Coping with Grief

Caregivers need to develop ways of coping with grief at both the personal and organizational levels. Regular opportunities to meet and talk together can help teams debrief about their experiences of grief when patients die and can also help them understand that not everyone grieves in the same way. Redinbaugh, Schuerger, Weiss, Brufsky, and Arnold (2001) note that physicians and nurses may prefer different coping strategies and may have different personality structures that lead to different responses to patient deaths. Individuals have natural propensities and aversions for minimizing grief reactions. Some caregivers are likely to talk with others about their grief. Others attempt to understand their grief through its depiction in literature and the arts. Some might dampen their grief with alcohol or drugs, while others use personal faith to resolve their grief. In a new book on palliative care teams, Speck (2006) speaks of valuing the people that you work with and attending to the dynamic processes which develop as a way of fostering mutual respect and achieving the desired outcome for the work of the team.

When caregivers begin to work in a setting where they will have regular exposure to dying persons, they should receive mentoring to help them to deal with their grief in a manner that is congruent with their personality and previous exposure to grief. Caregivers should be helped to recognize the feelings associated with grief that they experience when a patient dies, identify the source of these feelings, and share their feelings with a caring team.

Are these normal, straightforward feelings of grief because the caregiver was close to the person and will miss the person? If so, the following approaches might be helpful:

- Talking with colleagues about what was gained in the relationship with the person and what is lost with the person's death

- Recognizing what made the relationship with that person so special

- Journaling about the experience with the person

- Attending the person's wake, funeral, or memorial service

- Writing a card or letter to the bereaved relatives

- Taking the time to acknowledge whatever emotions are being experienced and reflecting what "connections" the caregiver might have with this person in the future—how will the experience with that person impact the caregiver's future care of other patients?

Are these feelings caused by identification or overidentification with the person who died? If so,

- The caregiver may need to speak with a more experienced colleague or supervisor to look at whether this identification with the patient reflects unresolved grief for a person in the caregiver's past who has died. If so, the caregiver might wish to deal with that grief with a therapist or grief counselor. Another approach that is often helpful is to write a letter to the person who has died, identifying the unresolved issues, expressing how much the caregiver misses the person, or saying whatever needs to be said. Then, on a new piece of paper, the caregiver can "let the person write back," letting the words that come into the caregiver's mind go onto the paper, without censoring the words in any way. This technique is often unexpectedly helpful.

Is the grief due to recognizing the caregiver's own mortality through identification with the patient?

- If so, the caregiver might find it helpful to speak with a trusted colleague or friend about ideas of personal mortality. What would it mean to be dying in the way this person has just died? Other caregivers might find that they reflect on healing relationships, or cherish the gift of being with family and friends, recognizing that "today is not my turn."

Does the caregiver frequently seem to experience more than the anticipated amount of grief when patients die, or does the caregiver never seem to really "connect" with patients enough to experience any grief? Does the caregiver have unresolved grief from the past that is unrecognized?

- If so, it might be helpful for the caregiver either to seek therapy or to attend a workshop dealing with grief issues.

- Consistent experiences with more than the usual amount of grief may also reflect a problem with boundary setting, or not having enough of a life outside of the professional setting, thereby trying to receive satisfaction through work alone. The caregiver needs to find satisfying interests and relationships outside of the work situation.

Are the feelings caused by the fact that this was not a "good death," or does the caregiver feel guilty about something that happened in the relationship or in the care of the person?

- The team might schedule a meeting to discuss the person's death, considering what lessons might be learned to improve the care of patients to follow.

- The caregiver might speak with colleagues, a manager, or a therapist about specific concerns about the care given, either letting go of unnecessary guilt or recognizing the mistakes and vowing not to make them again.

Medland, Howard-Ruben, and Whitaker (2004) describe an intervention to interrupt the cycle of turnover on a state-of-the-art oncology unit. The intervention involved a series of one day Circle of Care retreats that addressed specific concerns pertinent to improving the psychosocial wellness and skills of care providers. One hundred and fifty multidisciplinary team members attended this program over five sessions. These workshops were seen as the first phase of a comprehensive, ongoing psychosocial support program for staff, tailored to address the psychosocial demands of oncology nursing. The day included interactive and informal presentations about staying well, managing losses, developing stress management skills and strategies (e.g., relaxation, journaling), facilitating bereavement, cultivating team effectiveness, group support, storytelling, and an art therapy session called "All Gifts Differing" that offered a reflection of the unique attributes staff members bring to the work setting.

In addition, the program used the CARES philosophy to provide a framework for incorporating the stress management and self-care skills staff learned into their practice. This philosophy involves the following:

- **C** *creation* of a community of care as opposed to feeling solely responsible for meeting the needs of patients, caring for each team member unconditionally, being cognizant that the stress of the day depends more on work group than patient care assignment

- **A** *awareness* of the signs and symptoms of stress and burnout in self and others and a recognition that stress management needs to be as integral a competency as hanging chemotherapy

- **R** *reinforcement* of the importance of relaxation and rejuvenation as self-care skills so that the needs of others can be met effectively

- **E** *emphasis* on regular aerobic exercise and eating healthy

- **S** *spiritual* awareness and reconnection to whatever is personally meaningful—reconnecting to faith and being playful and attentive to the "spirit" at work (p. 52).

Following the Circle of Care retreat session, a Circle of Care Bereavement Council Group composed of alumni was convened to implement strategies discussed at the retreat and to develop rituals to be associated with bereavement care, for staff as well as bereaved families. Patient deaths are recognized by putting a placard on the door of the patient's room with the same artwork on a sympathy card that was sent to the family. An electric candle is illuminated in the nurses' station and kept burning for 24 hours after a death. Staff members on the two oncology units and palliative care unit let other involved staff know that the person has died. A memory board is kept in each of the report rooms, and the name of each person who dies is placed on a dove and put on the board for a week, after which time the dove is placed in a folder on the board. Family sympathy cards are kept on the board for several weeks so staff members can sign the card, which is sent to the family 3 to 4 weeks after the death. Additional strategies in the planning stage include providing increased chaplain support, educating interns on managing loss, creating an annual memorial service, and relying more on the services of the palliative care team.

Mindfulness Meditation (Cohen-Katz, Wiley, Capuano, Baker, & Shapiro, 2004) has been used with nurses and found to reduce burnout. Mindfulness is defined as being fully present to one's experience without judgment or resistance. Its emphasis is on self-care, compassion, and healing. As one cares for oneself, one has more energy to care for others. As one centers and becomes comfortable with meditation, one may become aware of an inner voice that helps one to make decisions. Furman (2006) suggests "to connect with your patients on the levels of physical presence, psychological presence, and therapeutic presence, look inside yourself for an inner reference and stability through meditation or listening to intuitive knowledge. In this personal space, you can be fully present for your patient without being overwhelmed by grief" (p. 56). This is similar to Harper's (1994) Stage VI, wherein the caregiver has inner knowledge and wisdom. For most caregivers, this will come only with time and through mentoring, group work, or personal psychotherapy.

Furman (2006) suggests that in dealing with grief, you must

- Confront your own mortality.
- Take care of yourself.

- Set realistic goals. If your goal is to "save" people with terminal illness, you'll fail every time. Redefine success to include a combination of results, processes, and relationships. Remember, your job isn't simply to save; it's also to care for and about your patients. You can always succeed in these things.

- Take time to grieve and mourn. Feeling acute grief isn't enough; you must also mourn. Mourning allows you to adapt to a loss and learn how to live while death surrounds you.

- Feel whole. When you talk about the experiences and express your feelings of loss, you'll feel better, more alive, and more whole for having done so. In the end you'll look back and remember the joy, the intimacy, and the privilege it was to help, to love, and to care. And you'll be able to give the same love and care to the next patient who needs you (p. 56).

Spirituality

Caregivers were asked about the role of spirituality in their work in palliative care and hospice (Vachon, 1987). More recently in research gathered for a chapter on nurse stress in palliative care (Vachon, 2006) the author spoke with and received e-mail responses from nurses in hospice palliative care settings in the United States and Canada. (This is the same study from which I referred to unpublished data above.) The following are their reflections on the importance of their spiritual belief systems for their lives and clinical practice. Although they were not asked specifically about grief, it can be assumed that the spiritual belief systems of these experienced palliative care nurses helped them with their grief when patients died.

- I feel like I do this work because I am supposed to do it. A Higher Something made me have the ability to do this—gave me a gift. I recognize when I am with patients and their families, when the patient is close to dying—I feel a presence of something greater than myself—a connectedness with that—I've always had that.

I've always believed in soul—something bigger than our bodies—but now it is more real. I've seen it, smelled it, felt others being with them when they are passing. I no longer wonder. I know there is something and that's comforting.

I have a much greater sense of intuition—gut, it comes from something not me, I listen in my professional life—I wish I did in my personal life—I'd be a free person.

- As a Seventh Day Adventist, I have God, I have others. I start the day with prayer and scriptures. It gives me a grounded center— the peace that passes all understanding.

- Spirituality is one of the reasons I am doing this work. Every once in a while, I get to see a miracle—that's why I am here. A man with lots of relationships came in saying, "I'm enlightened"— in one week he repaired relationships with his ex-wives and kids— the last one half an hour before he died—when he died everyone cried out of joy (unpublished research, Vachon, 2006).

CONCLUSION

Work with the dying is going to involve the experience of loss and grief if you connect with the people with whom you are working. However, through initially learning how to recognize and deal with loss and grief through a process of mentoring in a team of committed caregivers, taking the time to grow and reflect on your own mortality, acknowledging and dealing with loss and grief as it occurs, having a full life outside the work situation, engaging in self-care, and exploring meditation and spirituality, you can continue to grow and thrive in your work. ■

Mary Vachon, Ph.D., is a nurse, clinical sociologist, psychotherapist, researcher, educator, and cancer survivor. She is currently a consultant and psychotherapist in private practice, professor in the Departments of Psychiatry and Public Health Sciences at the University of Toronto, and clinical consultant at Wellspring. Dr. Vachon is the author of Occupational Stress in the Care of the Critically Ill, Dying and Bereaved. *She has published more than 150 scientific articles and book chapters and delivered more than 1,500 lectures around the world on topics related to bereavement, occupational stress, life-threatening illness, palliative care, survivorship, and spirituality. She is the recipient of many awards, including the Dorothy Ley Award for Excellence in Palliative Care received from the Ontario Palliative Care Association in April 1997 and is the recipient of the National Hospice and Palliative Care Organization's 2001 Distinguished Researcher Award. She is listed in* Who's Who of Canadian Women *and* Who's Who in Canada.

REFERENCES

Barnard, D., Towers, A., Boston, P., & Lambrinidou, Y. (2000). *Crossing over: Narratives of palliative care.* New York: Oxford.

Cho, C., & Cassidy, D. F. (1994). Parallel processes for workers and their clients in chronic bereavement resulting from HIV. *Death Studies,* 273-292.

Cohen-Katz, J., Wiley, S. D., Capuano, T., Baker, D., & Shapiro, S. (2004). The effects of mindfulness-based stress reduction on nurse stress and burnout: A quantitative and qualitative study. *Holistic Nursing Practice, 18*(6), 302-308.

Doka, K. J. (1989). *Disenfranchised grief.* New York: Lexington Books.

Escot, C., Artero, S., Gandubert, C., Boulenger, J. P., & Ritchie, K. (2001). Stress levels in nursing staff working in oncology. *Stress and Health, 17*(55), 273-279.

Furman, J. (2006). What you should know about chronic grief. *Nursing, 32*(2), 56-57.

Goleman, D., (2006). *Social Intelligence.* New York: Bantam Dell.

Harper, B. C. (1994). *Death: The coping mechanism of the health professional* (Rev. edition.). Greenville, SC: Southeastern University Press, Inc.

Kash, K. M., Holland, J. C., Breitbart, W., Berenson, S., Dougherty, J., Ouelette-Kobasa, S., & Lesko, L. (2000). Stress and burnout in oncology. *Oncology, 14*, 1621-1637.

Katz, R. (2006). When our personal selves influence our professional work: An introduction to emotions and countertransference in end of life care. In Katz, R. & Johnson, T. (Eds). *When professionals weep.* New York: Routledge, Taylor Francis Group.

Krikorian, D. A., & Moser, D. H. (1985). Satisfactions and stresses experienced by professional nurses in hospice programs. *American Journal of Hospice Care, I*(1), 25-33.

Lev, E. (1989). A nurse's perspective on disenfranchised grief. In K. Doka (Ed.), *Disenfranchised grief: Recognizing hidden sorrows.* Lexington, MA: Lexington Books. 289-300.

Marino, P. A. (1998). The effects of cumulative grief in the nurse. *Journal of IV Nursing, 21*, 101-104.

Maslach, C. (1982). *Burnout—The cost of caring.* New York: Prentice Hall.

Medland, J., Howard-Ruben, J., & Whitaker, E. (2004). Fostering psychosocial wellness in oncology nurses: Addressing burnout and social support in the workplace. *Oncology Nursing Forum, 31*(1), 47-54.

Mills, J., & Aubeeluck, A. (2006). Nurses' experiences of caring for their own family members. *British Journal of Nursing, 15*(3), 160-165.

Mount, B. M. (1986). Dealing with our losses. *Journal of Clinical Oncology, 4*, 1127-1134.

Papadatou, D. (2000). A proposed model of health professionals' grieving process. *Omega, 41*, 59-77.

Papadatou, D., Martinson, I. M., & Chung, P. M. (2001). Caring for dying children: A comparative study of nurses' experiences in Greece and Hong Kong. *Cancer Nursing, 24*(5), 402-412.

Payne, N. (2001). Occupational stressors and coping as determinants of burnout in female hospice nurses. *Journal of Advanced Nursing, 33*, 396-405.

Rando, T. A. (1984). *Grief, dying and death: Clinical interventions for caregivers.* Champaign, IL: Research Press.

Redinbaugh, E. M., Schuerger, J. M., Weiss, L., Brufsky, A., & Arnold, R. (2001). Health care professionals' grief: A model based on occupational style and coping. *Psycho-Oncology, 10*, 187-198.

Russ, A. J. (2005). Love's labor paid for: Gift and commodity at the threshold of death. *Cultural Anthropology, 20*(1), 128-155.

Saunders, J. M., & Valente, S. M. (1994). Nurses' grief. *Cancer Nursing,* 318-325.

Selwyn, P. A. (1998). *Surviving the fall.* New Haven, CT: Yale University Press.

Speck, P. (Ed.) (2006). *Teamwork in Palliative Care.* Oxford University Press.

Strazdins, L. (2002). Emotional work and emotional contagion. In N. Ashkanasy et al. (Eds.) *Managing emotions in the workplace.* Armonk, NY: ME Sharp.

Vachon, M. L. S. (1987). *Occupational stress in the care of the critically ill, dying and bereaved.* New York: Hemisphere.

Vachon M. L. S. (2006). The experience of the nurse in end-of-life care in the 21st century. In B. R. Ferrell, & N. Coyle (Eds.) *Textbook of palliative nursing.* Oxford: Oxford University Press.

Wakefield, A. (2000). Nurses' responses to death and dying: A need for relentless self-care. *International Journal of Palliative Nursing, 6*(5), 245-251.

Woolley, H., Stein, A., Forrest, G. C., & Baum, J. D. (1989). Staff stress and job satisfaction at a children's hospice. *Archives of Disease in Childhood, 64,* 114-118.

CHAPTER 19

Selected Resources

Lisa McGahey Veglahn

The Hospice Foundation of America recognizes that dealing with grief and bereavement is a difficult and personal journey. The following list of selected resources can serve as a guide, whether you are a consumer or a professional helping someone facing grief. While the list is divided for consumers and professionals, many organizations provide information and support for both. And as always, your local hospice can serve as an excellent community resource. While the list below provides useful resources, be sure to look to those who have helped you in the past—friends and family, coworkers, your faith community, your family physician, and other care professionals. Whether you are facing these situations as a family member or as a professional caregiver, you don't need to struggle alone.

ASSOCIATIONS FOR CONSUMERS

AARP

www.aarp.org
601 E Street, NW
Washington, DC 20049
888-OUR-AARP

AARP is dedicated to enhancing quality of life for all as we age. We lead positive social change and deliver value to members through information, advocacy and service. AARP's website includes information and publications about grief and loss.

The Candlelighters Childhood Cancer Foundation

www.candlelighters.org
PO Box 498
Kensington, MD 20895-0498
800-366-CCCF (2223) or 301-962-3520
staff@candlelighters.org

CCCF provides support, information, and advocacy to families of children with cancer (at any stage of the illness or who are bereaved), to professionals in the field, and to adult survivors, through local groups, newsletters, and other services.

The Compassionate Friends, Inc.

www.thecompassionatefriends.org
PO Box 3696
Oak Brook, IL 60522-3696
630-990-0010 or 877-969-0010
nationaloffice@compassionatefriends.org

The Compassionate Friends is a national nonprofit, self-help support organization that offers friendship, understanding, and hope to bereaved parents, grandparents, and siblings. Chapters across the country provide monthly meetings, phone contacts, lending libraries, and a local newsletter. The national organization provides newsletters, distributes grief-related materials, and answers requests for referrals and information.

The Dougy Center

www.dougy.org
PO Box 86852
Portland, OR 97286
503-775-5683
Help@dougy.org

The Dougy Center, The National Center for Grieving Children and Families, provides support groups for grieving children that are age specific (3-5, 6-12, teens) and loss specific (parent death, sibling death, survivors of homicide/violent death, survivors of suicide). Additional services include national trainings, consultations to schools and organizations, crisis-line information, and referrals. The Dougy Center has served as a model for support groups nationwide.

GriefNet.org

www.griefnet.org

cendra@griefnet.org

GriefNet.org is an Internet community of persons dealing with grief, death, and major loss. GriefNet.org has more than 40 e-mail support groups and two websites. GriefNet's integrated approach to on-line grief support provides help to people working through loss and grief issues of many kinds. Its companion site, KIDSAID.com, provides a safe environment for kids and their parents to find information and ask questions.

Tragedy Assistance Program for Survivors, Inc. (TAPS)

www.taps.org

910 17th Street, NW Suite 800

Washington, DC 20006

202-588-TAPS (8277)

info@taps.org

TAPS is a national non-profit organization made up of, and providing services at no cost to, all those who have suffered the loss of a loved one in the Armed Forces. The heart of TAPS is its national military survivor peer support network called SurvivorLINK, which links together the families, friends, and coworkers of those who are grieving. TAPS also offers bereavement counseling referral, hosts the nation's only annual National Military Survivor Seminar and Kids Camp, publishes a quarterly journal, and offers a toll-free crisis and information line available 24 hours a day.

Young Widow.org

www.youngwidow.org

webmaster@ywbb.org

Young Widow.org provides a forum for young widows and widowers to connect online. Through these connections, young widows and widowers find understanding and validation of their feelings so that they are able to recover their joy for life, reclaim their identities, and rebuild their futures.

ASSOCIATIONS FOR PROFESSIONALS

American Association of Pastoral Counselors

www.aapc.org
9504A Lee Highway
Fairfax, VA 22031-2303
703-385-6967
info@aapc.org

The American Association of Pastoral Counselors (AAPC) was organized in 1963 to promote and support the ministry of pastoral counseling within religious communities and the field of mental health in the United States and Canada.

American Foundation for Suicide Prevention

www.afsp.org
120 Wall Street, 22nd Floor
New York, NY 10005
1-888-333-AFSP or (212) 363-3500

AFSP works closely with support group facilitators, first responders, clergy members, mental health professionals, and others in the community, to help survivors cope with their loss, their pain, their questions, and their journey of healing. In addition, AFSP has taken the leading role in developing an agenda for research on survivors of suicide loss.

Association for Death Education and Counseling

www.adec.org
60 Revere Drive, Suite 500
Northbrook, IL 60062
847-509-0403
adec@adec.org

The Association for Death Education and Counseling (ADEC) is one of the oldest interdisciplinary organizations in the field of dying, death, and bereavement. Its nearly 2,000 members include a wide array of mental and medical health personnel, educators, clergy, funeral directors, and volunteers. ADEC offers numerous educational opportunities through its annual conference, courses and workshops, its certification program, and via its acclaimed newsletter, *The Forum.*

Association for Clinical Pastoral Education

www.acpe.edu

1549 Clairmont Road, Suite 103

Decatur, GA 30033-4611

404-320-1472

acpe@acpe.edu

The ACPE is a multicultural, multifaith organization devoted to providing education and improving the quality of ministry and pastoral care offered by spiritual caregivers of all faiths through the clinical educational methods of Clinical Pastoral Education.

Association of Professional Chaplains

www.professionalchaplains.org

1701 E. Woodfield Road, Suite 400

Schaumburg, IL 60173

847-240-1014

info@professionalchaplains.org

As a national, not-for-profit professional association, the APC advocates for quality spiritual care of all persons in healthcare facilities, correctional institutions, long term care units, rehabilitation centers, hospice, the military, and other specialized settings.

The End-of-Life Nursing Education Consortium

c/o American Association of Colleges of Nursing

One Dupont Circle, NW, Suite 530

Washington, DC 20036

www.aacn.nche.edu/elnec

202-463-6930

The ELNEC project is a comprehensive, national education program to improve end-of-life care by nurses. ELNEC brings together leading nursing groups and perspectives to form a collaborative approach to improve end-of-life education and care.

End of Life/Palliative Education Resource Center (EPERC)

www.eperc.mcw.edu

This site offers resources to support individuals involved in the design, implementation, and/or evaluation of End-of-Life/Palliative education for physicians, nurses, and other health care professionals. The site includes Fast Facts, downloadable educational materials, and links to clinical and educational Web resource centers.

The Foundation for End of Life Care

www.vitascharityfund.org
100 South Biscayne Boulevard, Suite 1500
Miami, FL 33133
877-800-2951 or 305-350-6978

The Foundation for End-of-Life Care, a not-for-profit organization established by VITAS Healthcare Corporation, was created to improve end-of-life care for individual patients and their families, while supporting fundamental societal change. The Foundation provides resources to advance the quality of end-of-life care through support of the Duke Institute on Care at the End of Life, as well as through research grants, partnerships, and individual grants.

Growth House

www.growthhouse.org
415-863-3045
info@growthhouse.org

Growth House, Inc. serves as a portal to resources for life-threatening illness and end-of-life care. Its primary mission is to improve the quality of compassionate care for people who are dying through public education and global professional collaboration. Growth House has an excellent search engine that offers access to the Internet's most comprehensive collection of reviewed resources for end-of-life care and grief and bereavement.

Hospice Foundation of America

www.hospicefoundation.org
1621 Connecticut Avenue, NW, Suite 300
Washington, DC 20009
800-854-3402
hfaoffice@hospicefoundation.org

Hospice Foundation of America provides leadership in the development and application of hospice and its philosophy of care with the goal of enhancing the American health care system and the role of hospice within it. Hospice Foundation of America meets its mission by conducting programs of professional development, public education and information, research, publications, and health policy issues. HFA's programs for heath care professionals assist those who cope either personally or professionally with terminal illness, death, and the process of grief, and are offered on a national or regional basis. HFA's programs for the public assist individual consumers of health care who are coping with issues of caregiving, terminal illness, and grief.

Hospice and Palliative Nurses Association

www.hpna.org
One Penn Center West, Suite 229
Pittsburgh, PA 15276-0100
412-787-9301
hpna@hpna.org

The purpose of the Hospice and Palliative Nurses Association (HPNA) is to exchange information, experiences, and ideas; to promote understanding of the specialties of hospice and palliative nursing; and to study and promote hospice and palliative nursing research.

National Association of Social Workers
www.naswdc.org
750 First Street, NE, Suite 700
Washington, DC 20002-4241
202-408-8600
membership@naswdc.org

The National Association of Social Workers (NASW) is the largest membership organization of professional social workers in the world. NASW works to enhance the professional growth and development of its members, to create and maintain professional standards, and to advance sound social policies.

National Hospice and Palliative Care Organization
www.nhpco.org
1700 Diagonal Road, Suite 625
Alexandria, VA 22314
703-837-1500
Consumer HelpLine: 800-658-8898
Nhpco_info@nhpco.org

National Hospice and Palliative Care Organization (NHPCO) is the largest non-profit membership organization representing hospice and palliative care programs and professionals in the United States. The organization is committed to improving end-of-life care and expanding access to hospice. NHPCO offers educational programs and materials for professionals and the public.

▪ INDEX ▪

D

E

F

G

guiding paradoxes, 32–41
life cycle periods and, 27
the metaphysical self, 38–41
paradoxical wordplay, 32–36
progress measurement, 31
retirement and, 28
self-esteem and, 27–28, 30–31
Lifton, R.J.
connecting help to transition, 184–186
Lindemann, E.
acute grief reactions, 215
anticipatory grief concept, 5, 216
complicated grief description, 140
cultural relevance of grief, 123
importance of remembrance to the grieving process, 77
manifestations of grief, 92
Living eulogies, 2
Ludwig, Robert
children and anticipatory mourning, 217
children's understanding of death, 210
Lund, D.A.
social support programs for widows, 180

M

MacPherson, M.
survivors and "unpleasant details," 58
Maercker, A.
internet-based complicated grief therapy, 146–147
Malinowski, B.
death rituals, 65
Malkinson, R.
mutual help programs, 187
Mandelbaum, D.G.
death rituals, 65–66
Marks, I.M.
"guided mourning therapy," 145
Marshall, H.
death of a parent of an adult child, 265
Martin, T.L.
grieving styles, 92, 291–292
problem-solving activities for disenfranchised grief, 296
Martinson, I.M.
losses that extend beyond the deaths of patients, 313
Mawson, D.
"guided mourning therapy," 145
McBride, A.
rumination effect on grief, 92
Medland, J.
Circle of Care workshops, 324–325
Men. *See also* Women
reactions to a parent's death, 261–262

N

S